INTRODUCTION

Welcome to a rich collection of tattoo inspiration, designed with the artist in mind. This book features over 2,000 diverse tattoo designs, thoughtfully assembled to spark your creativity and enhance your craft.

Here, you'll find a variety of styles and motifs, presented in a random order to encourage spontaneous exploration and new ideas. Each page offers a fresh perspective, inviting you to discover unique patterns, refine your technique, and fuel your artistic vision.

As you dive into these pages, let the diversity of designs inspire you and the randomness spark your imagination. This book is your canvas of possibilities—embrace the journey and let your creativity guide the way.

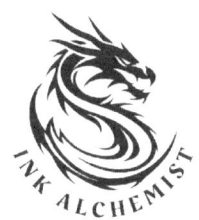

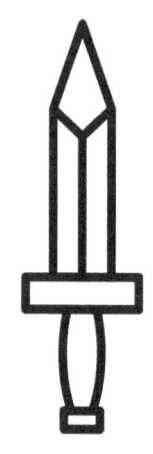

BOMB

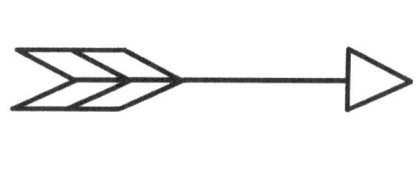

"Street Art"

GANG

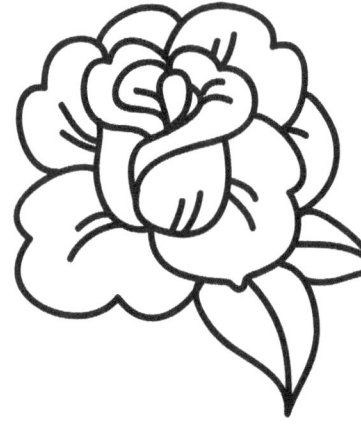

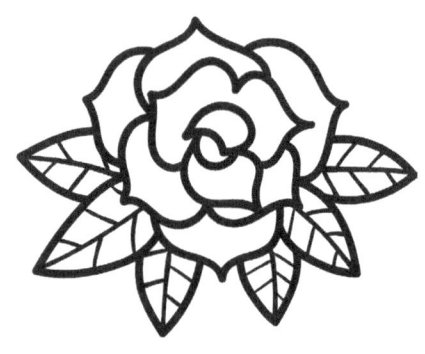

VANDAL

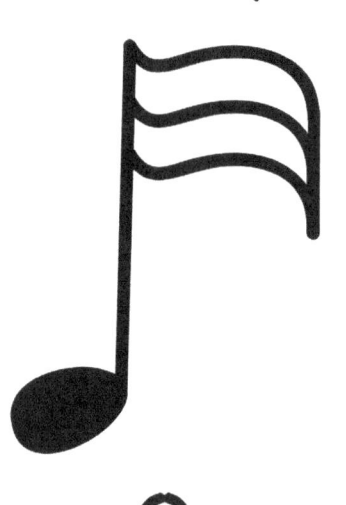

MUSIC

HIP HOP

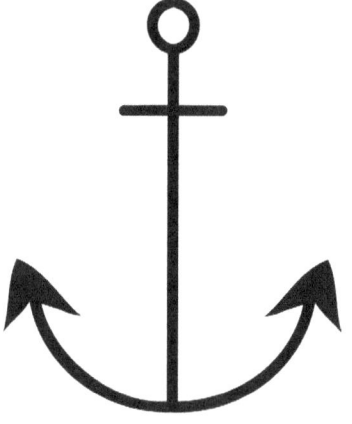

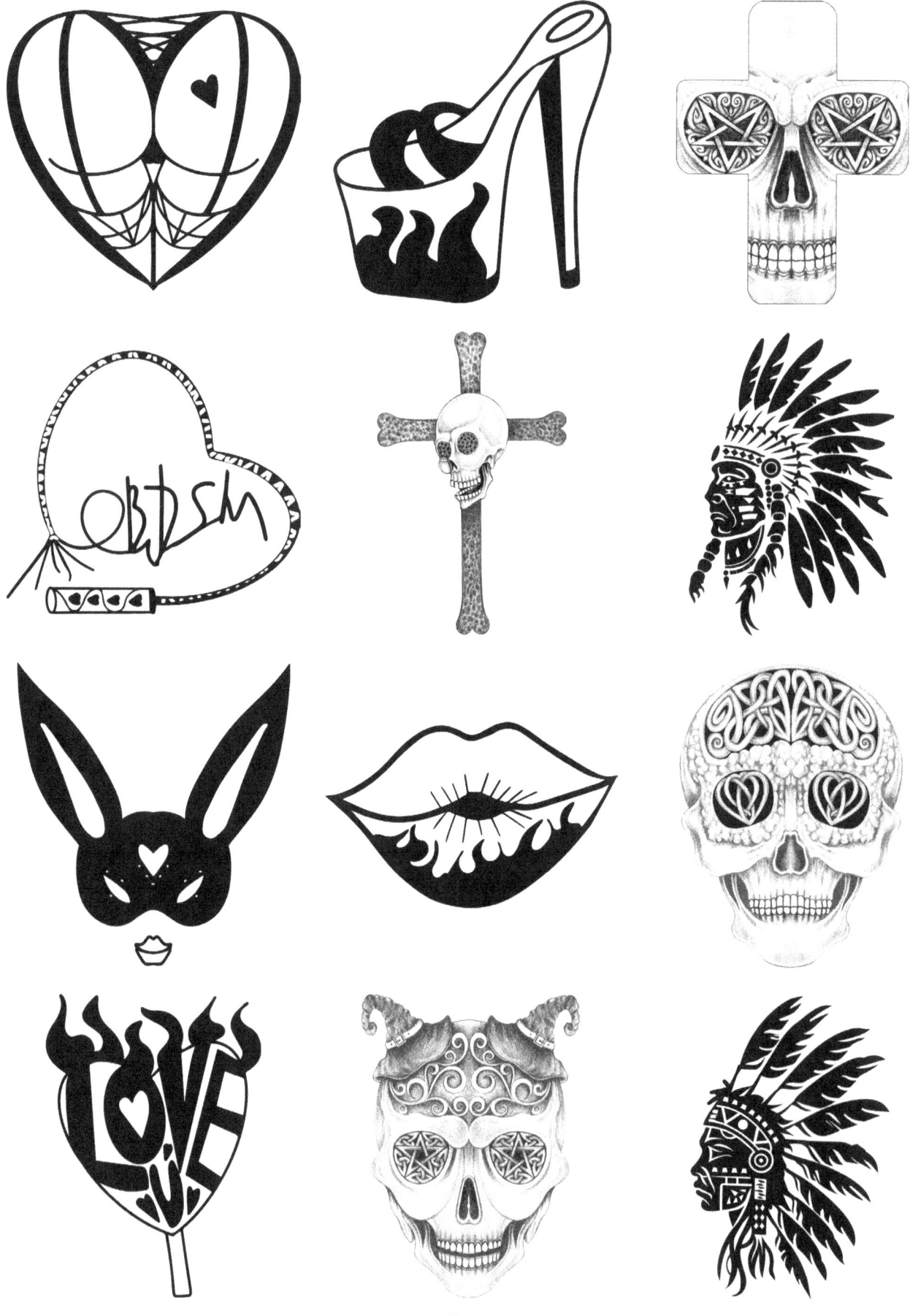

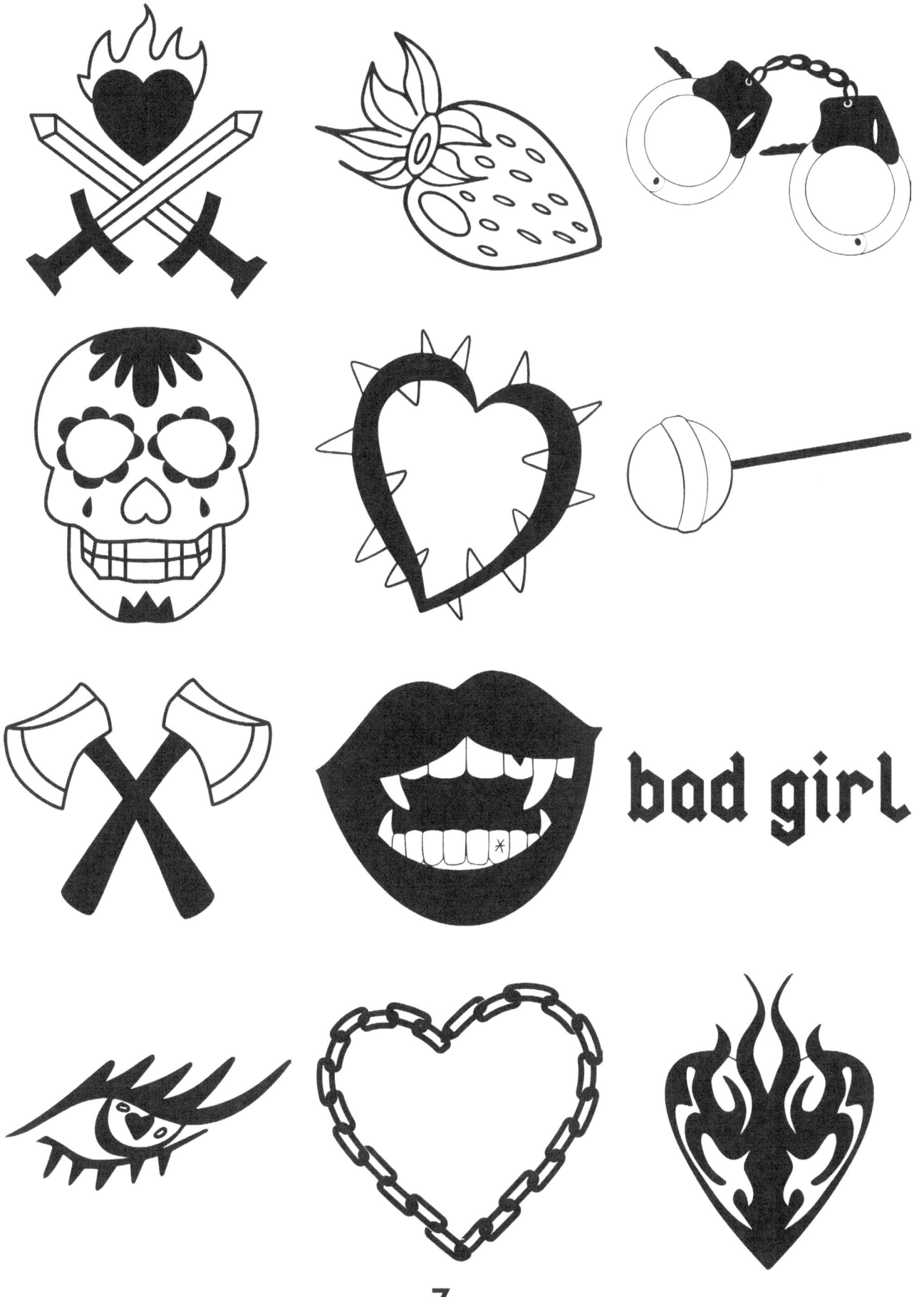

bad girl

7

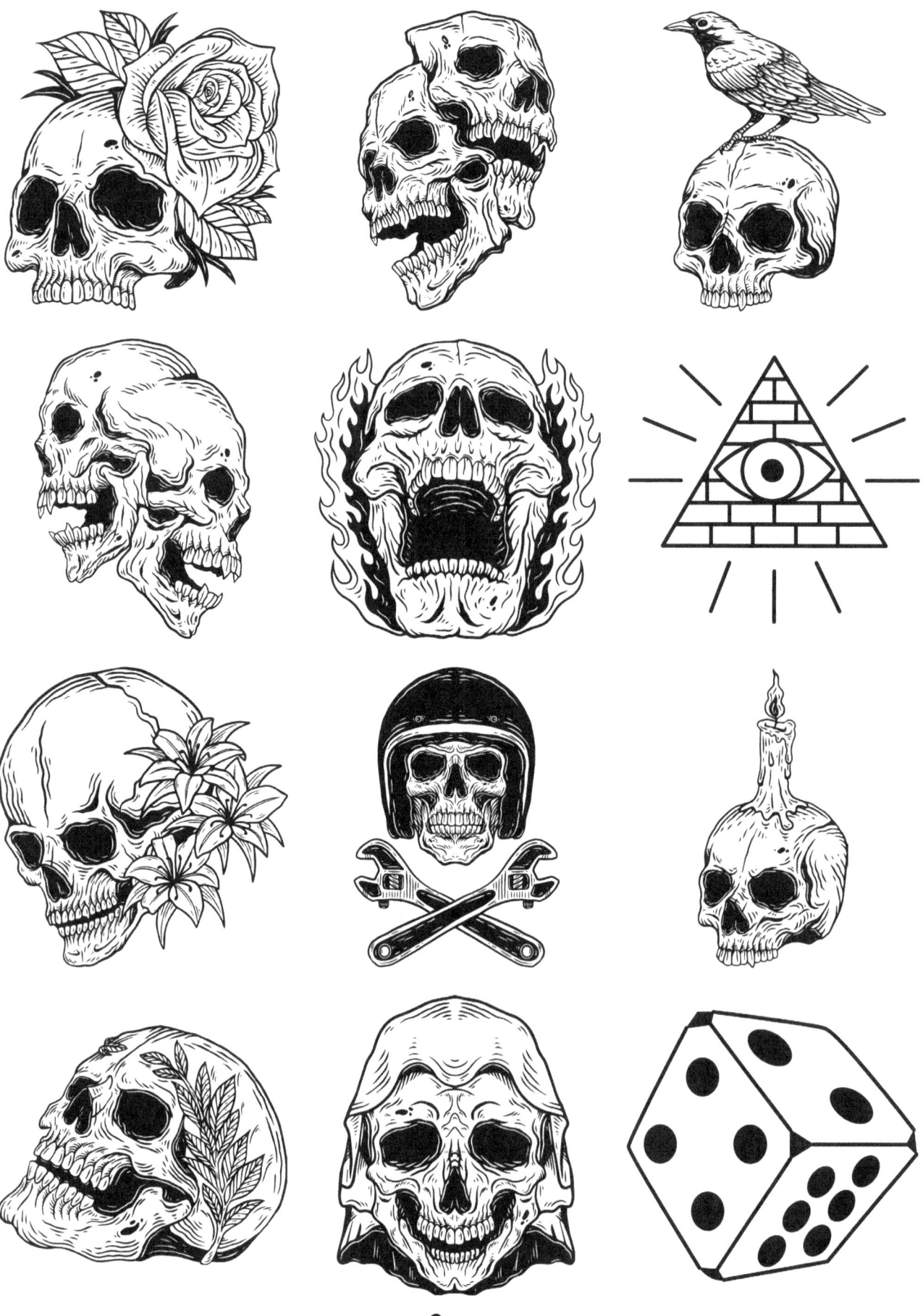

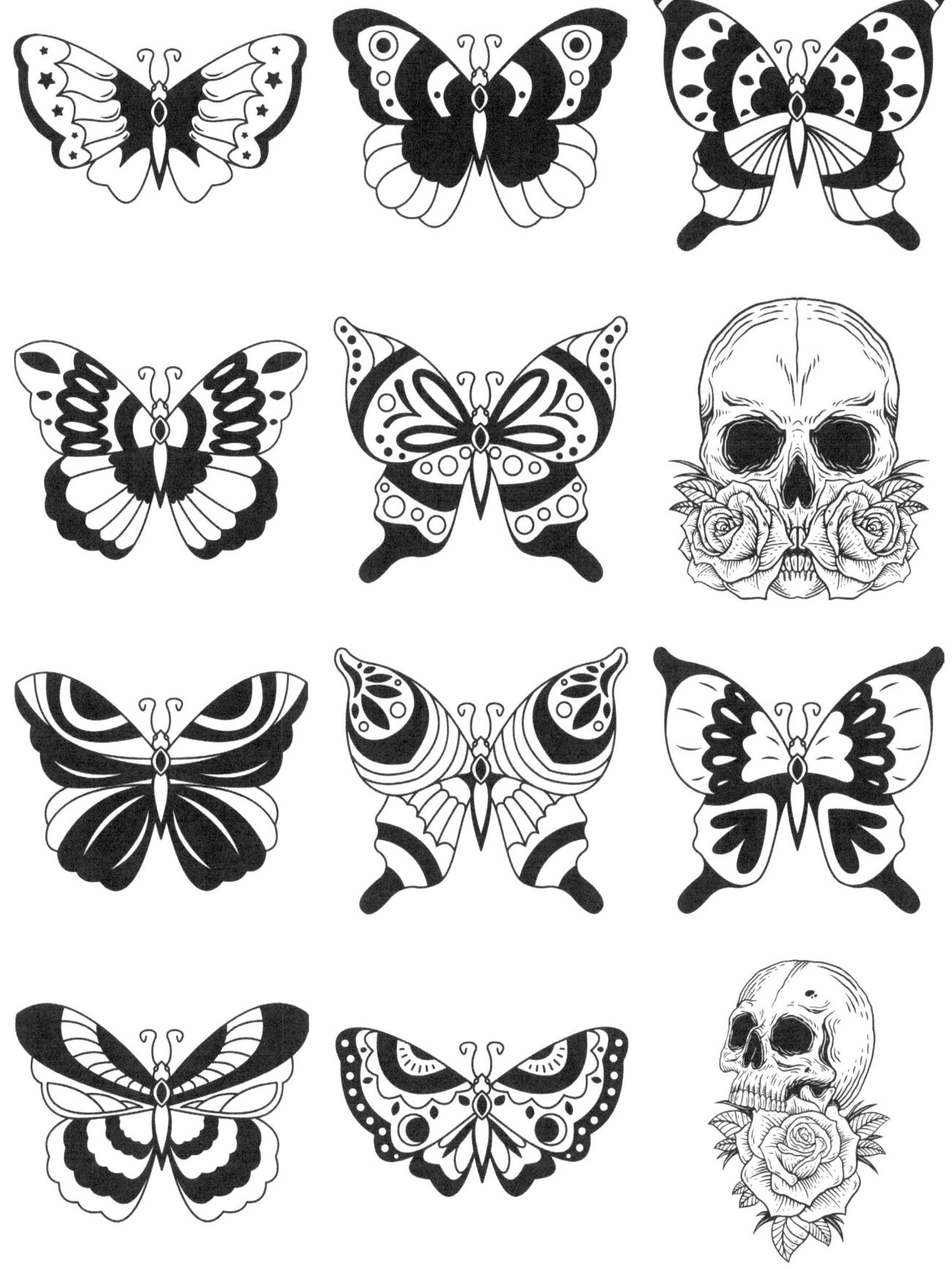

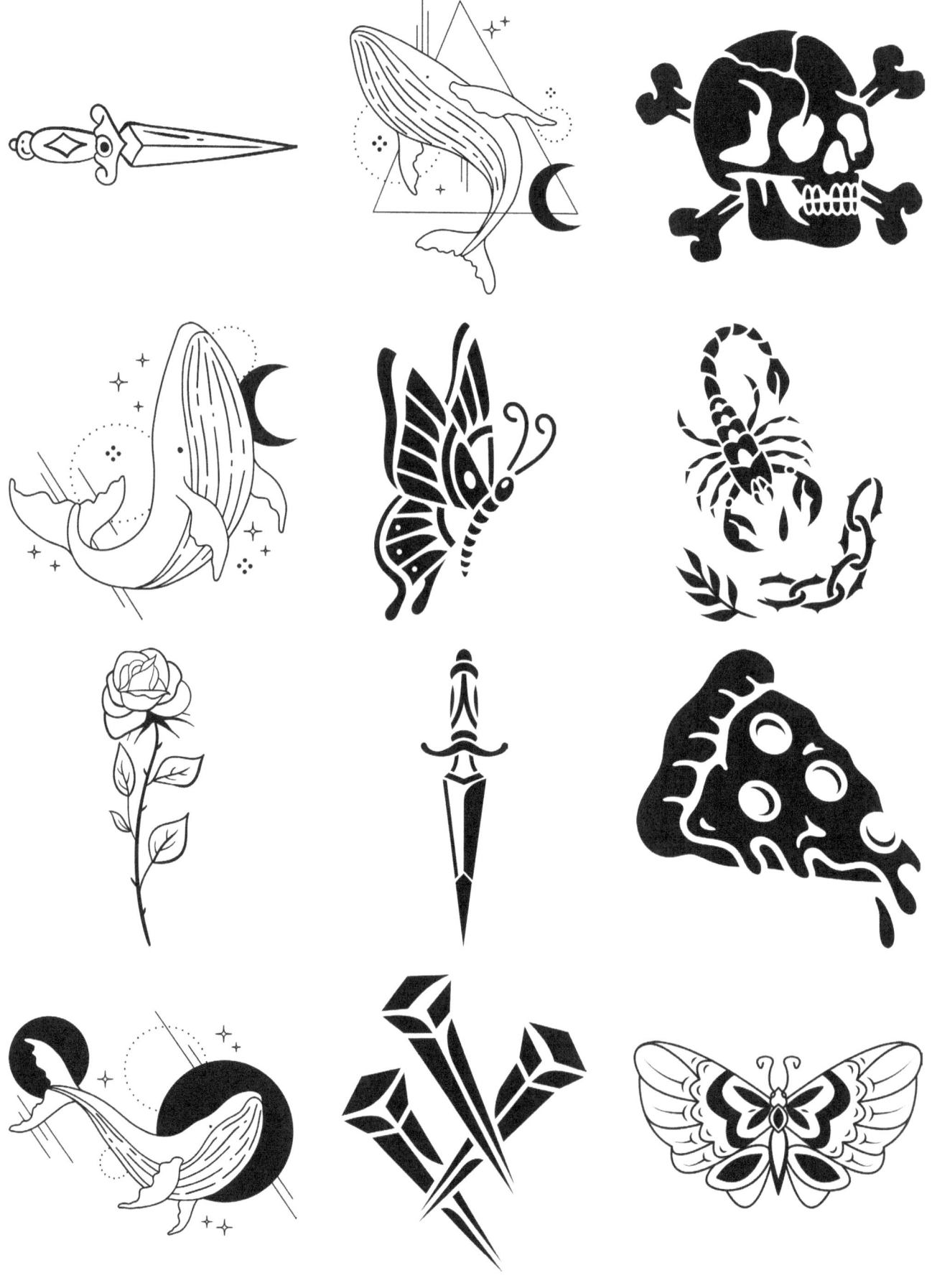

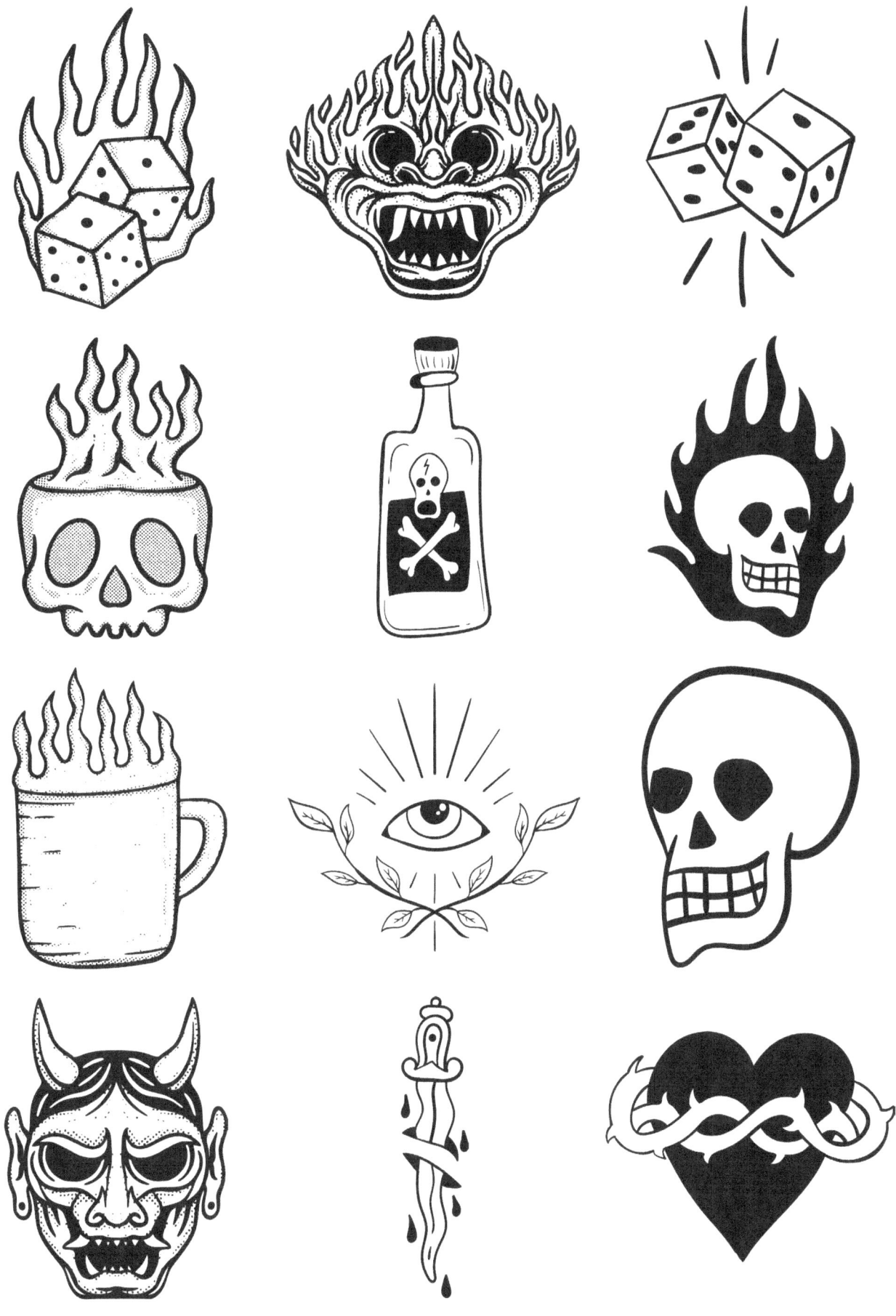

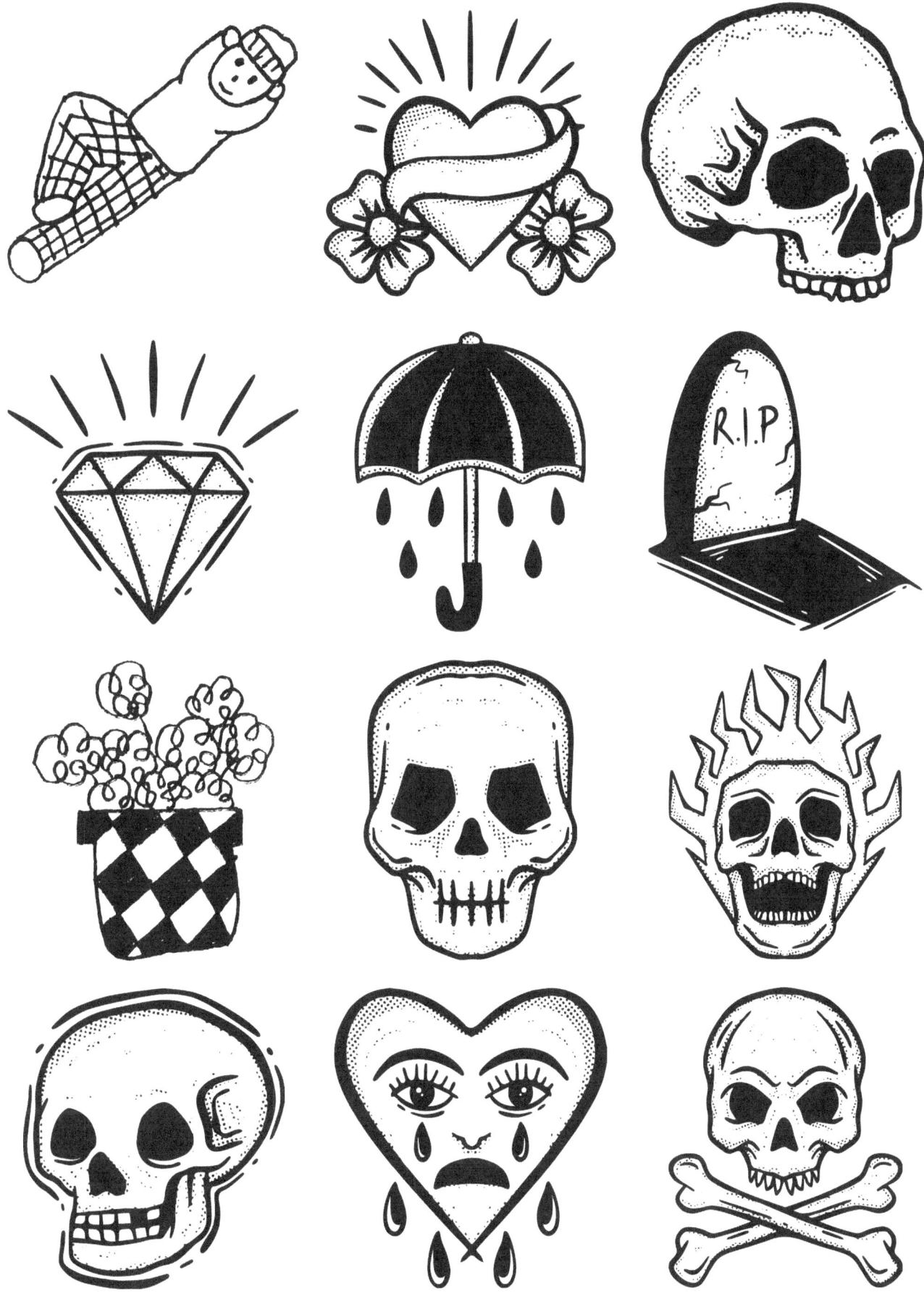

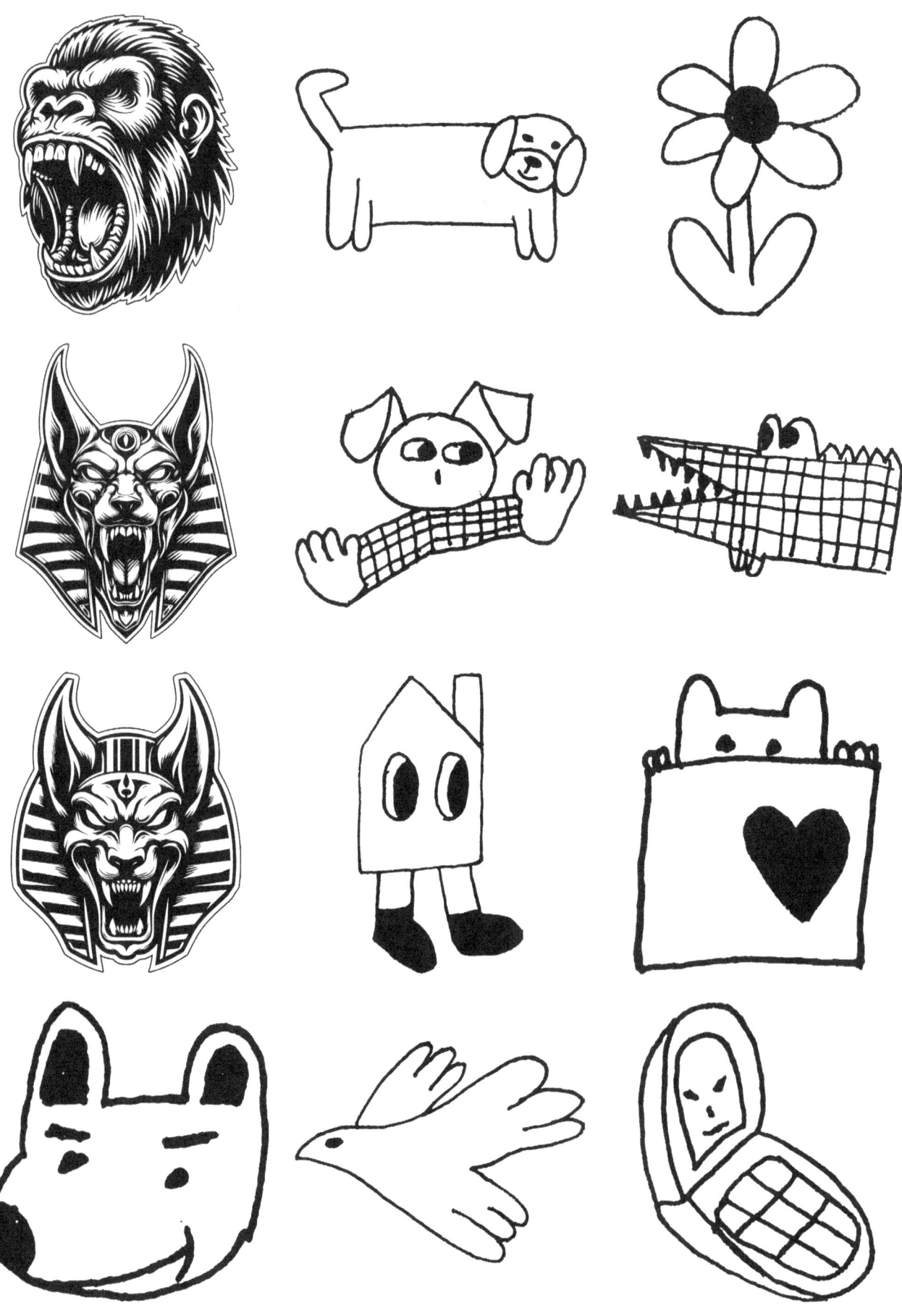

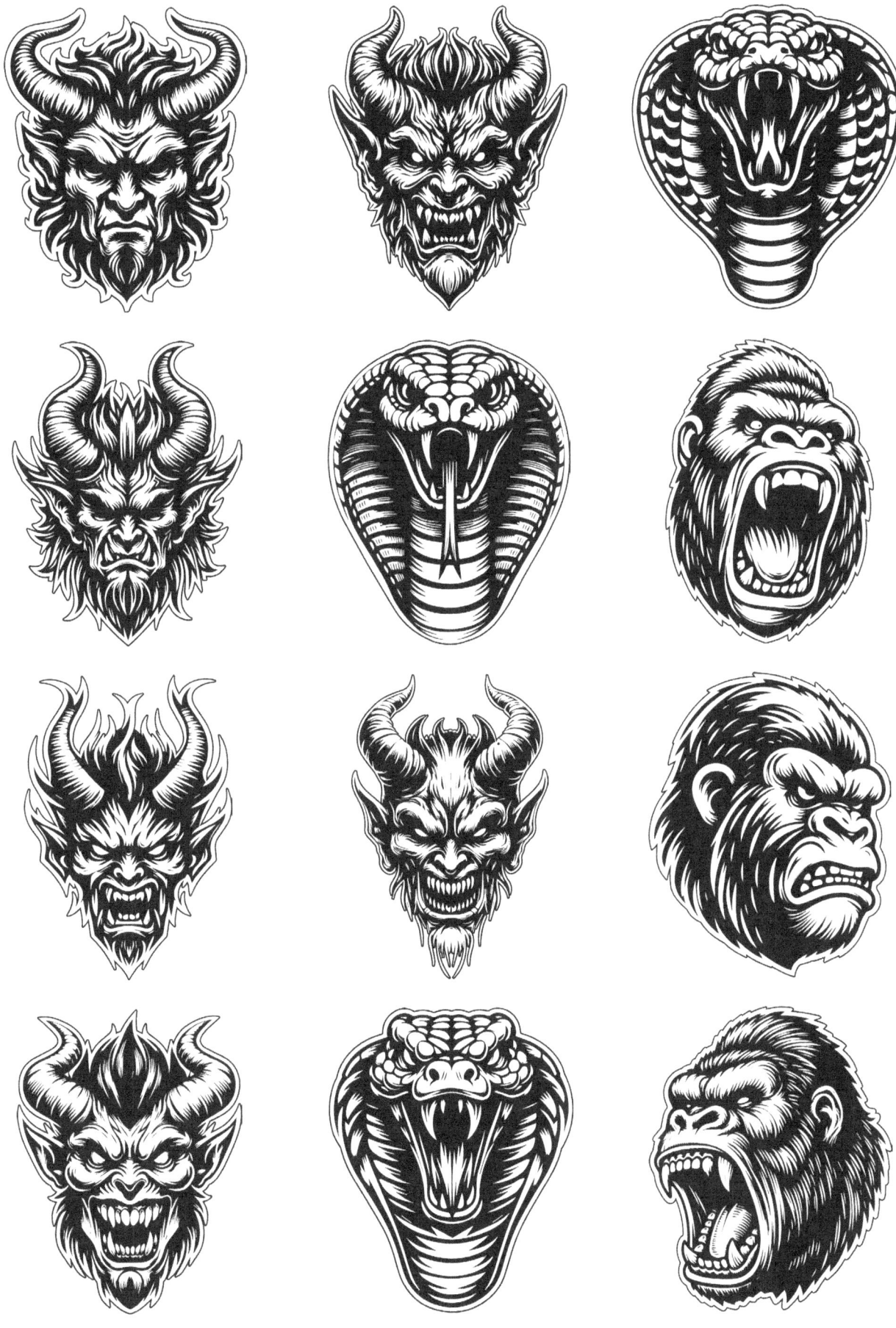

15

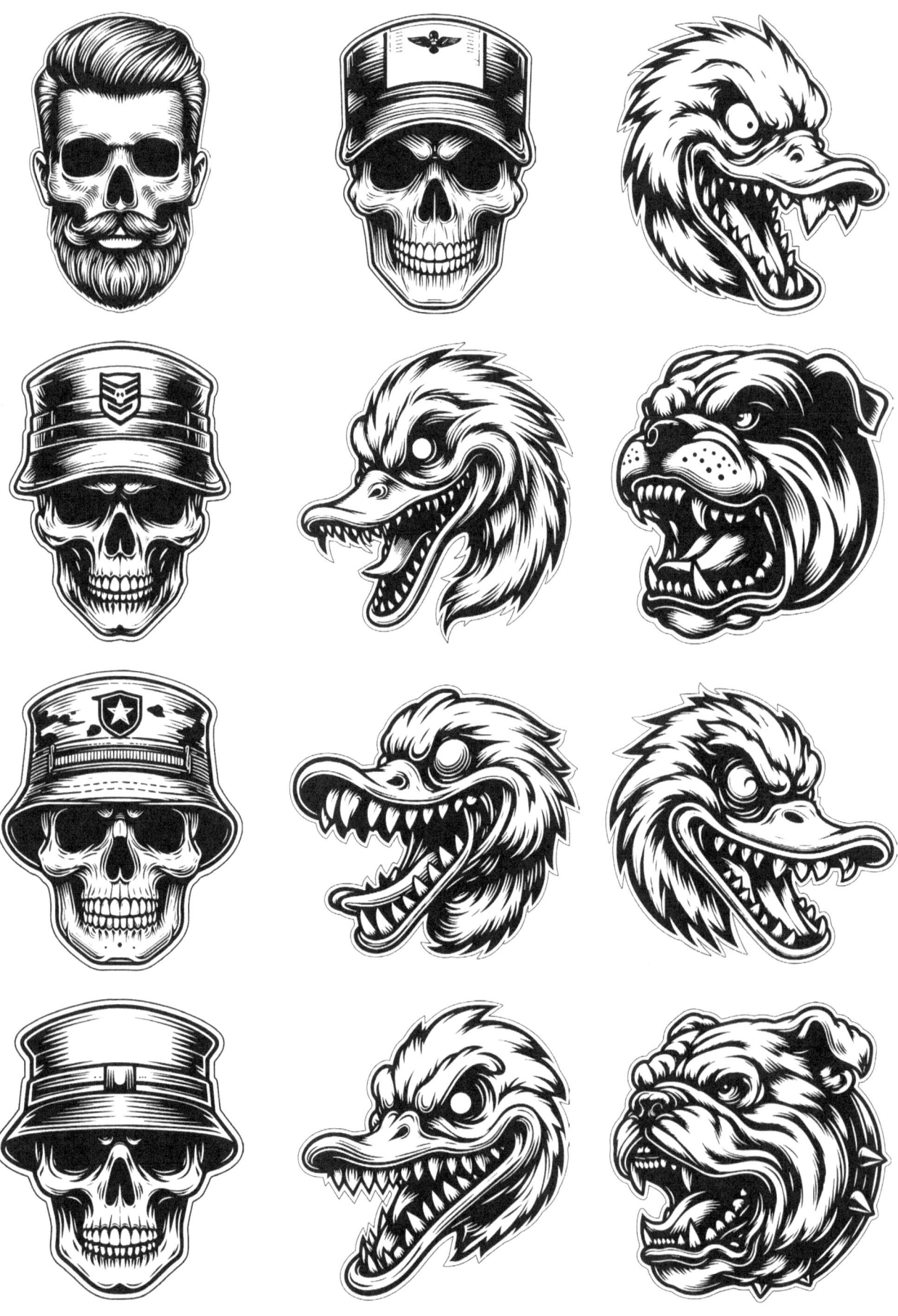

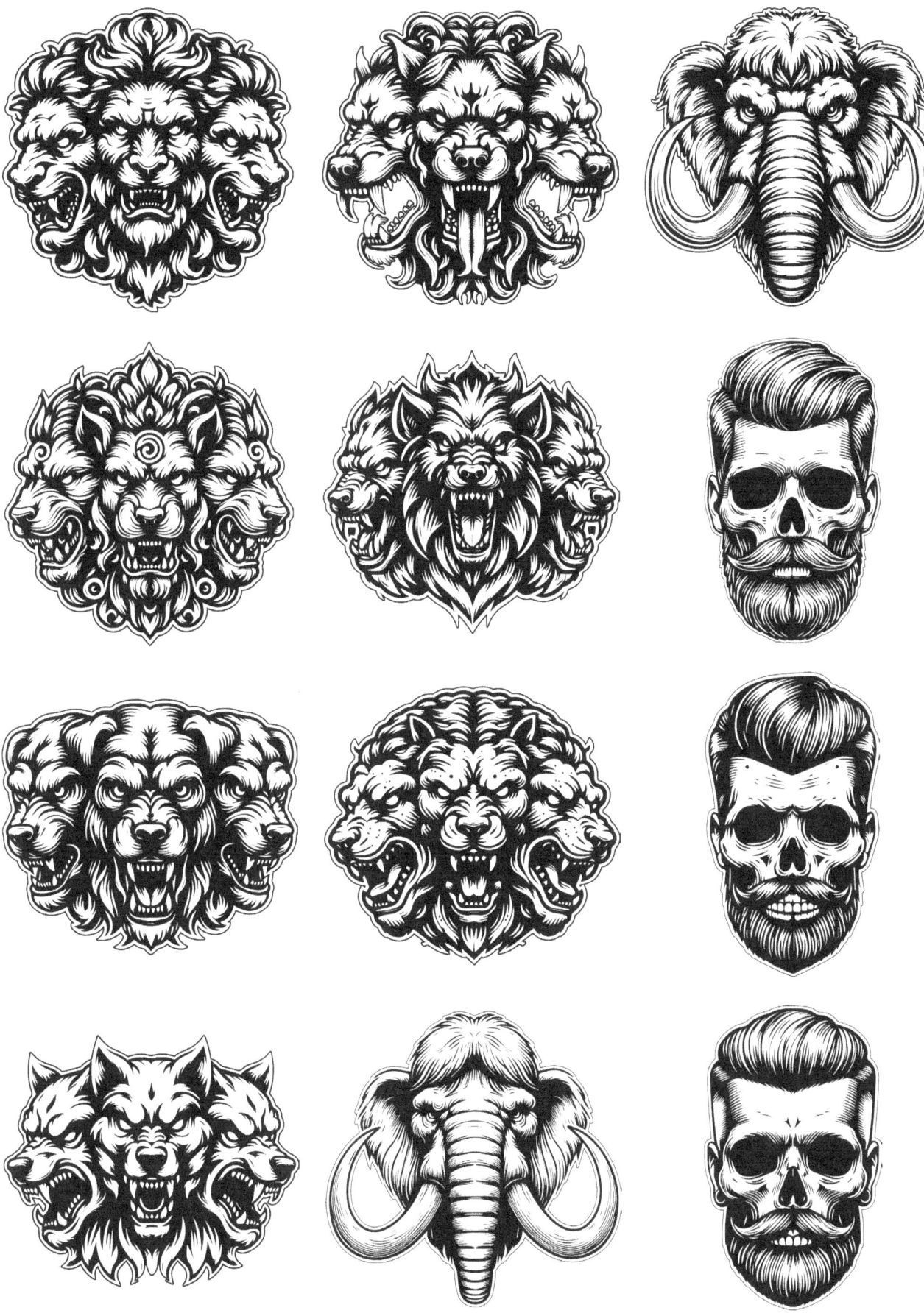

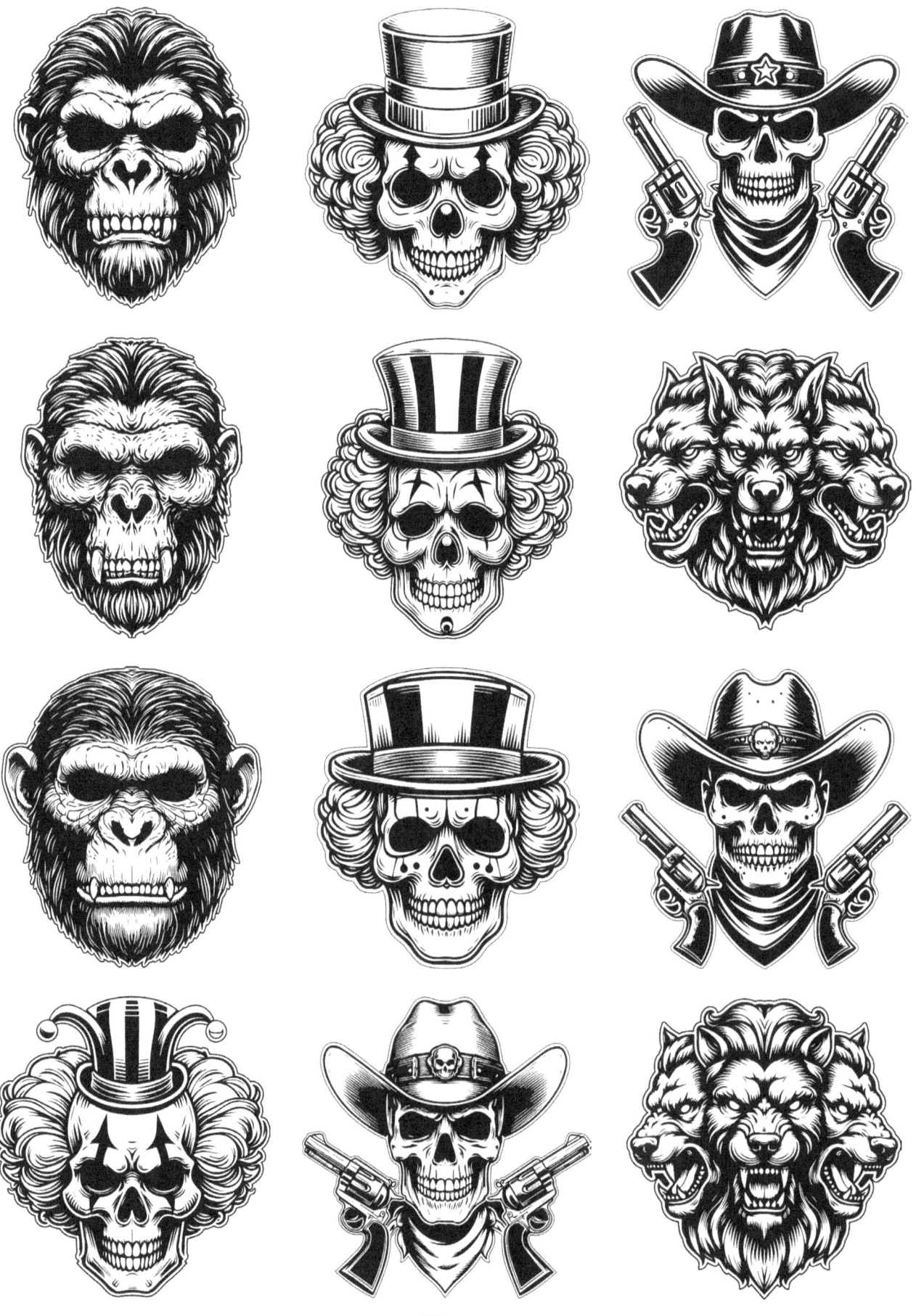

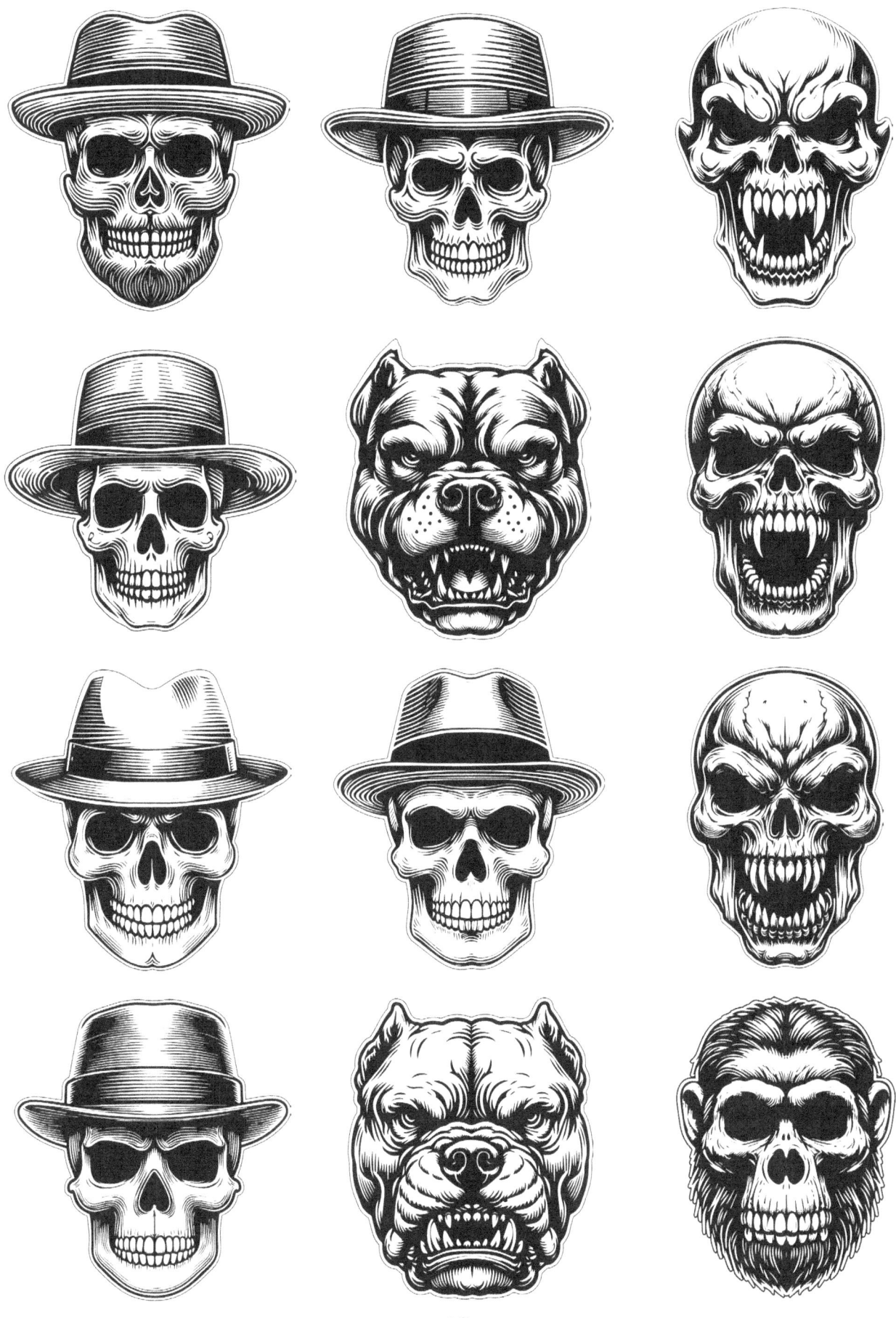

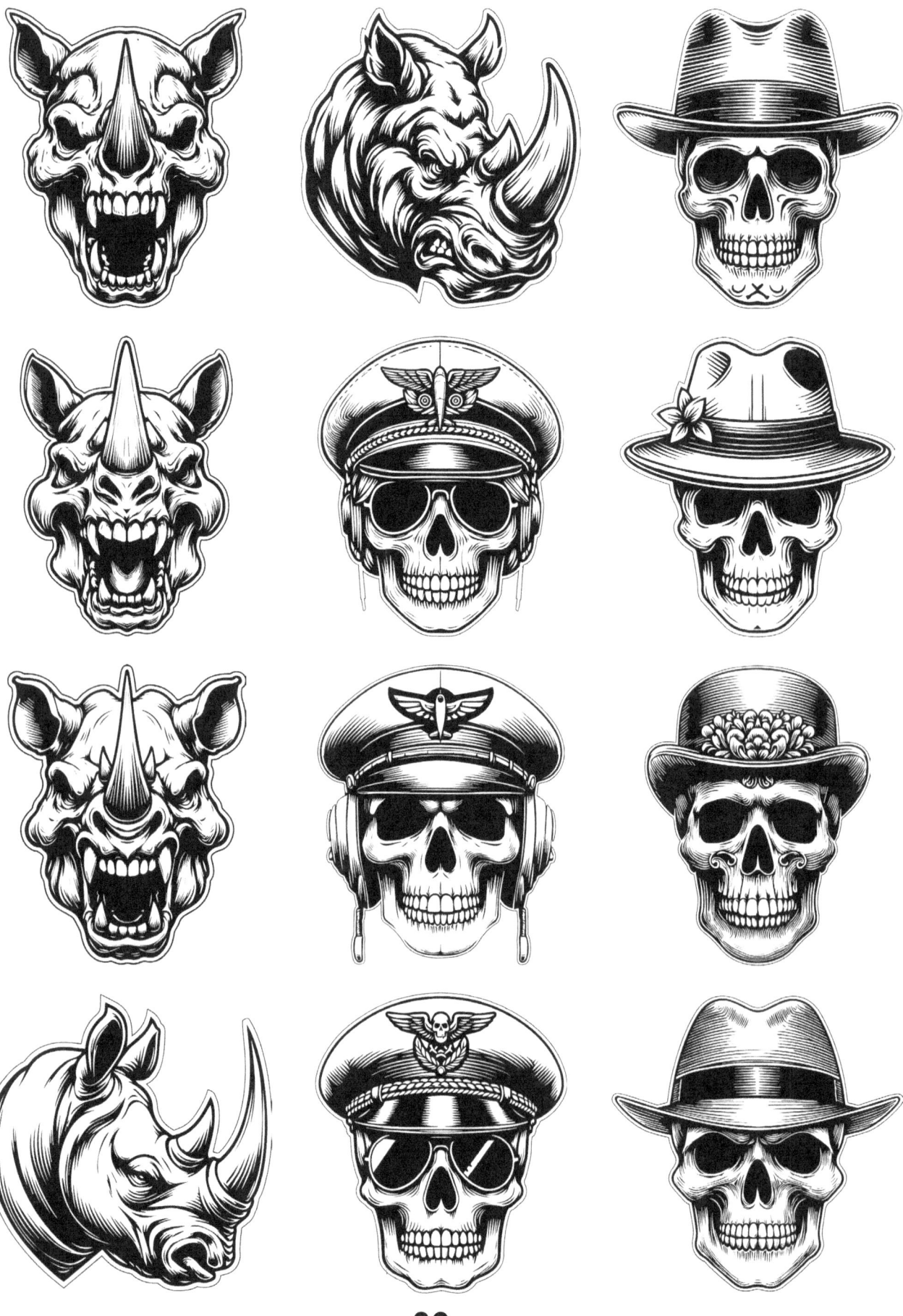

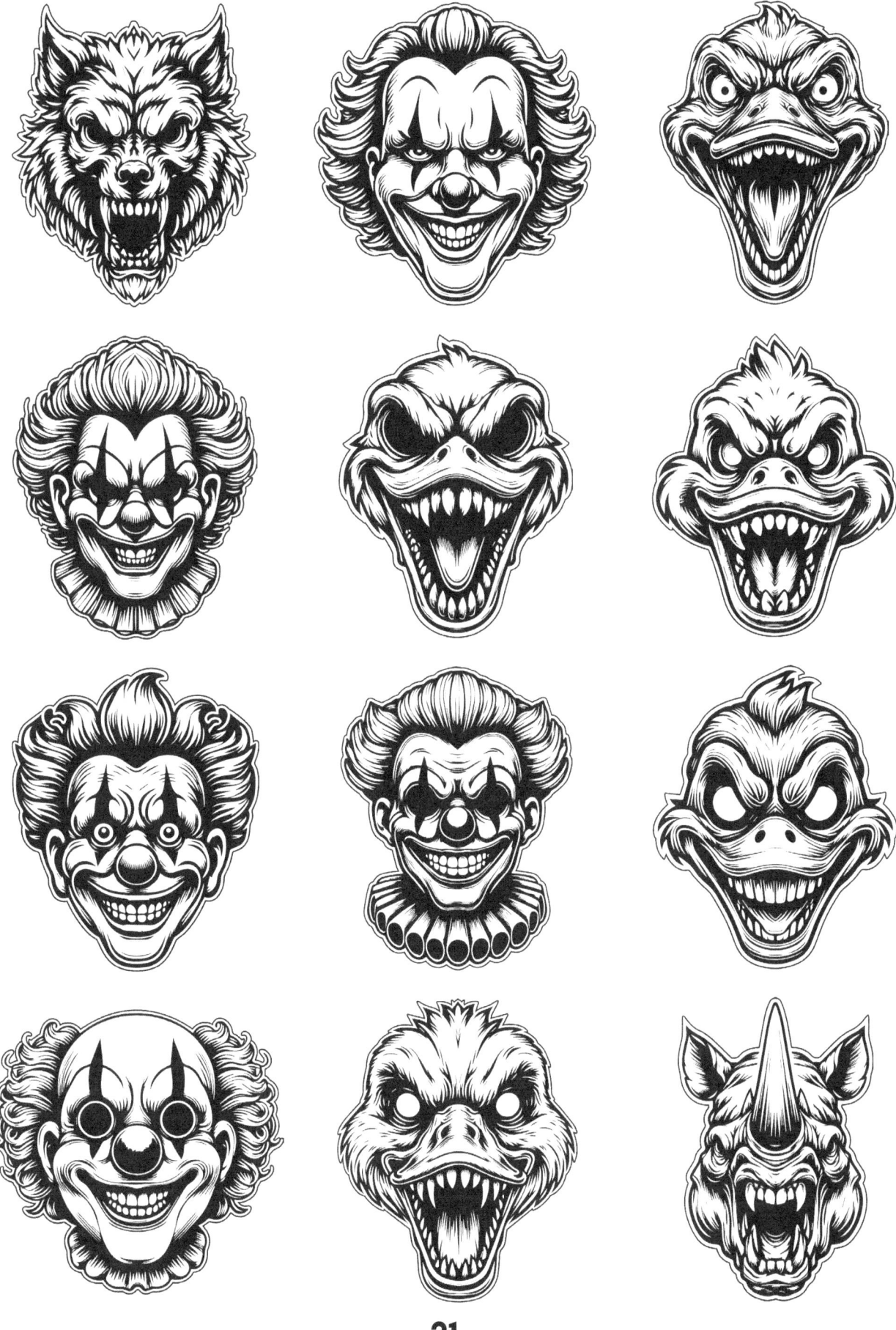

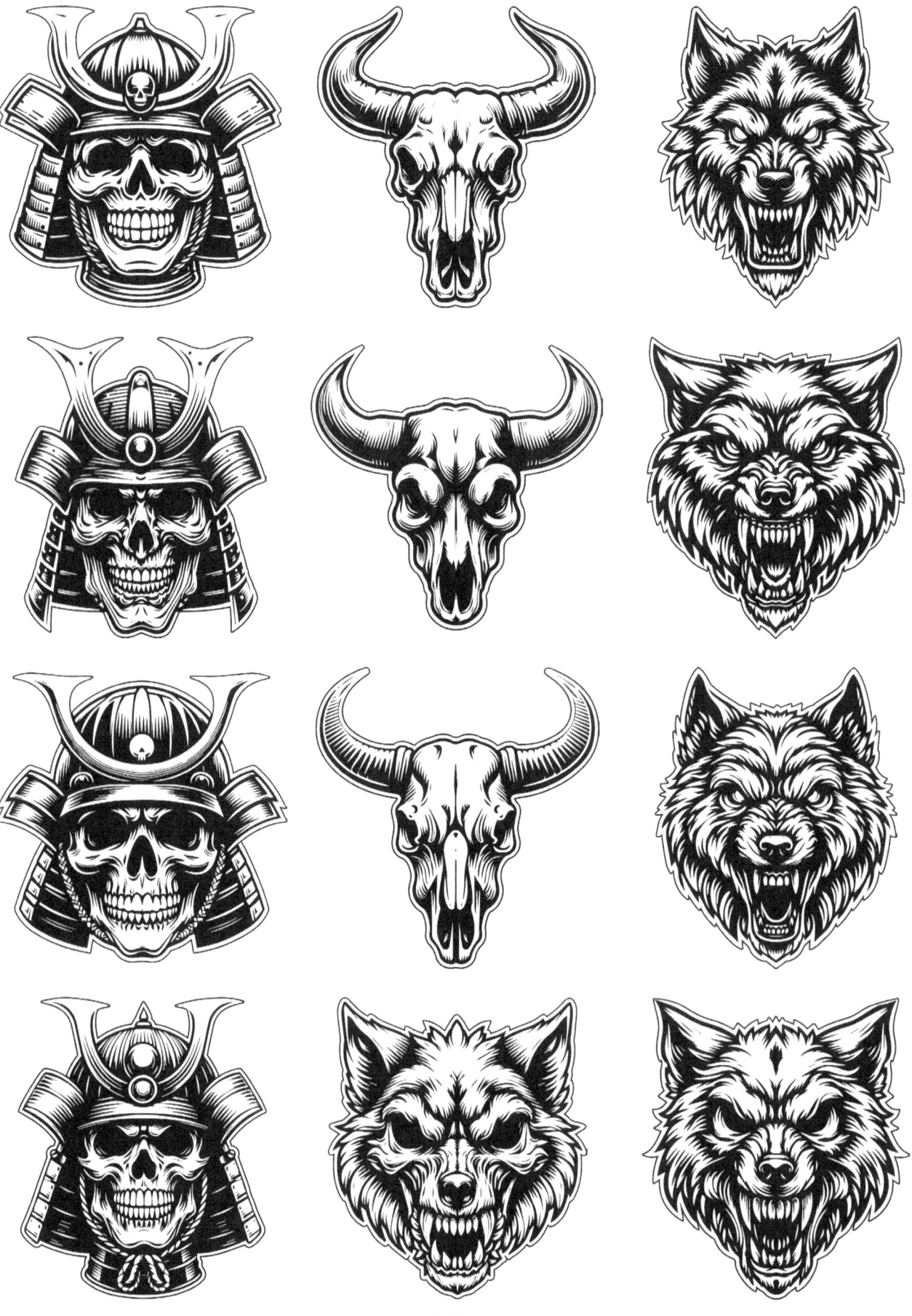

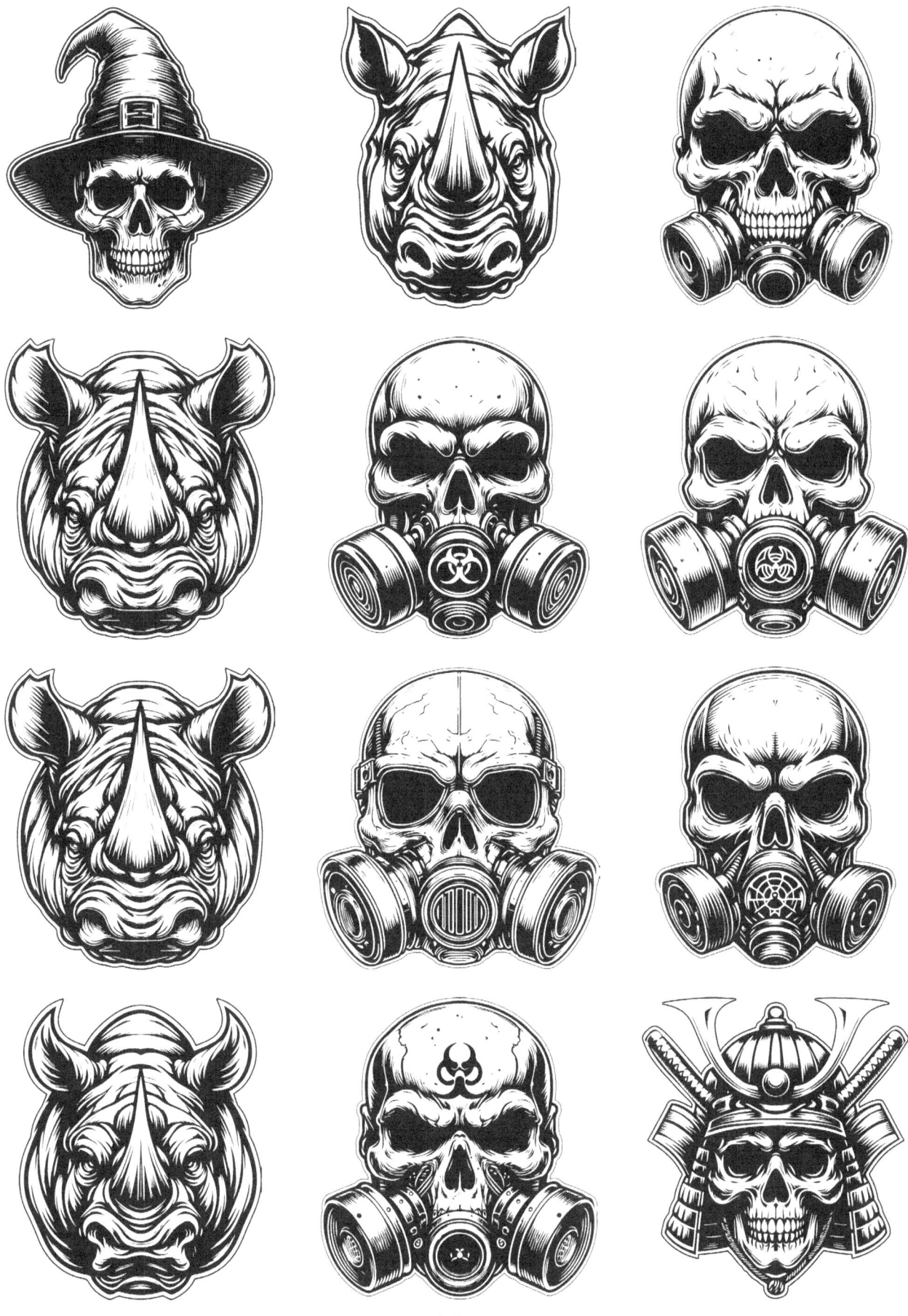

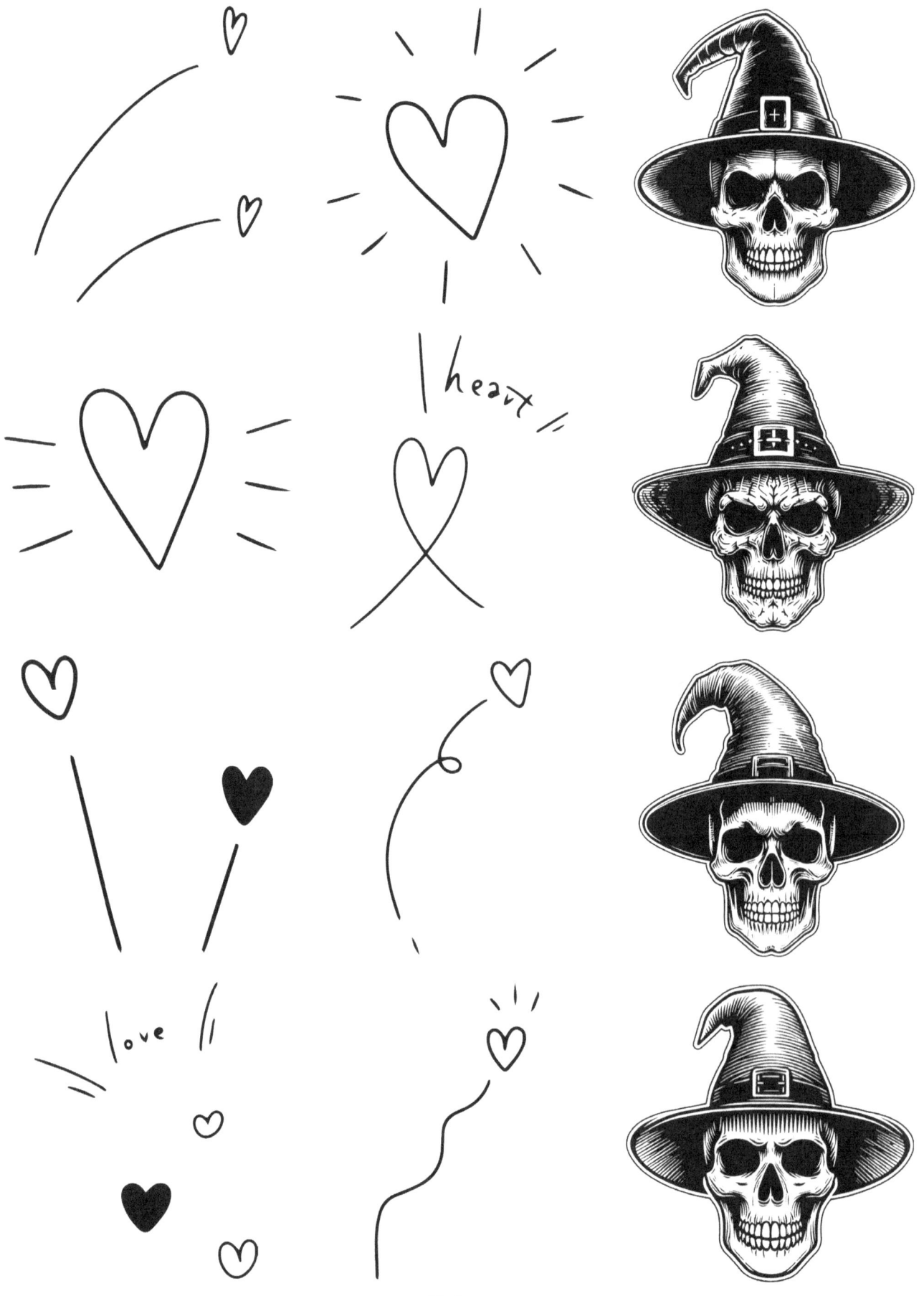

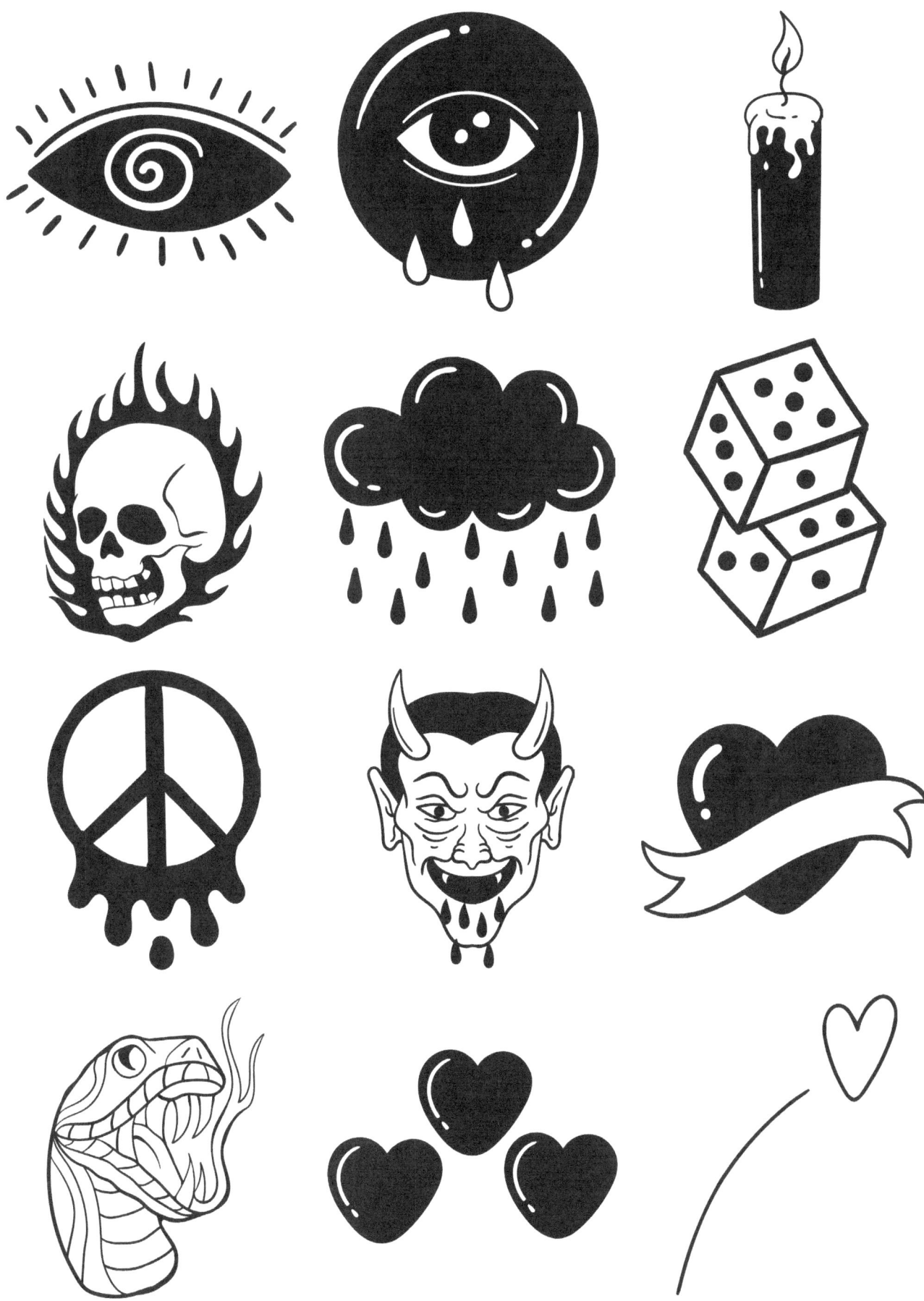

Alone

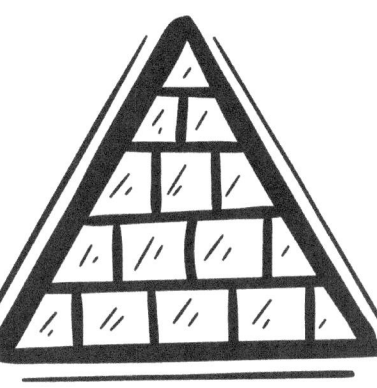

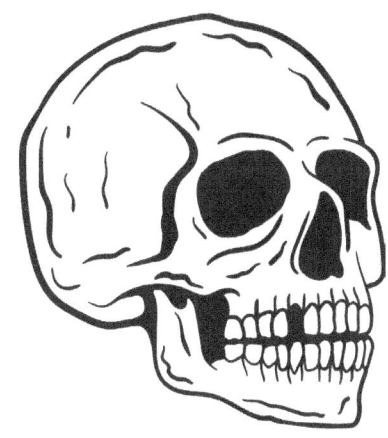

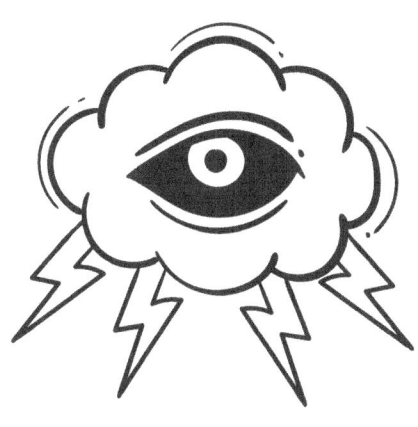

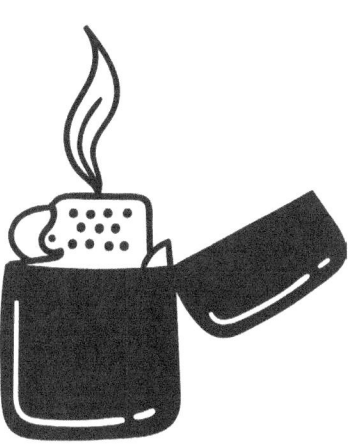

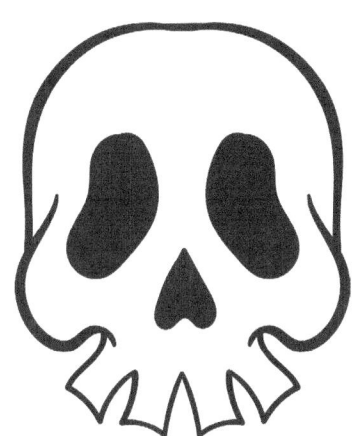

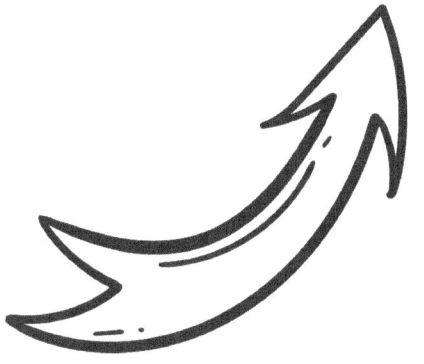

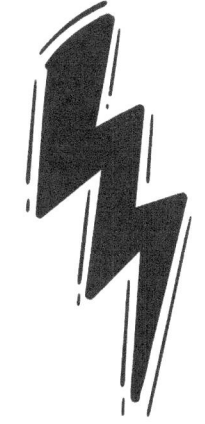

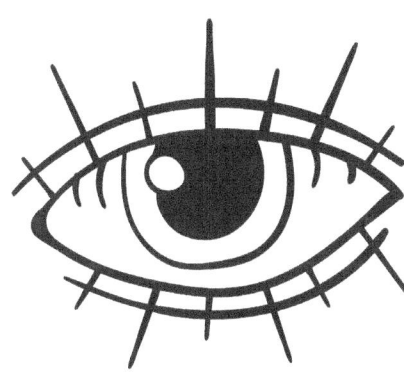

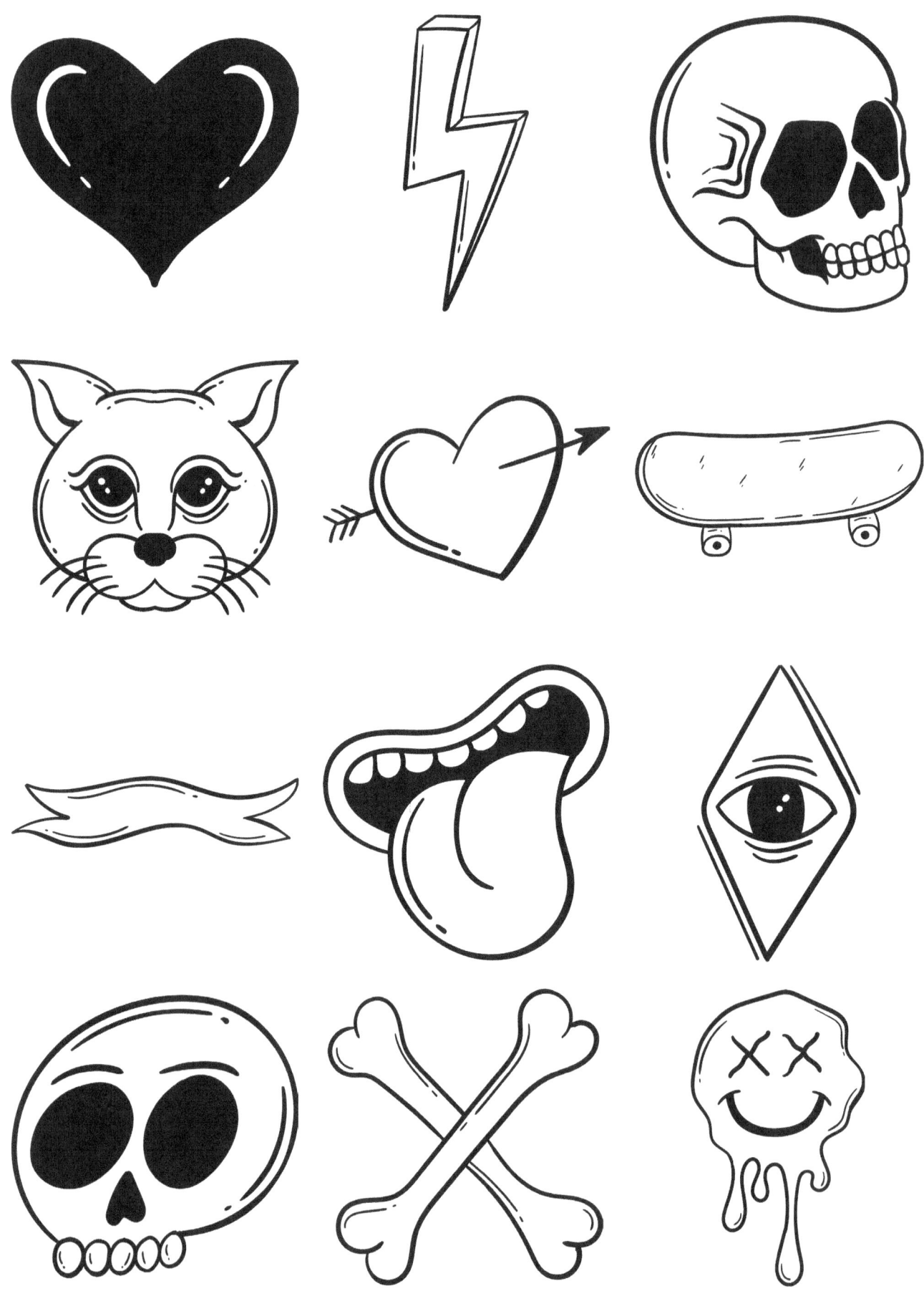

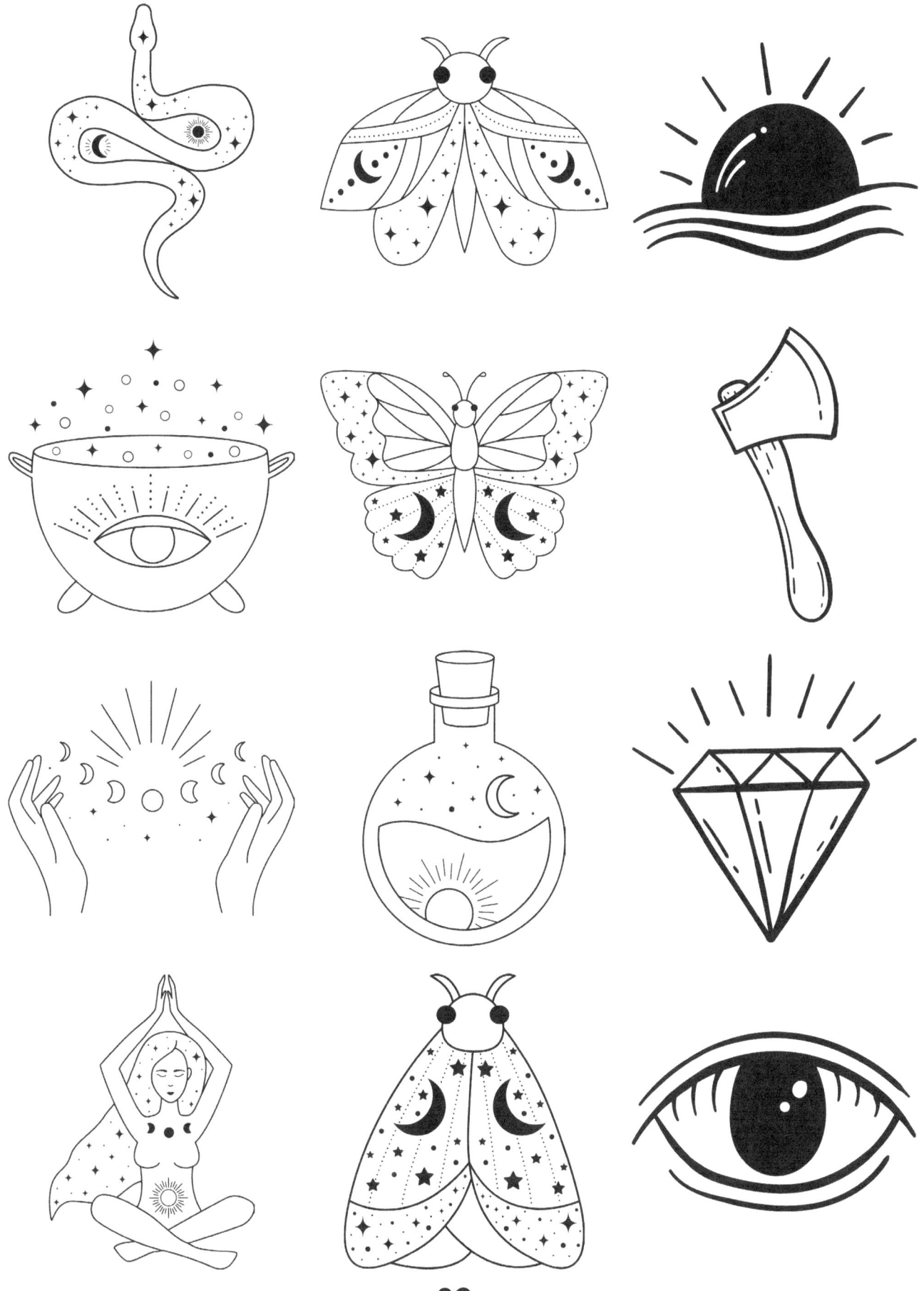

29

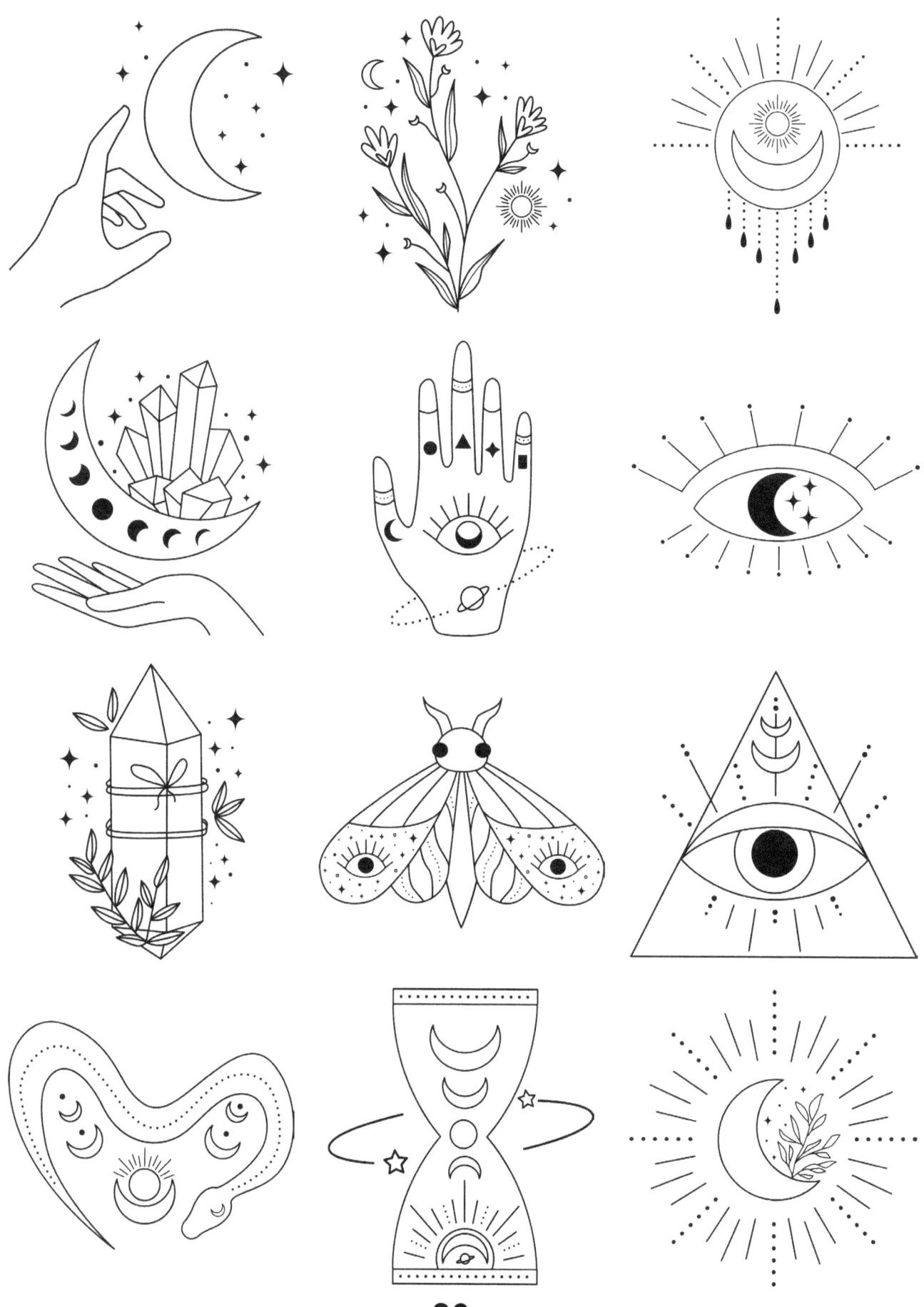

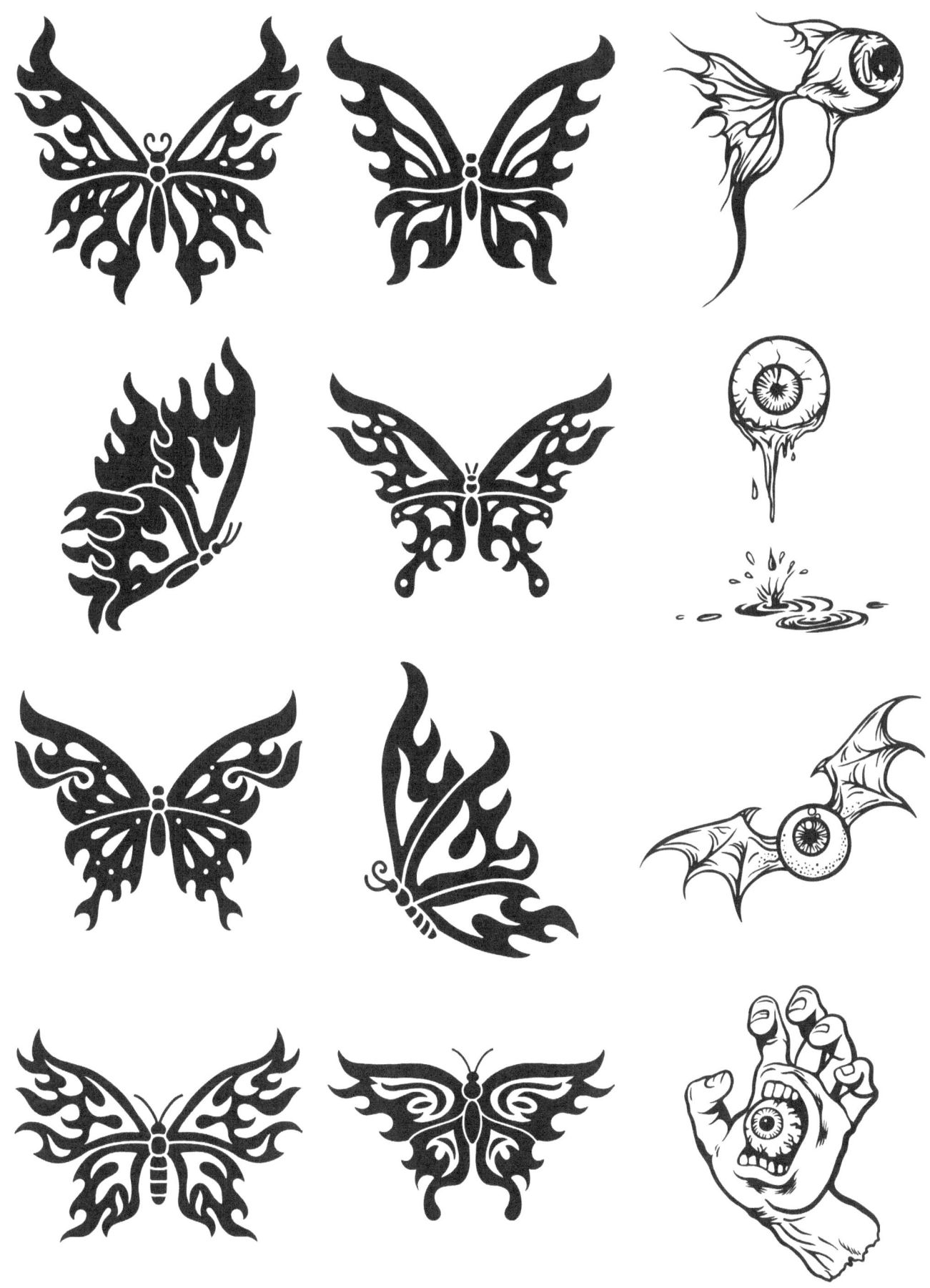

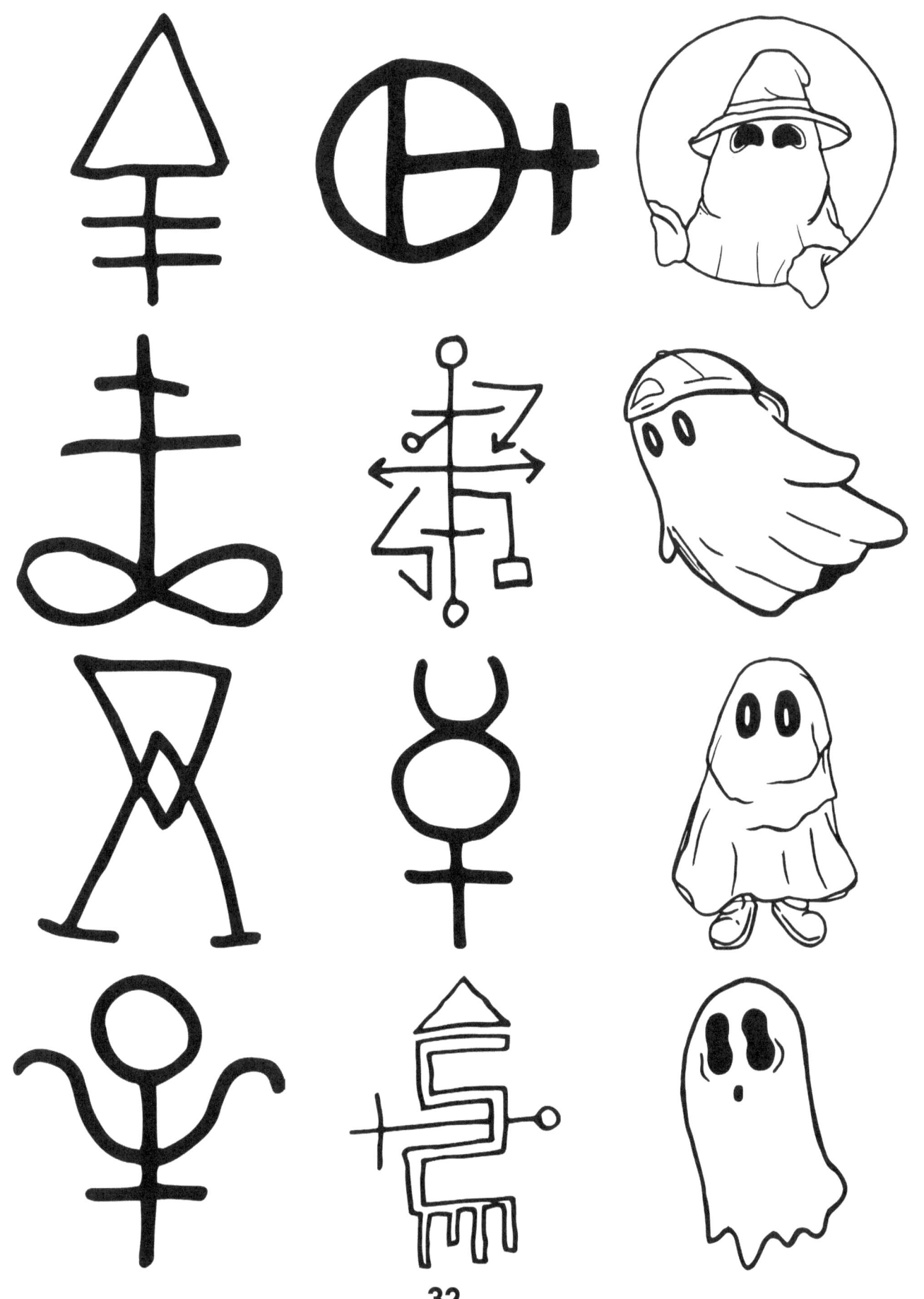

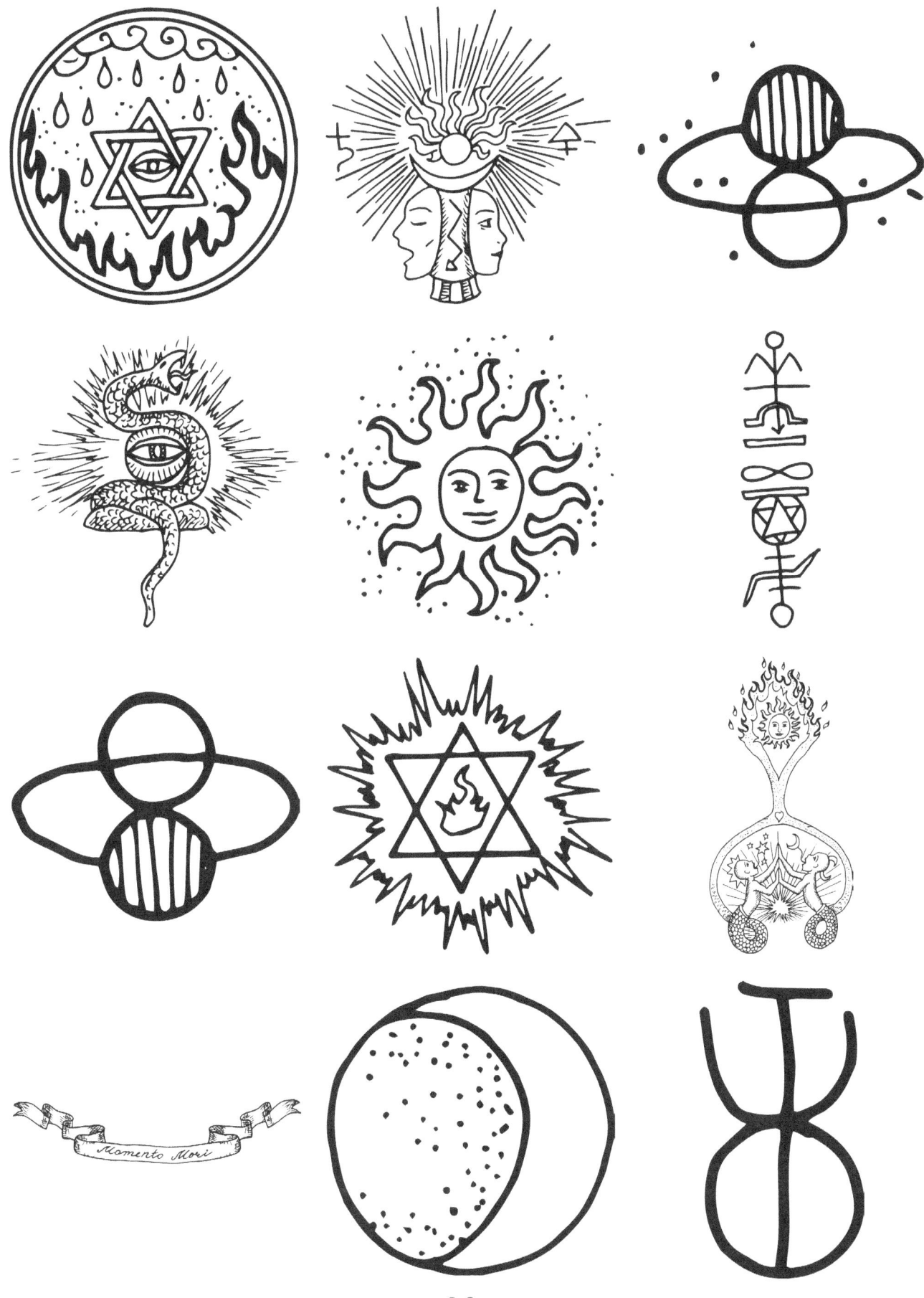

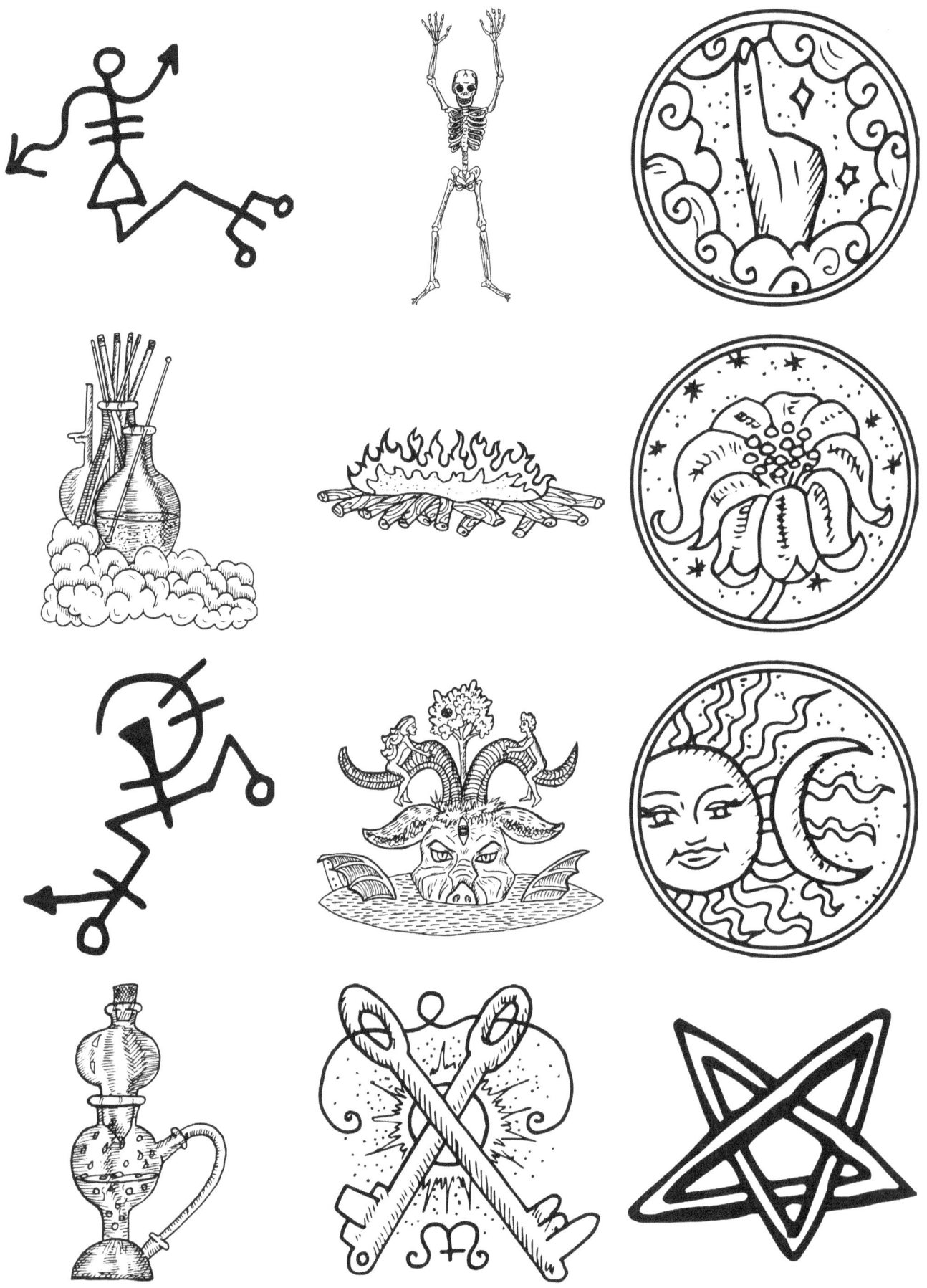

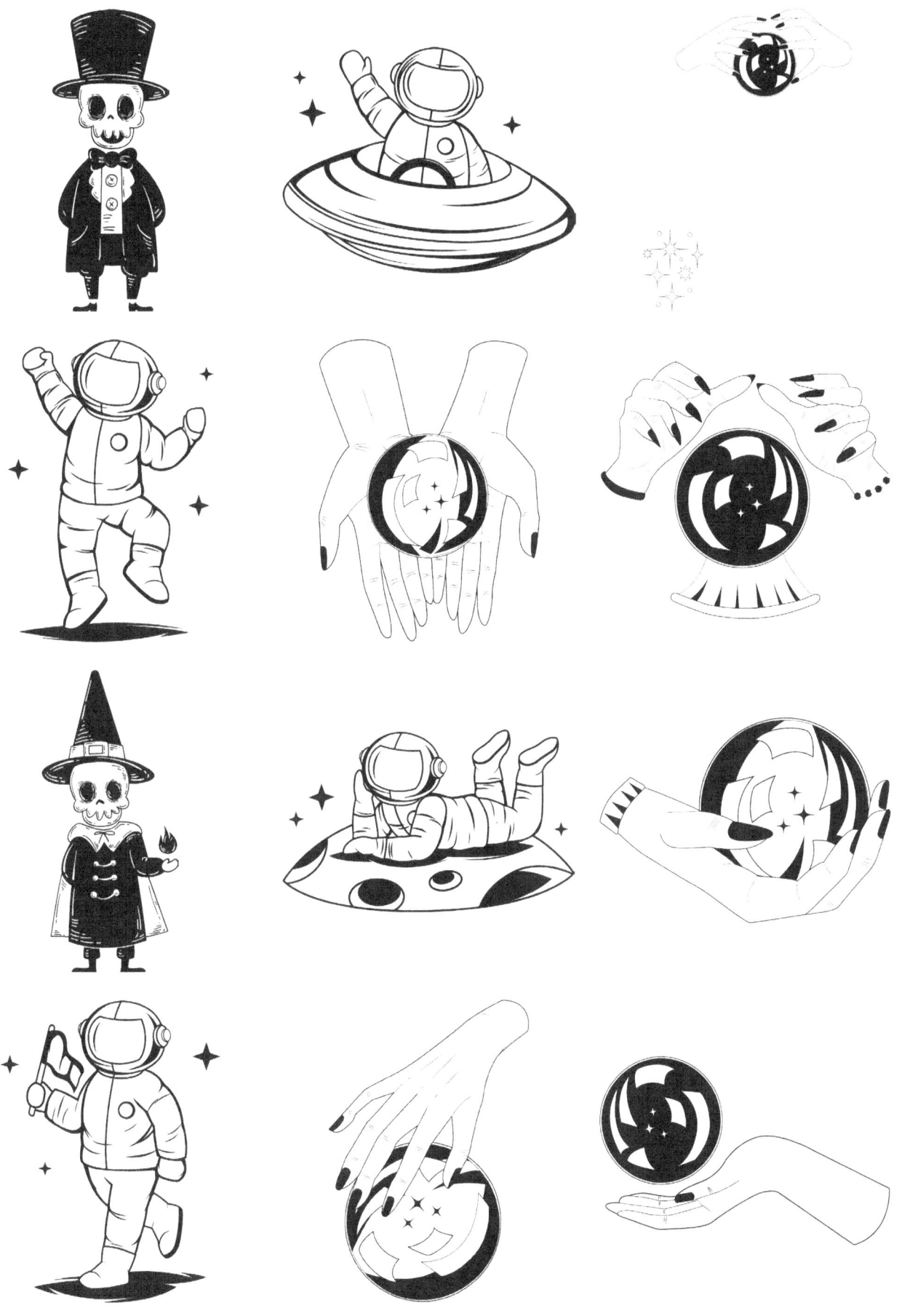

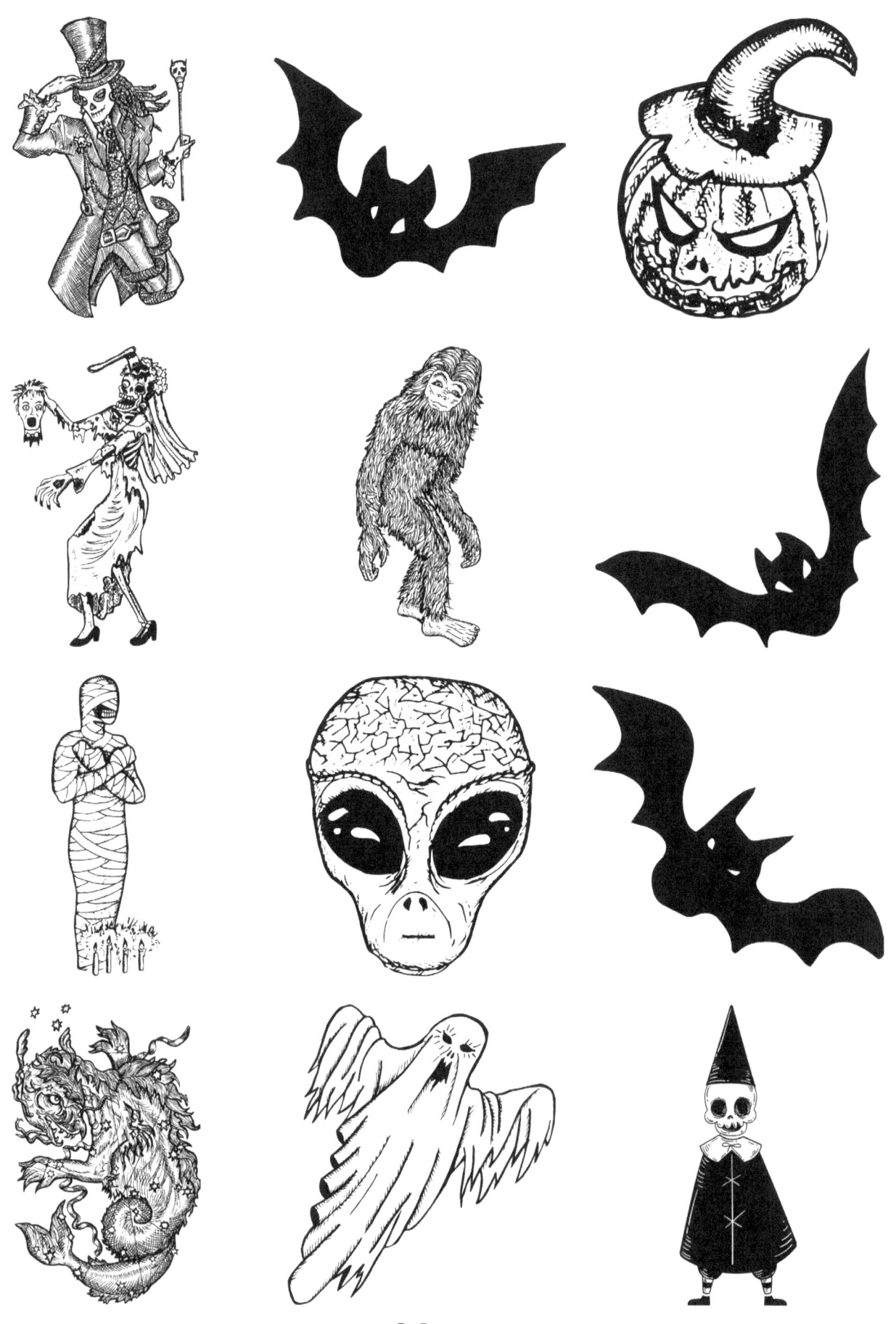

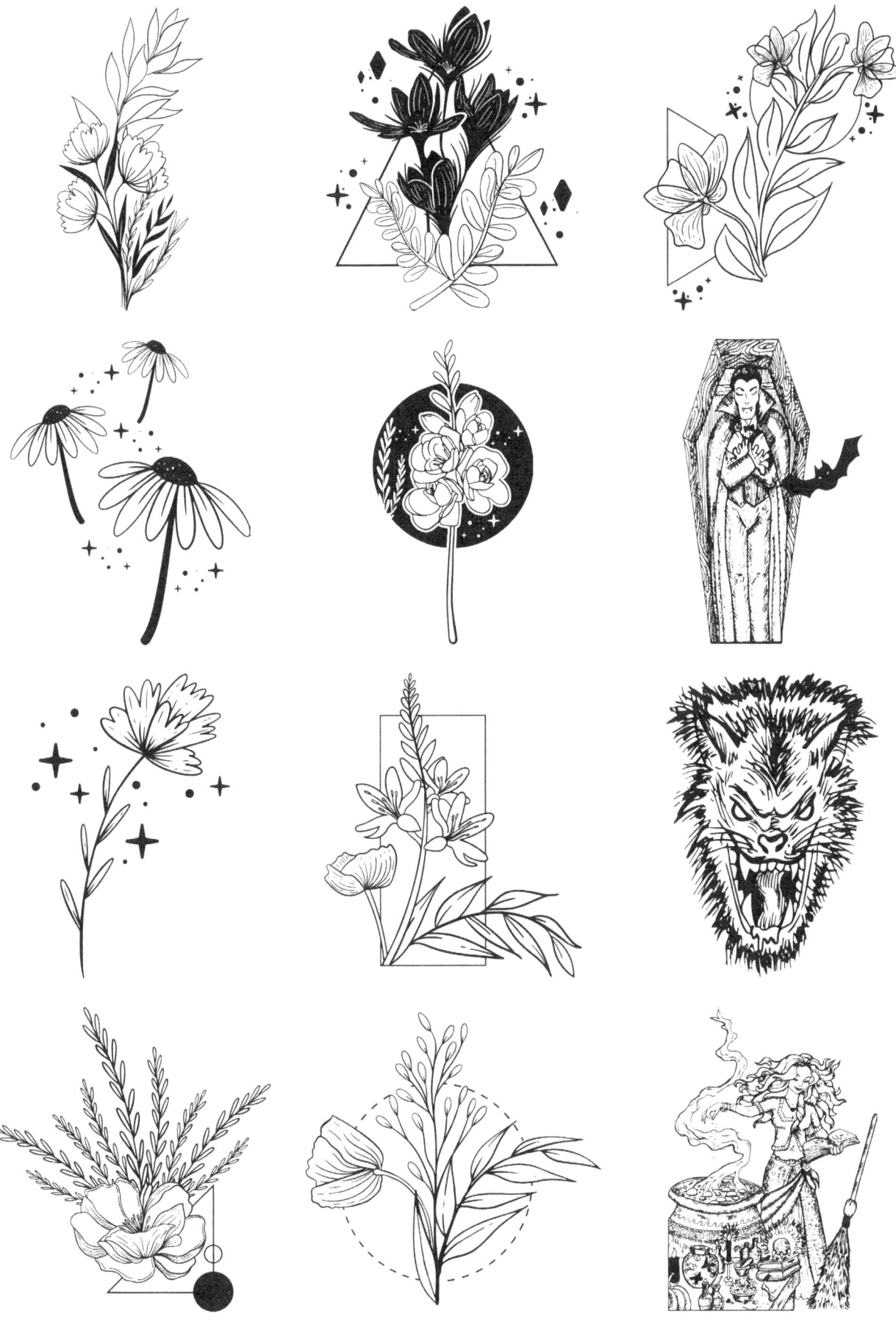

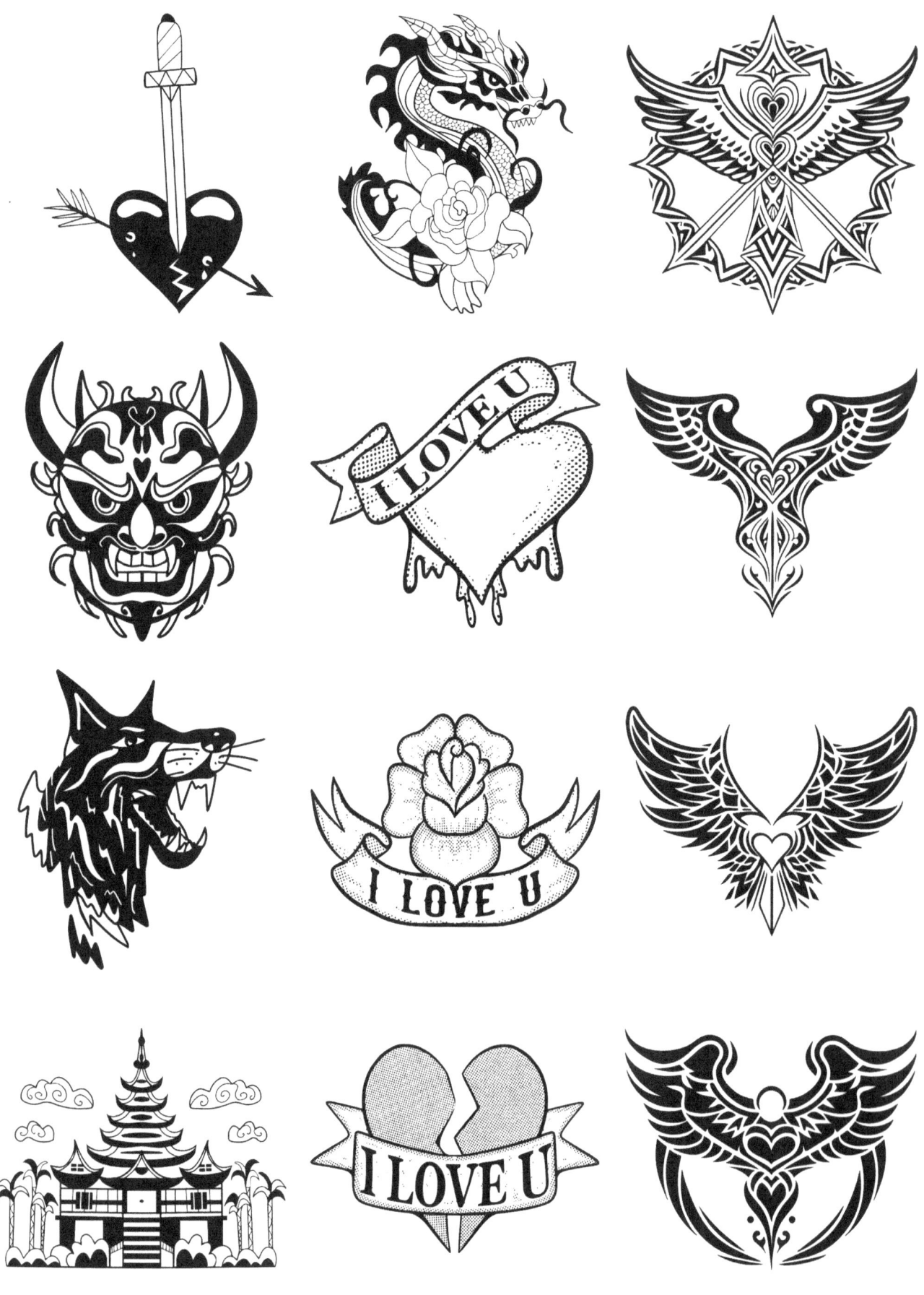

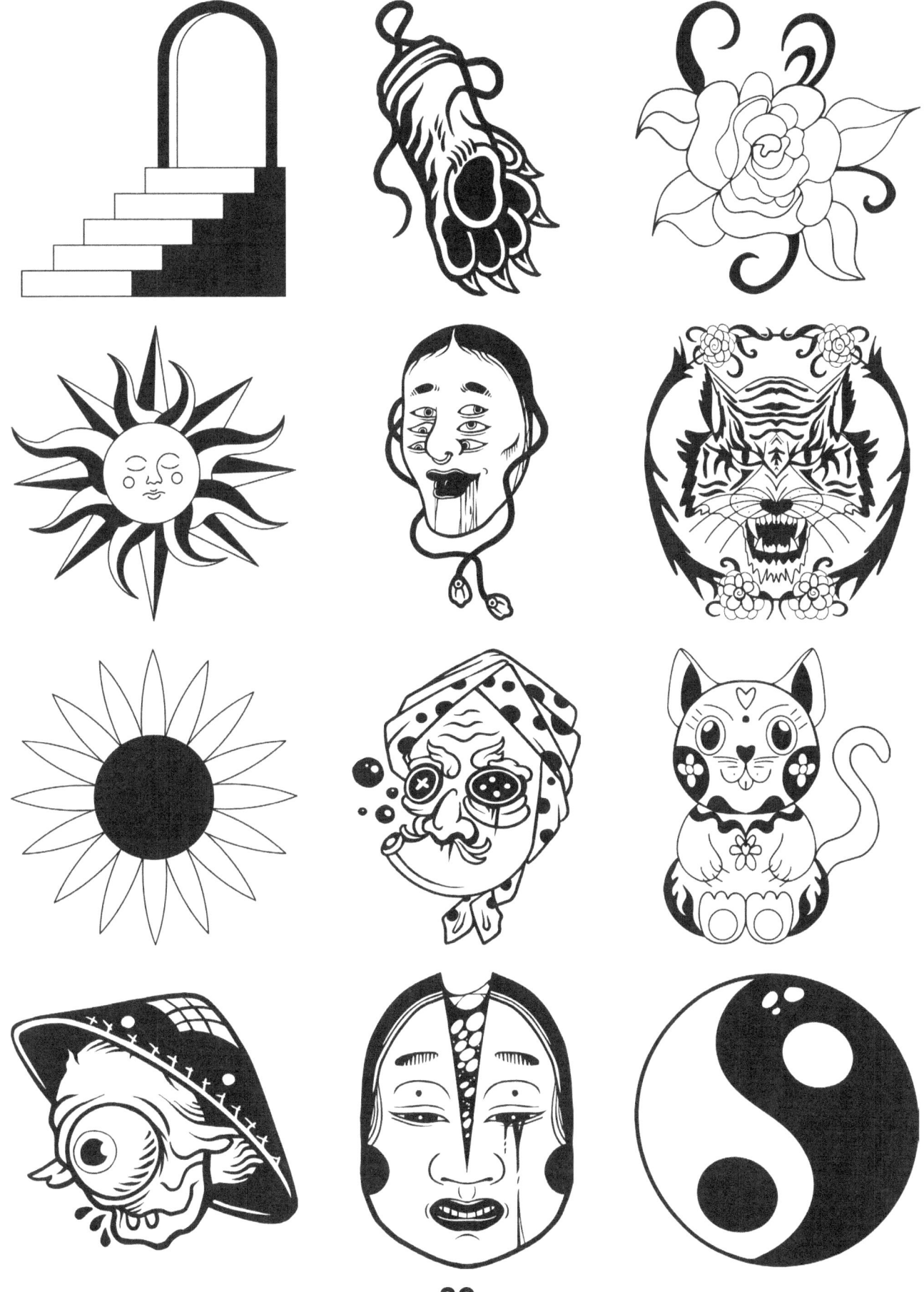

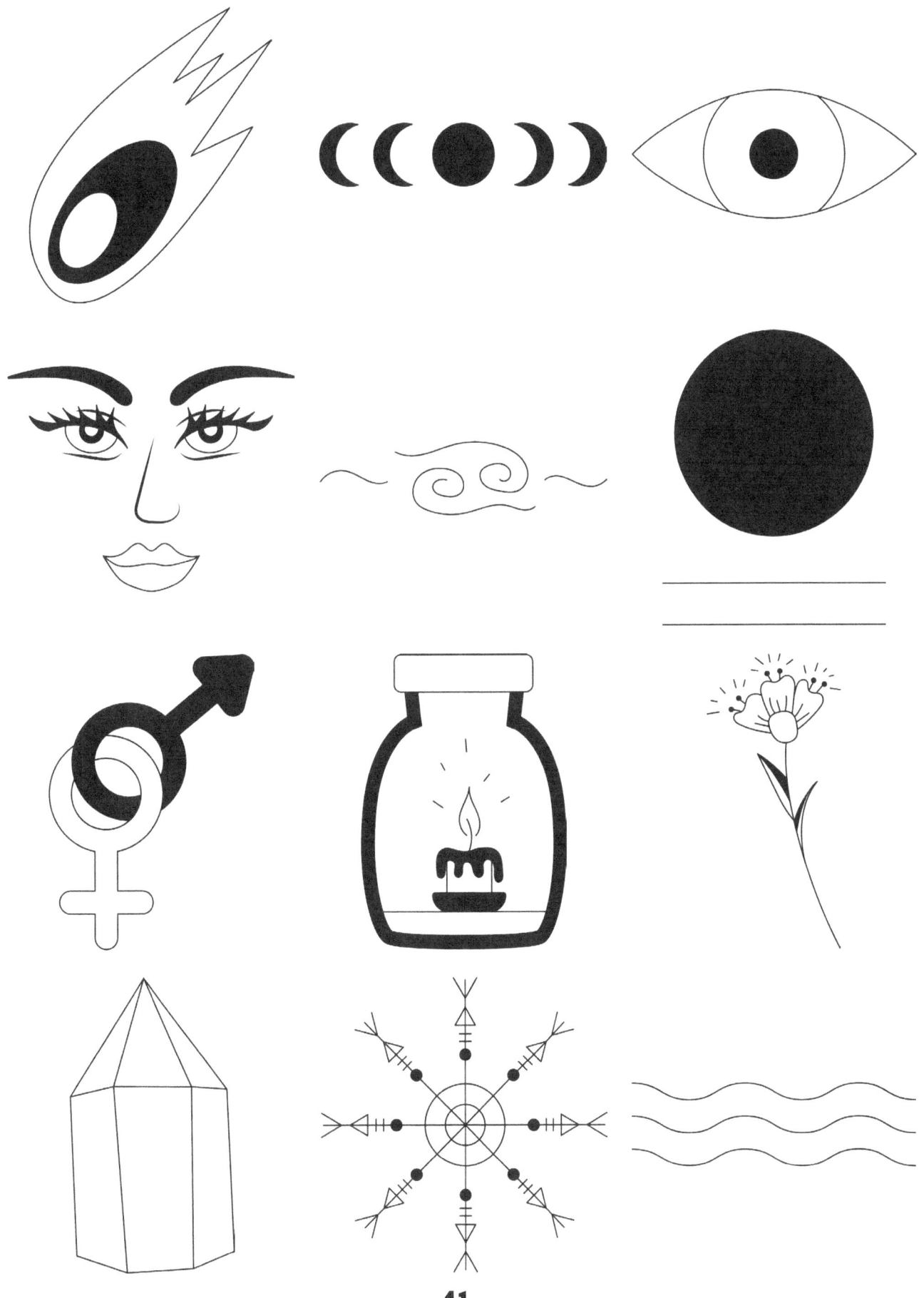

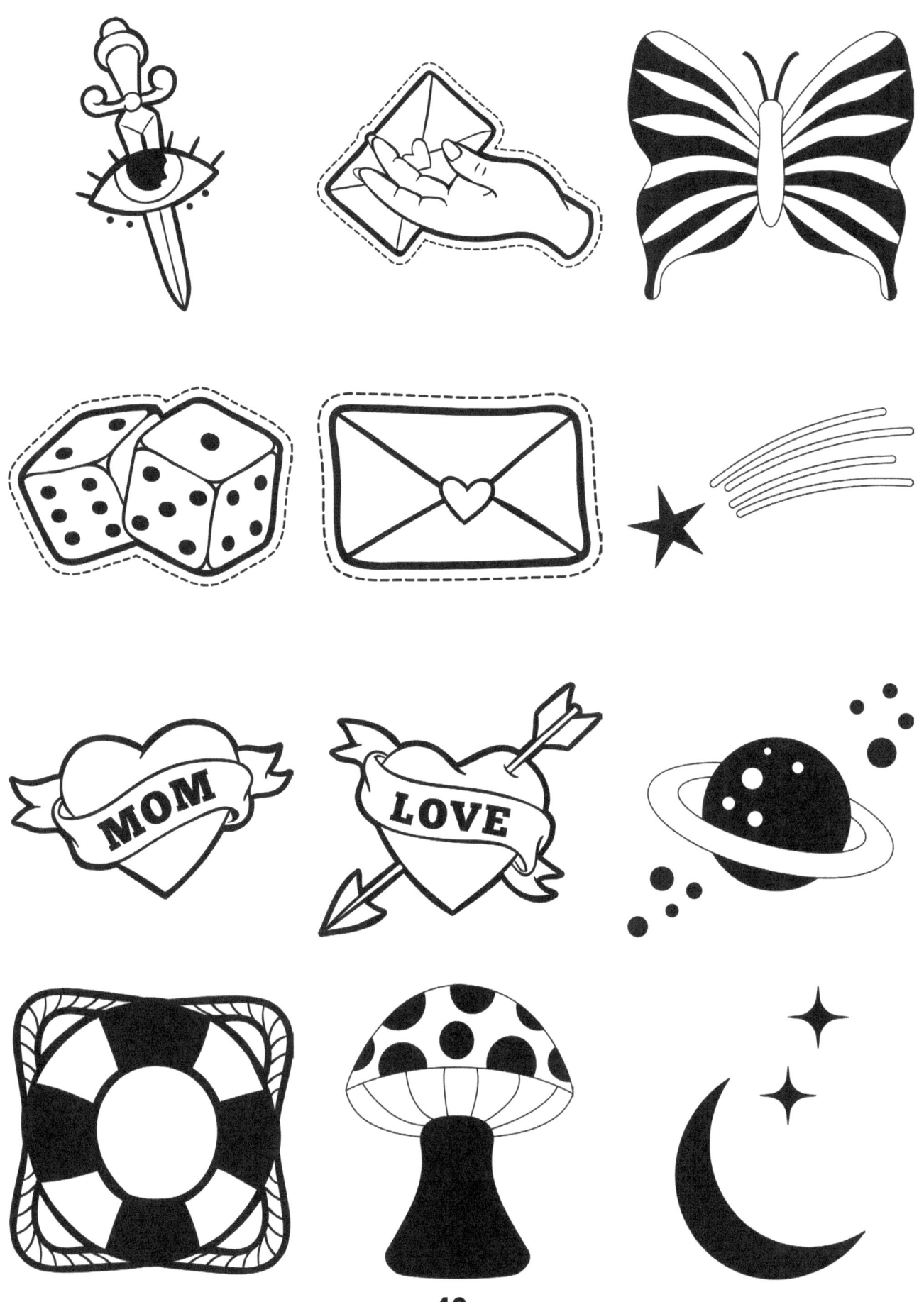

43

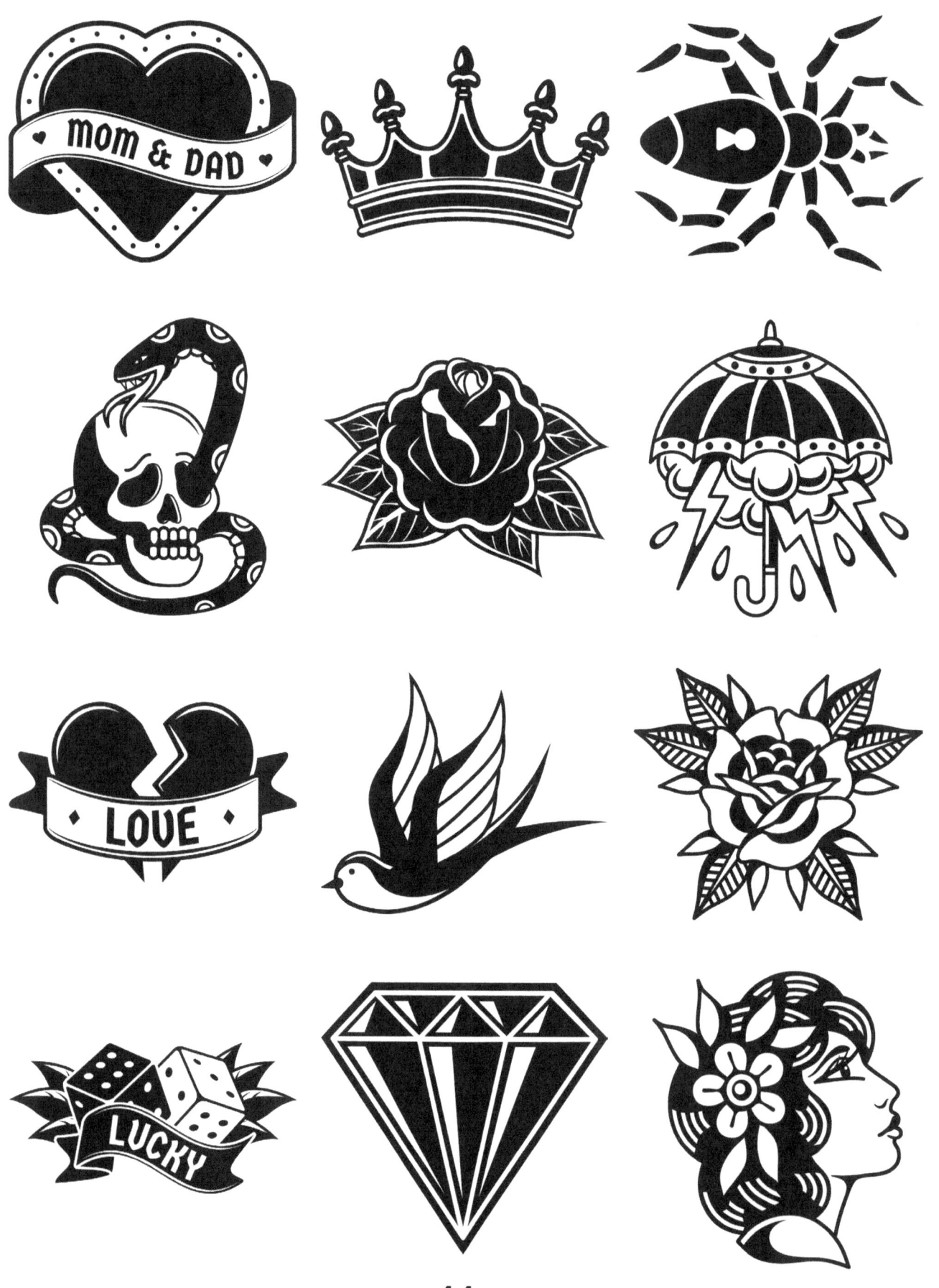

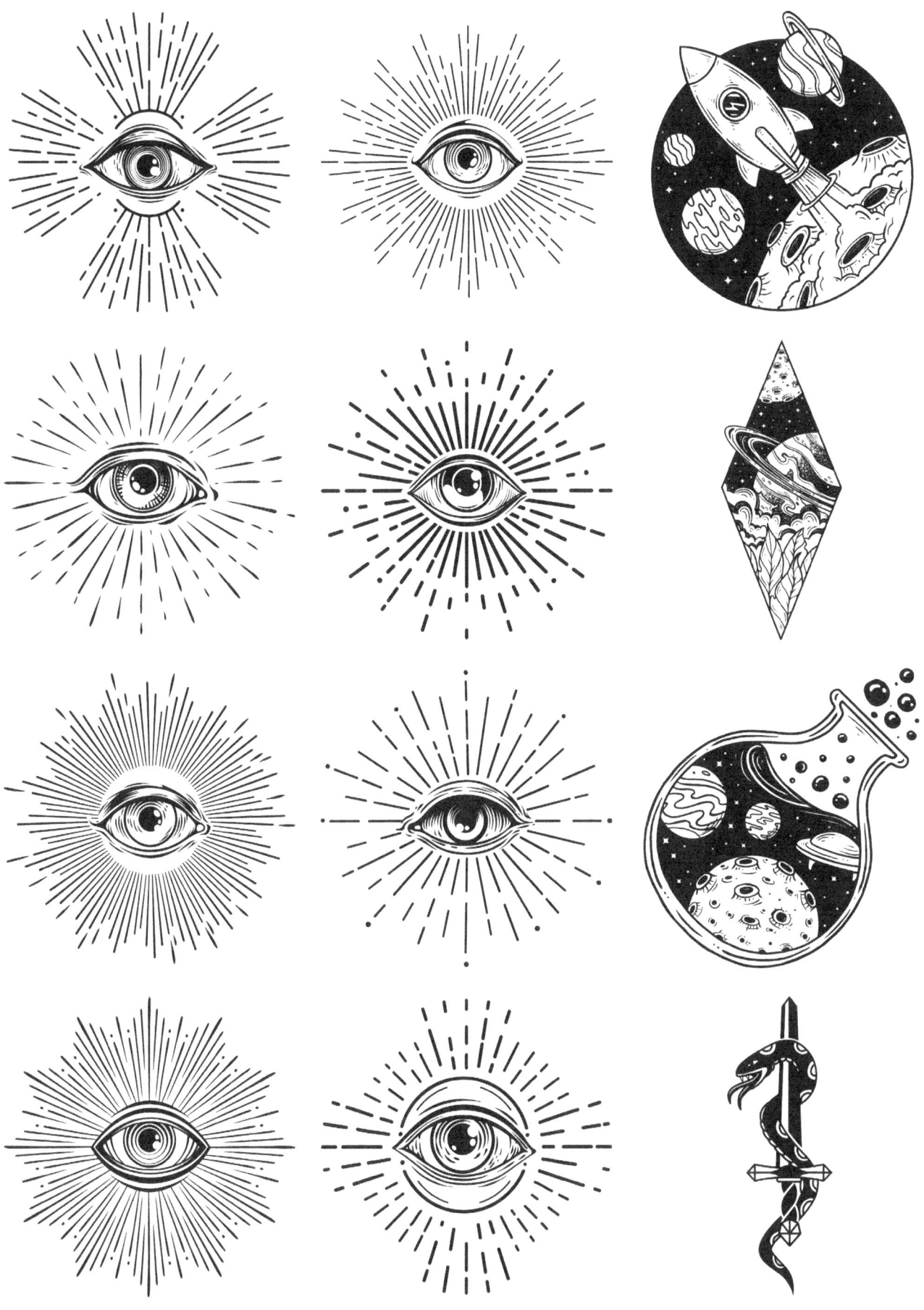

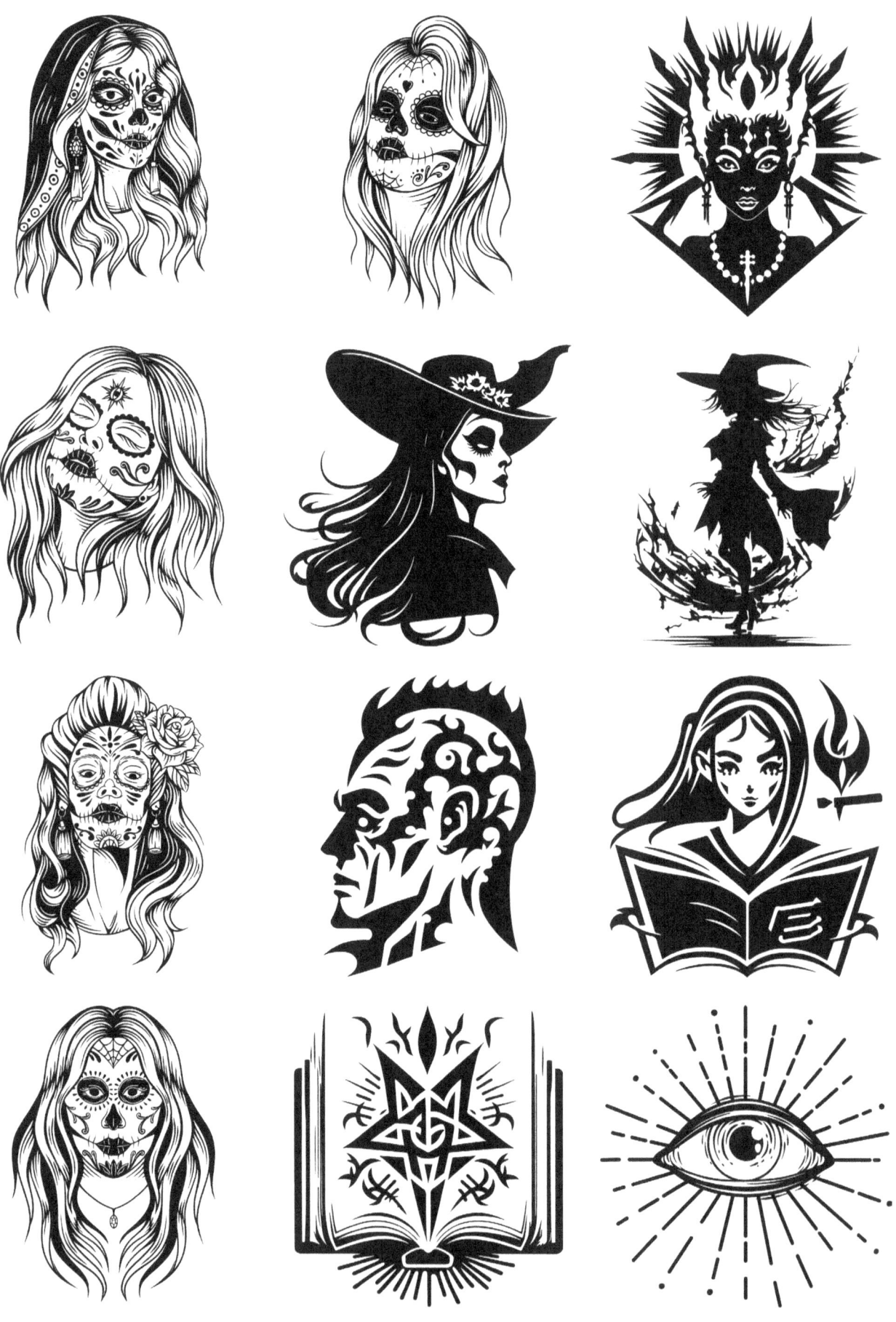

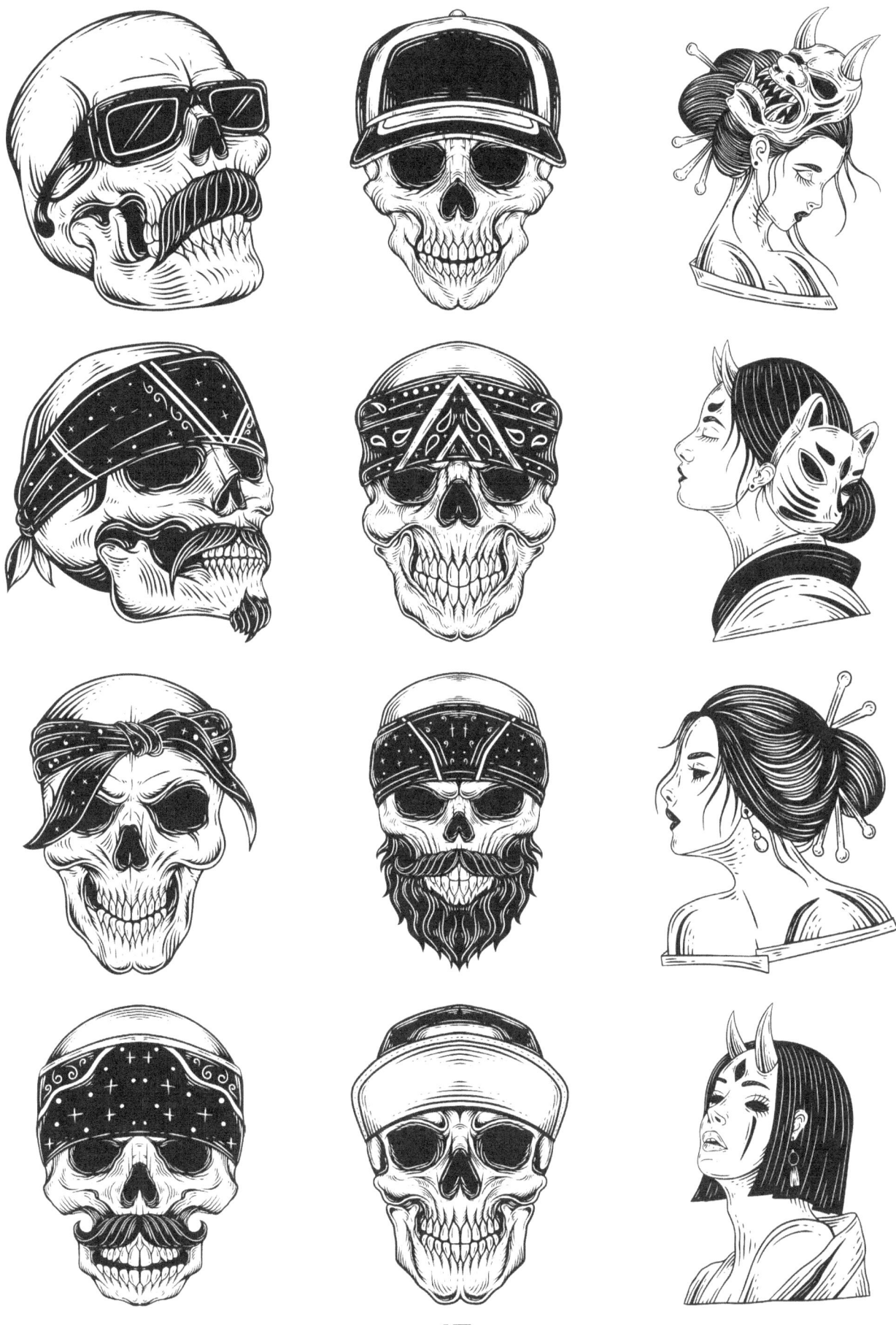

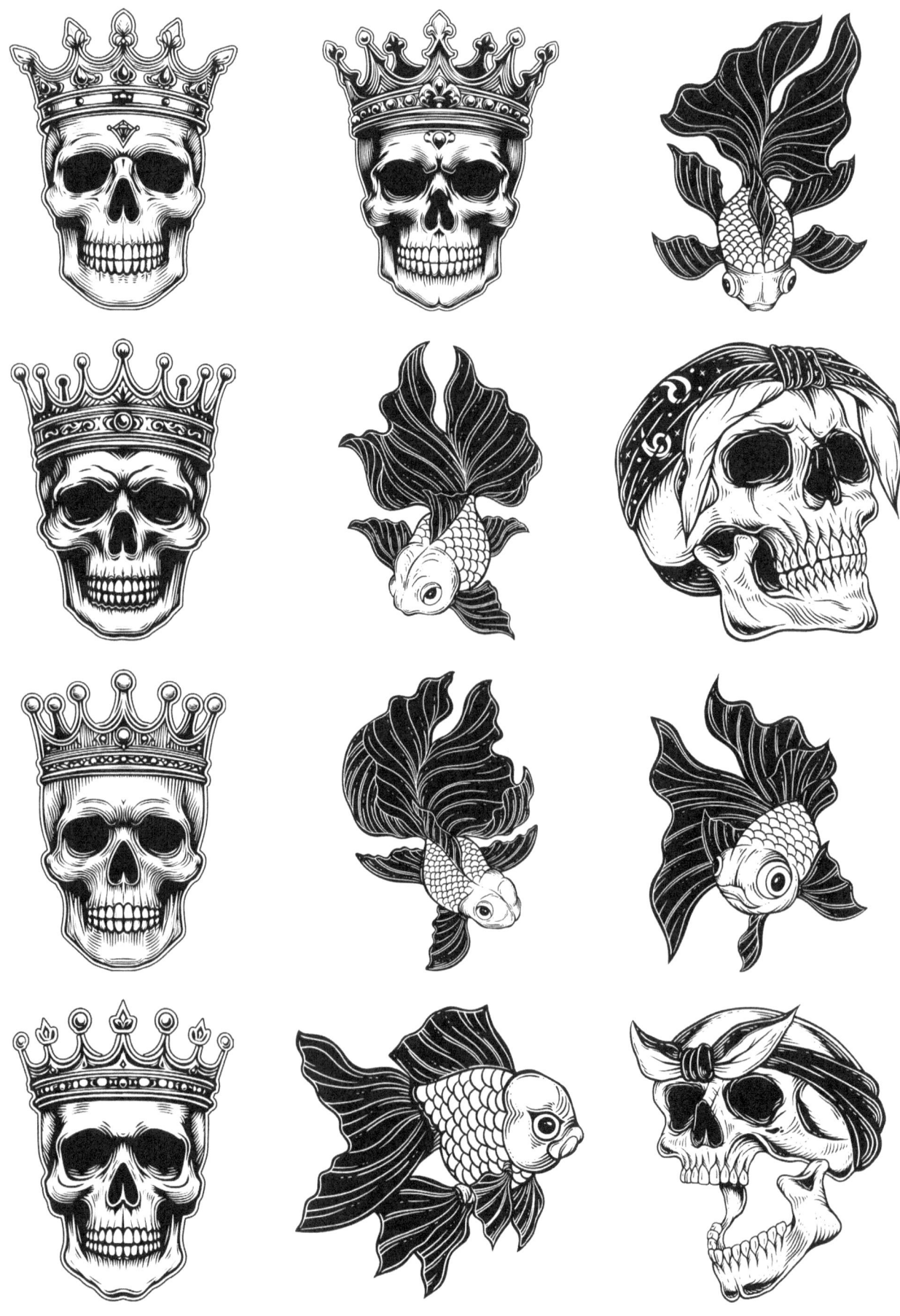

48

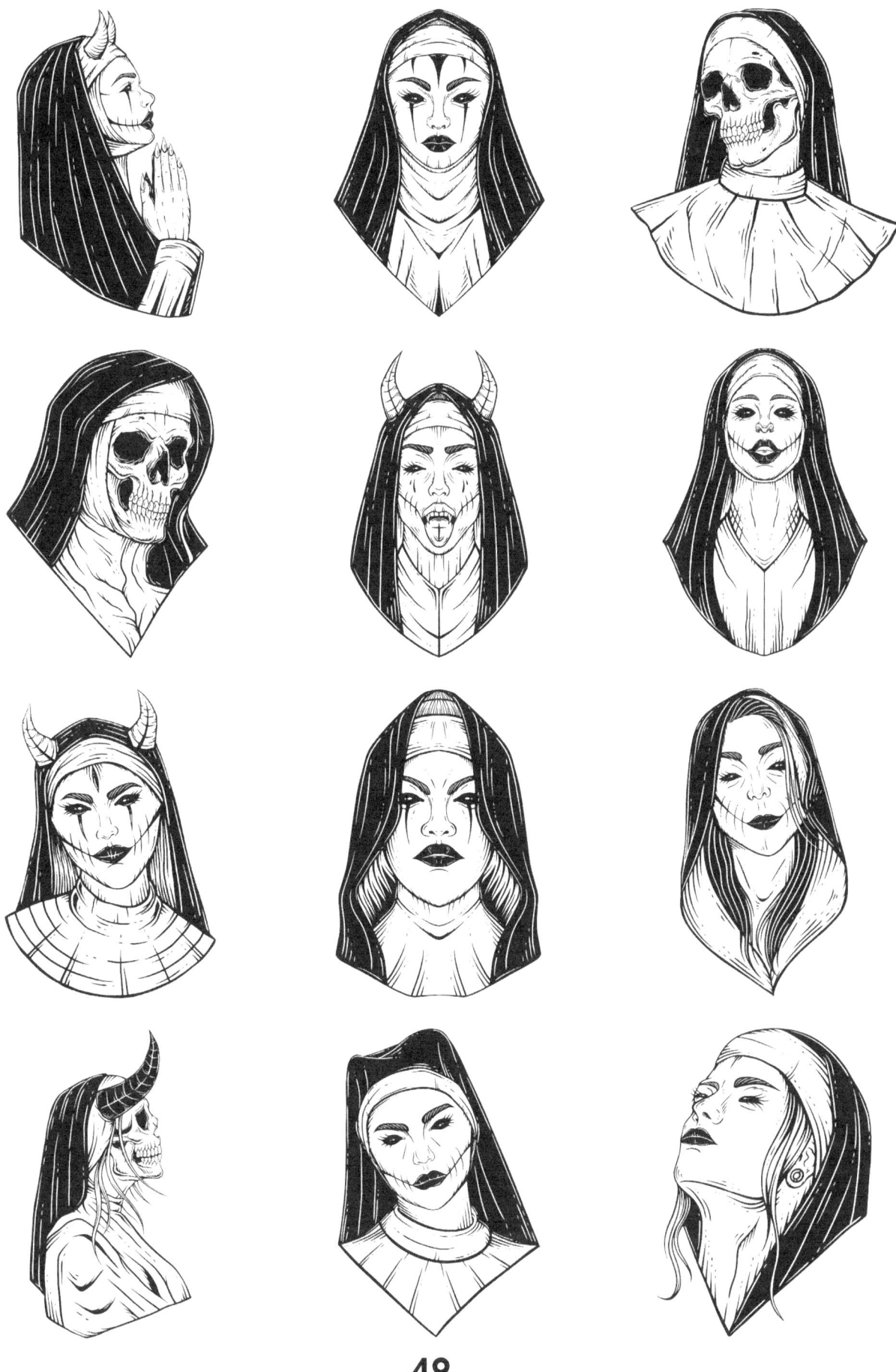

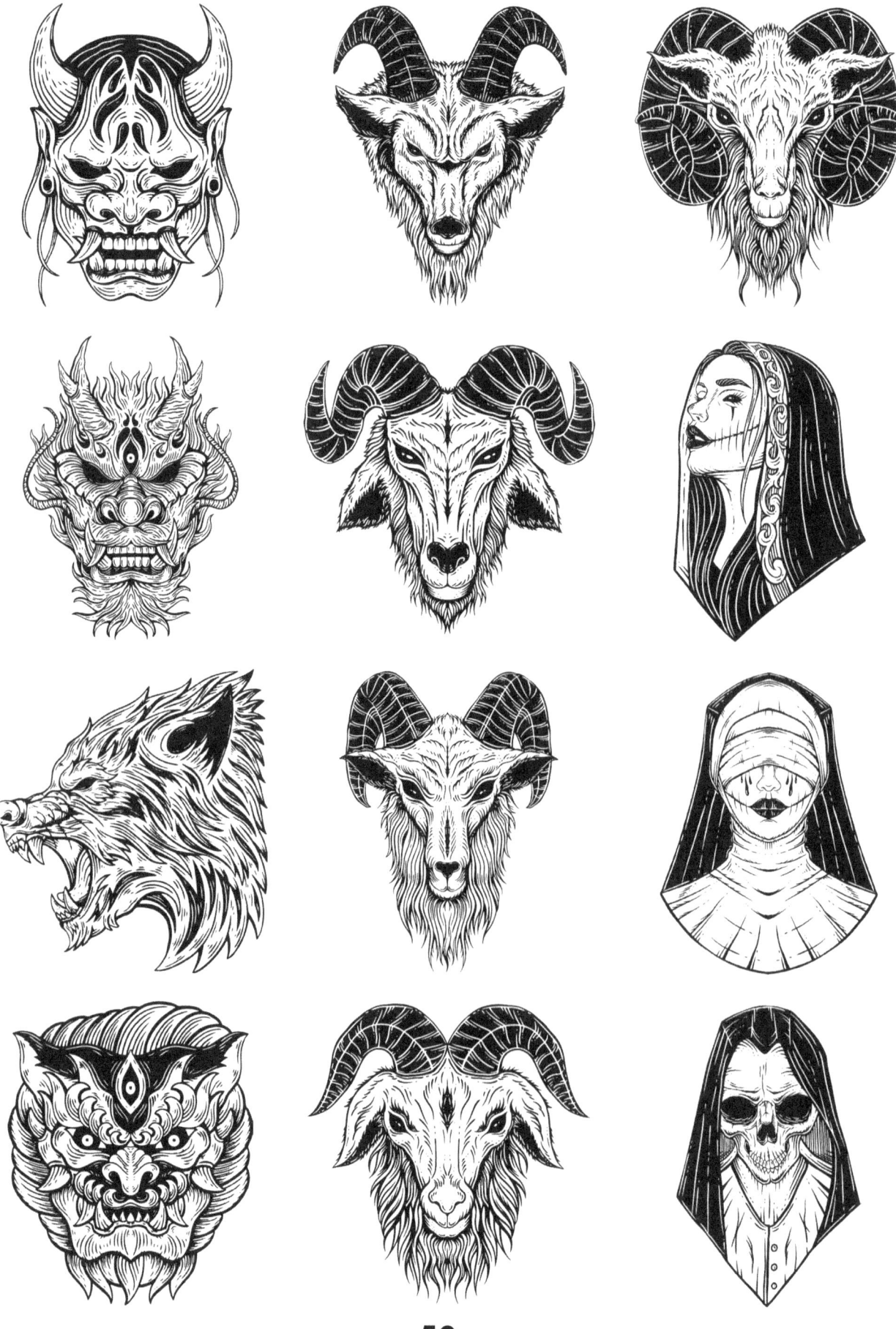

50

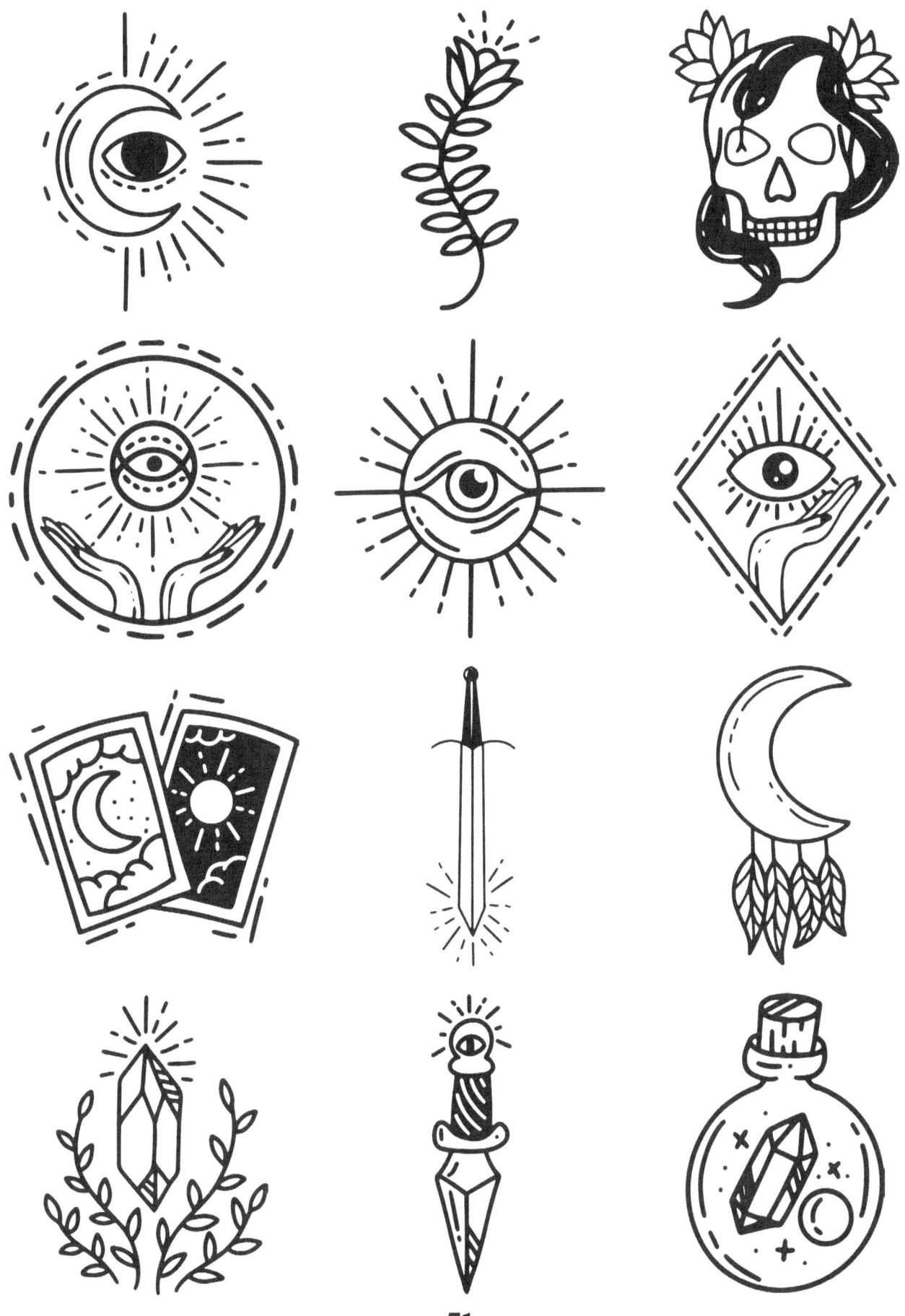

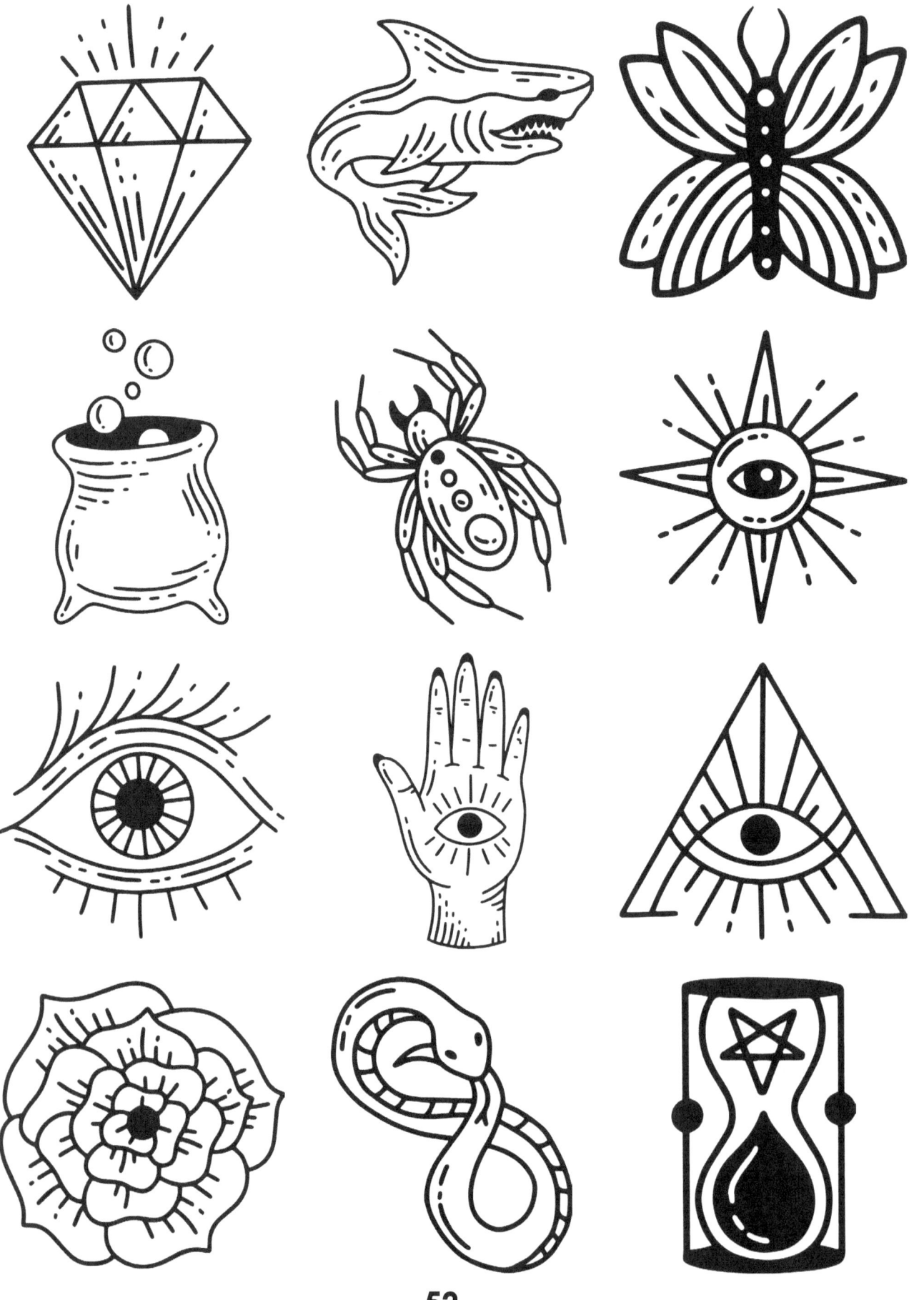

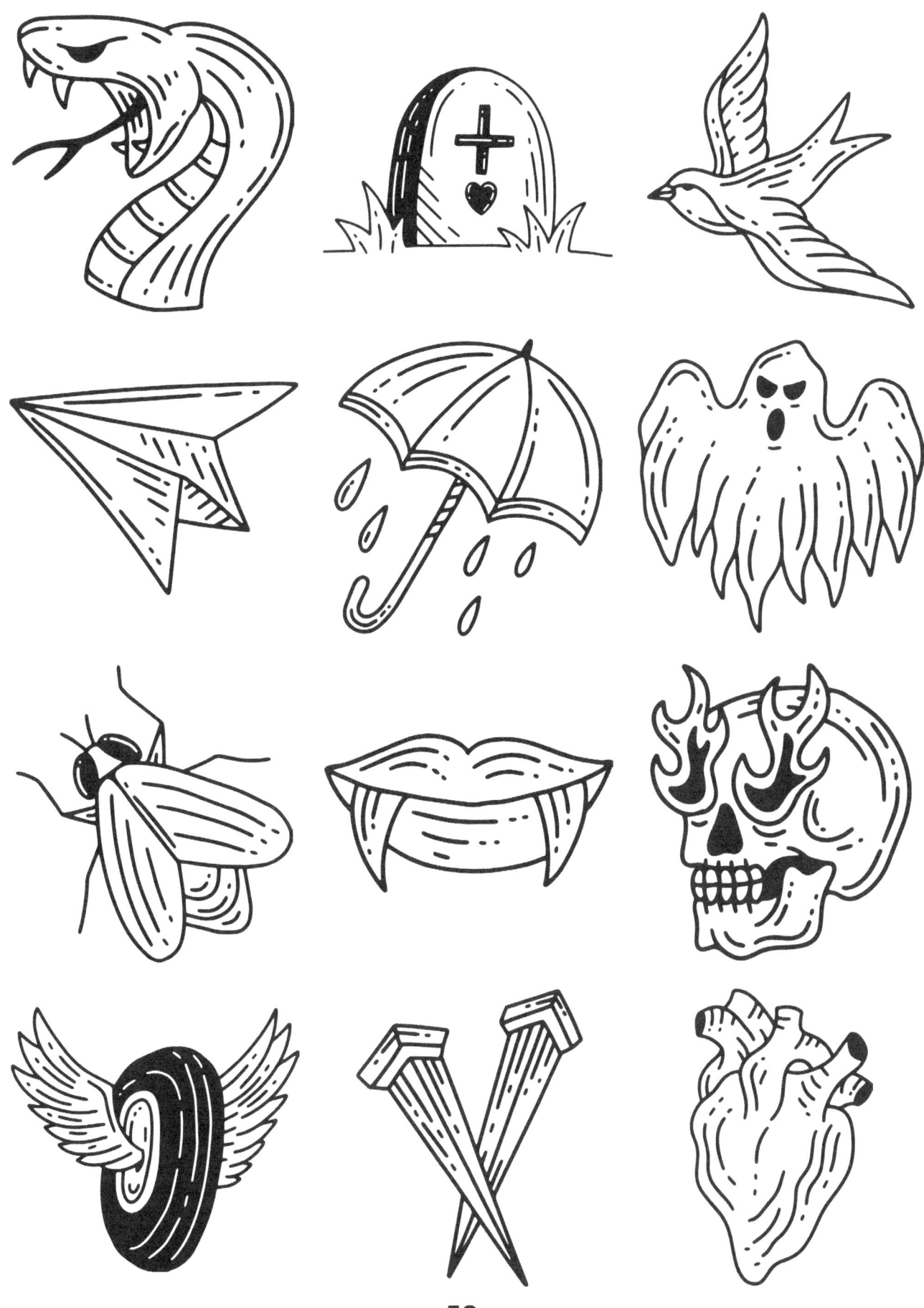

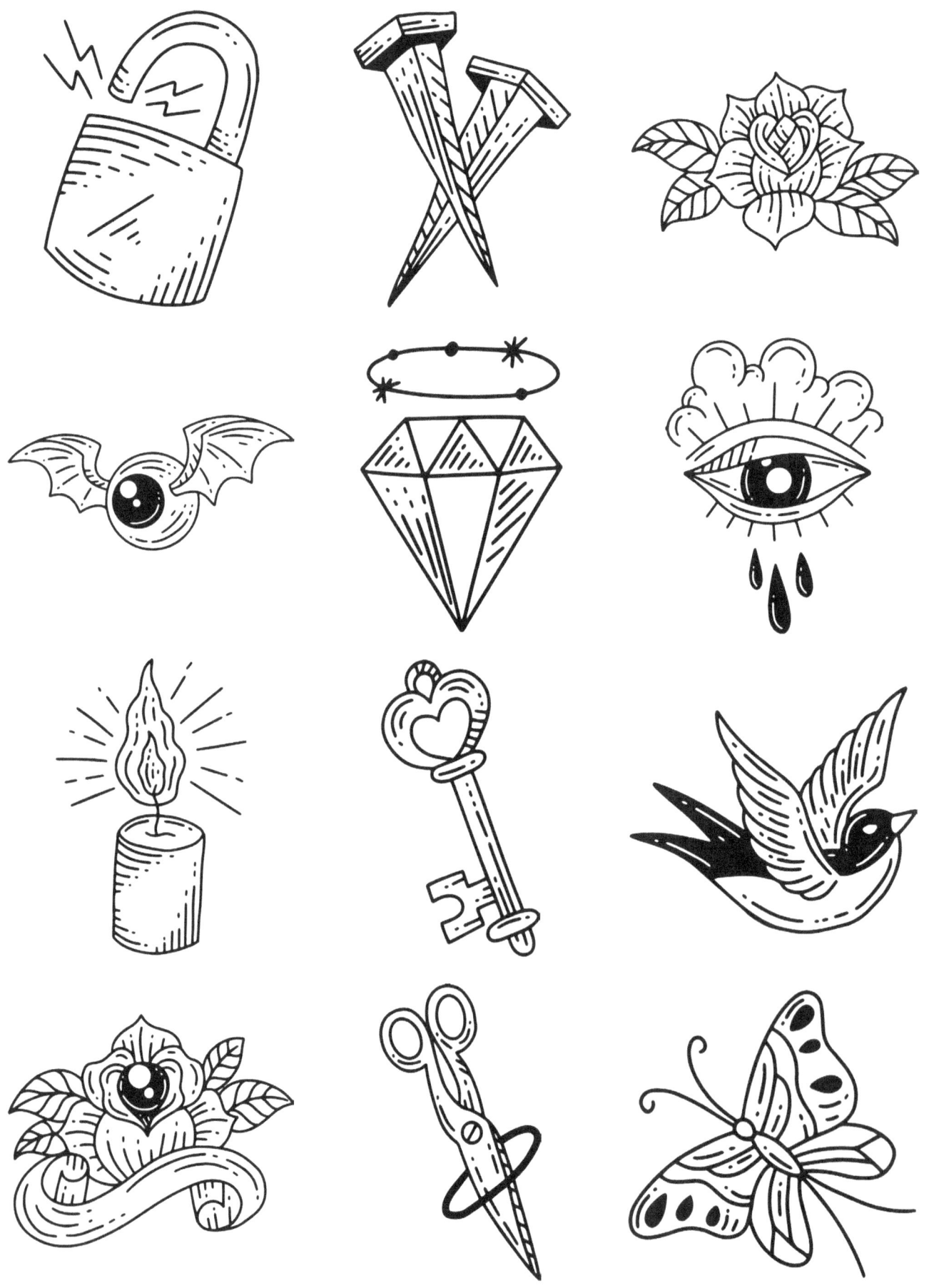

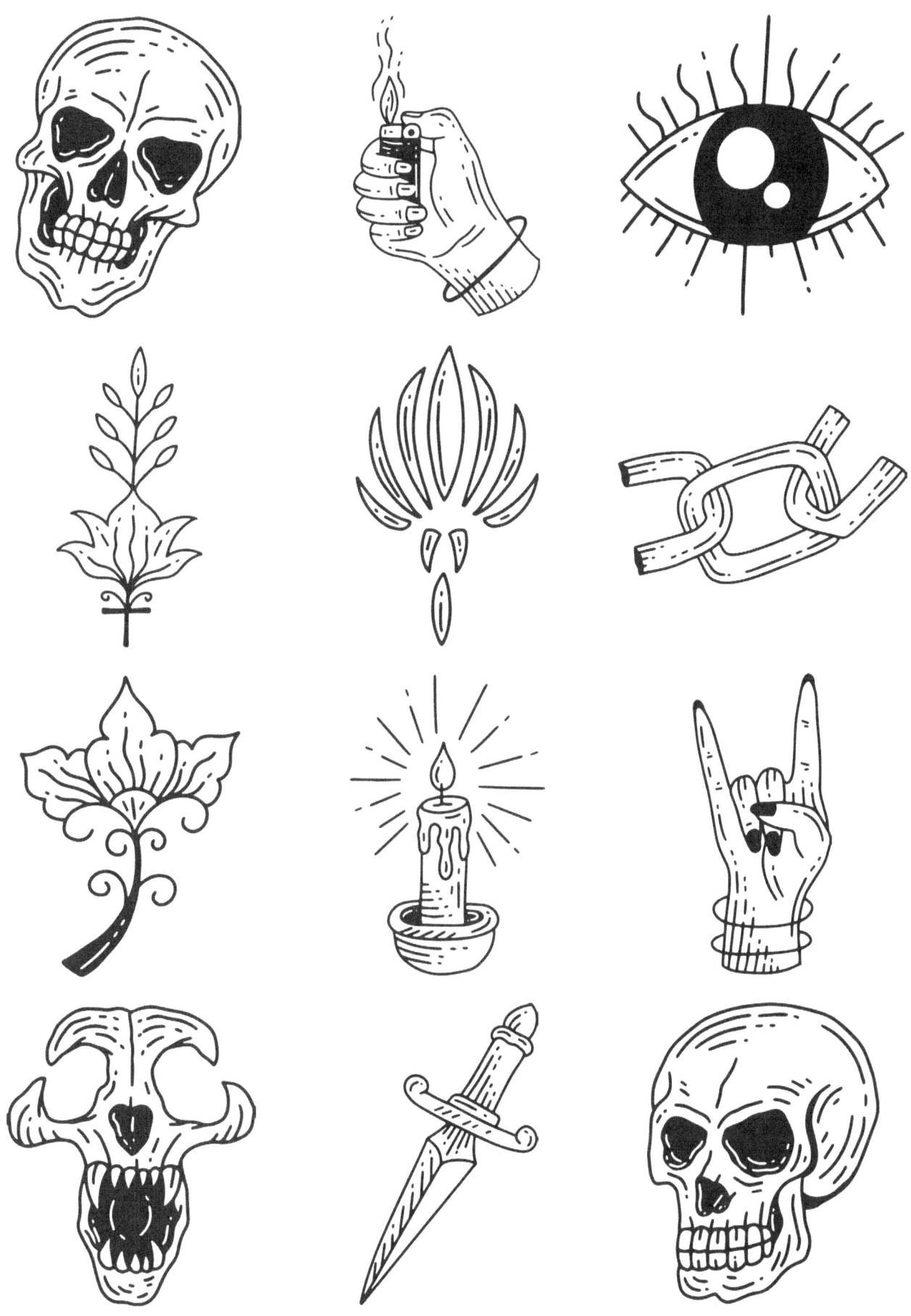

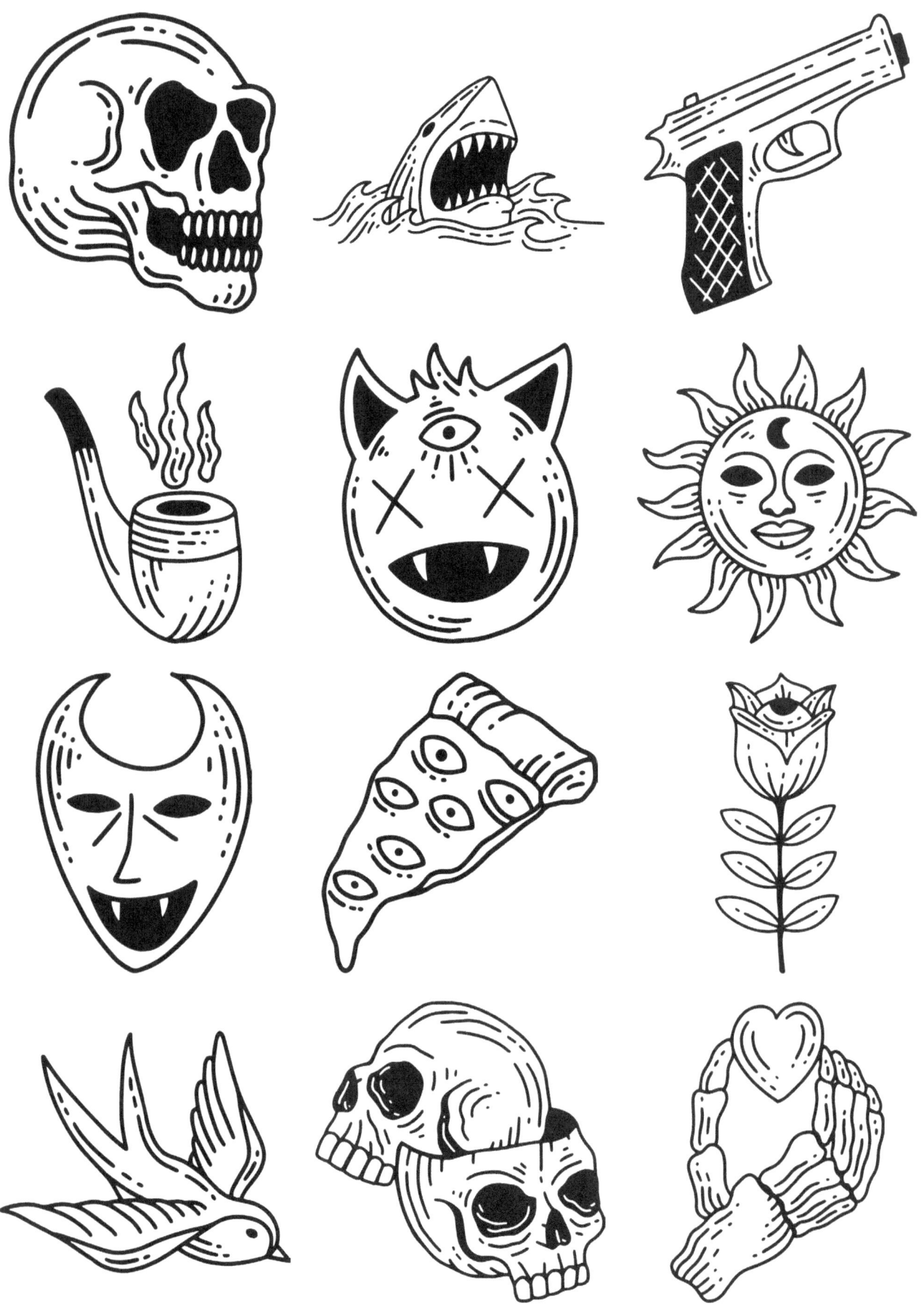

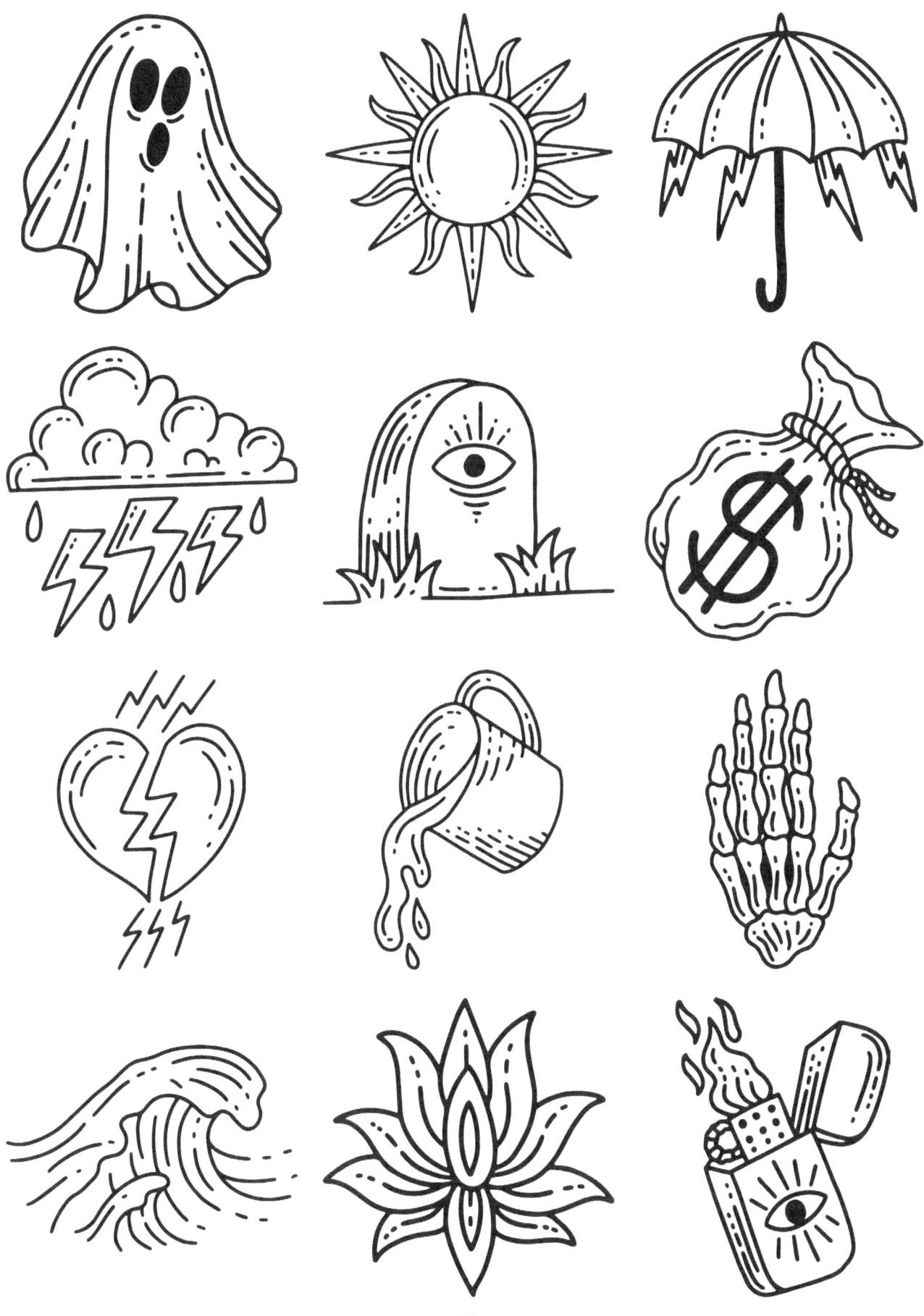

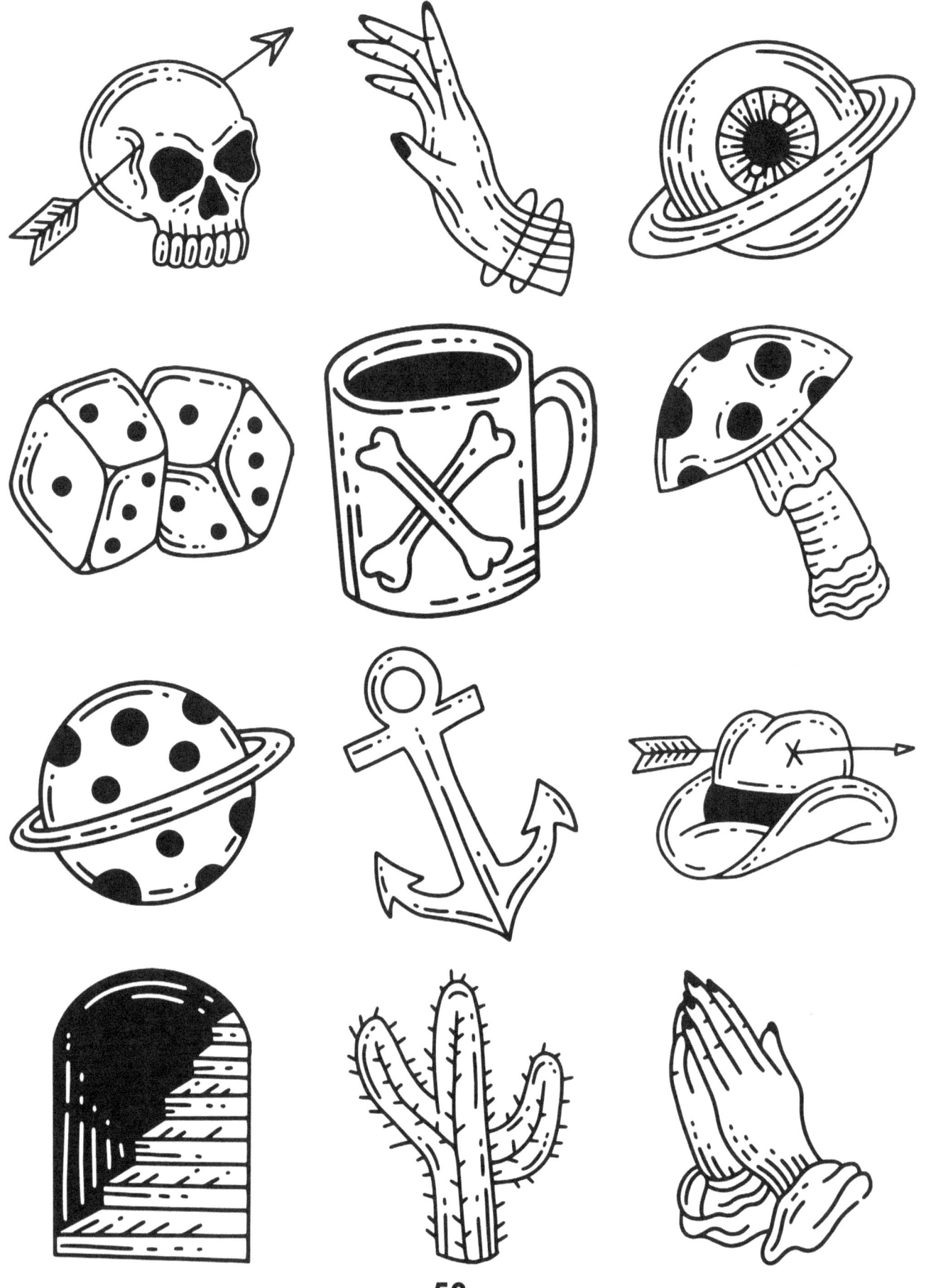

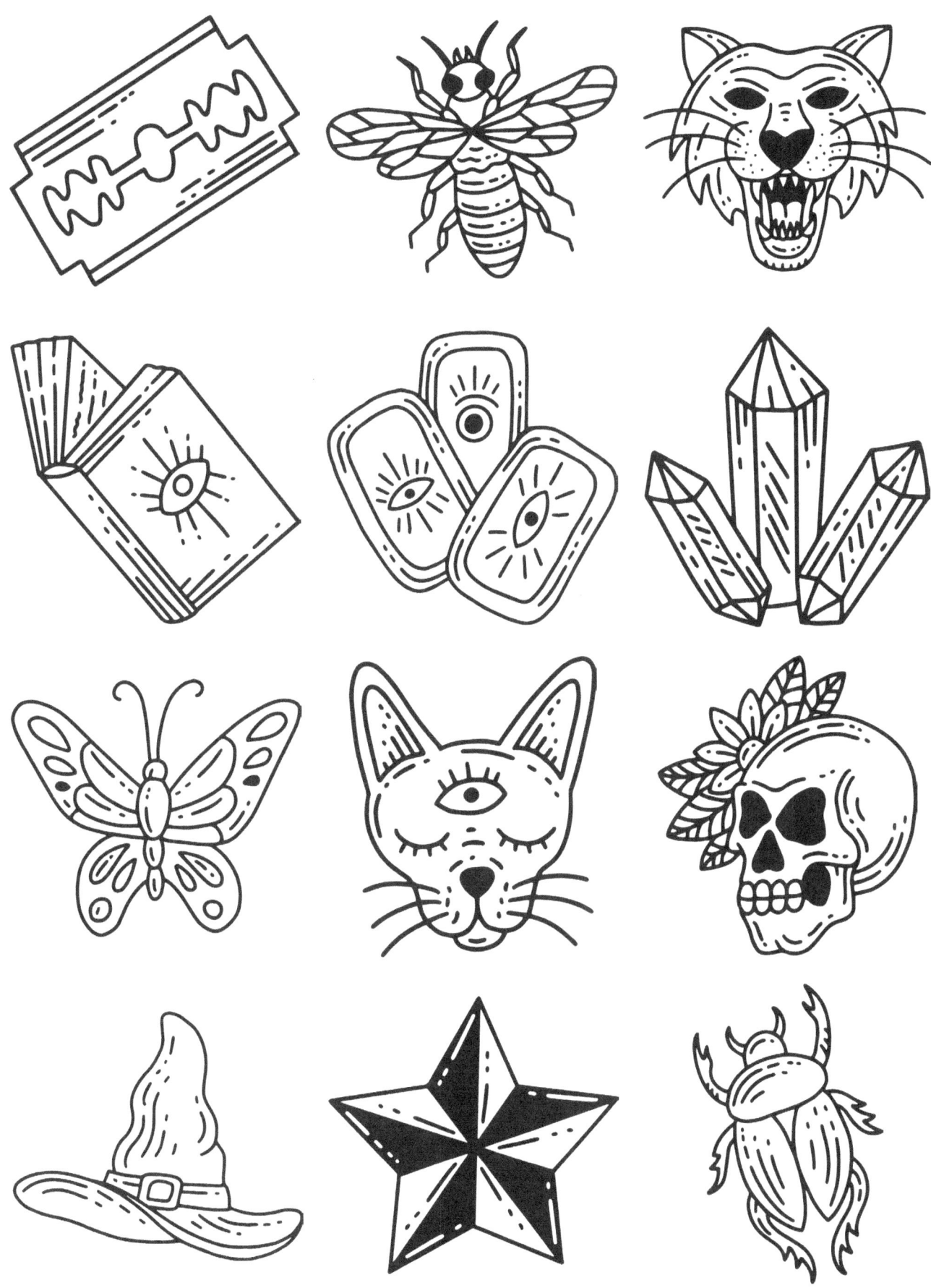

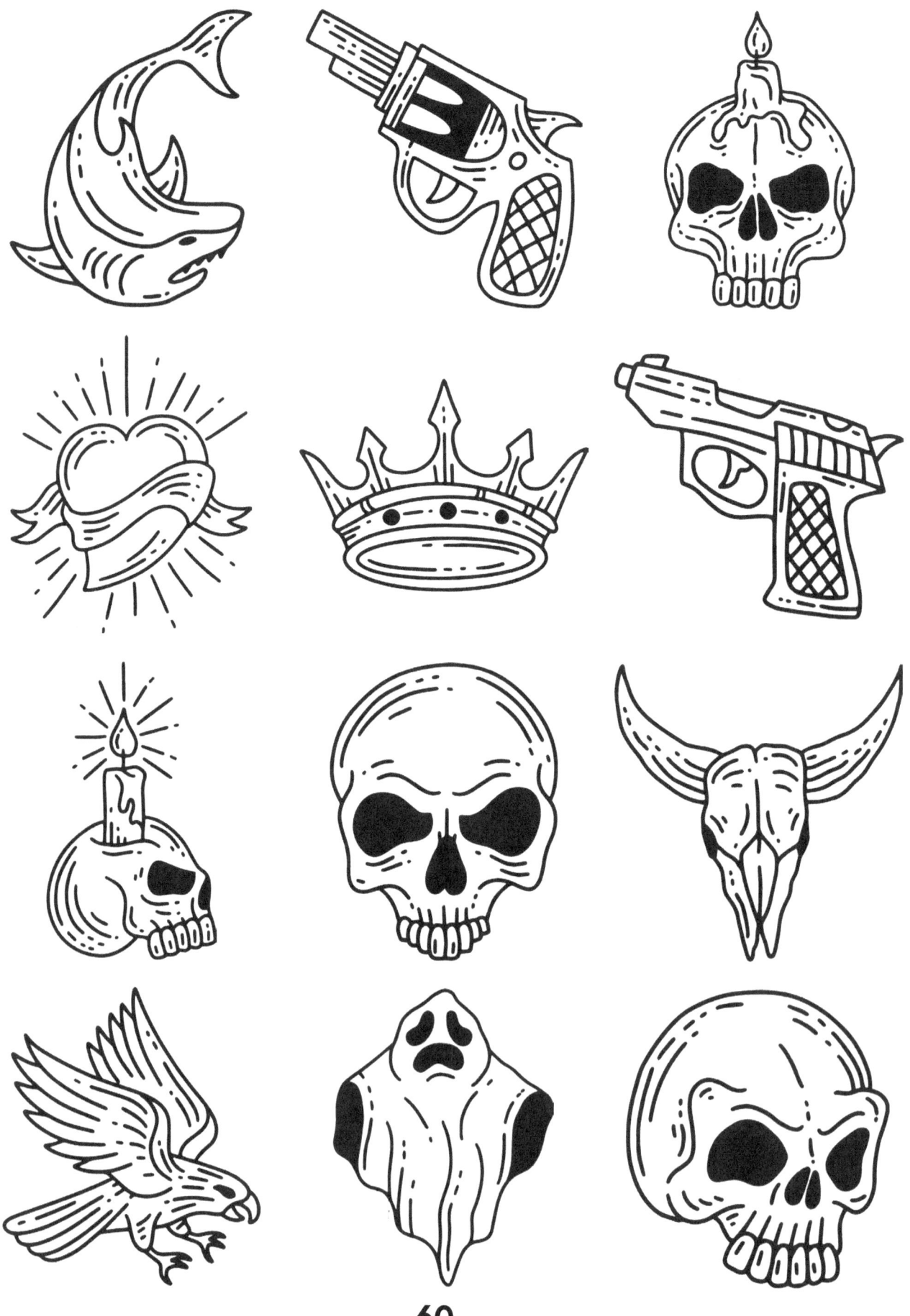

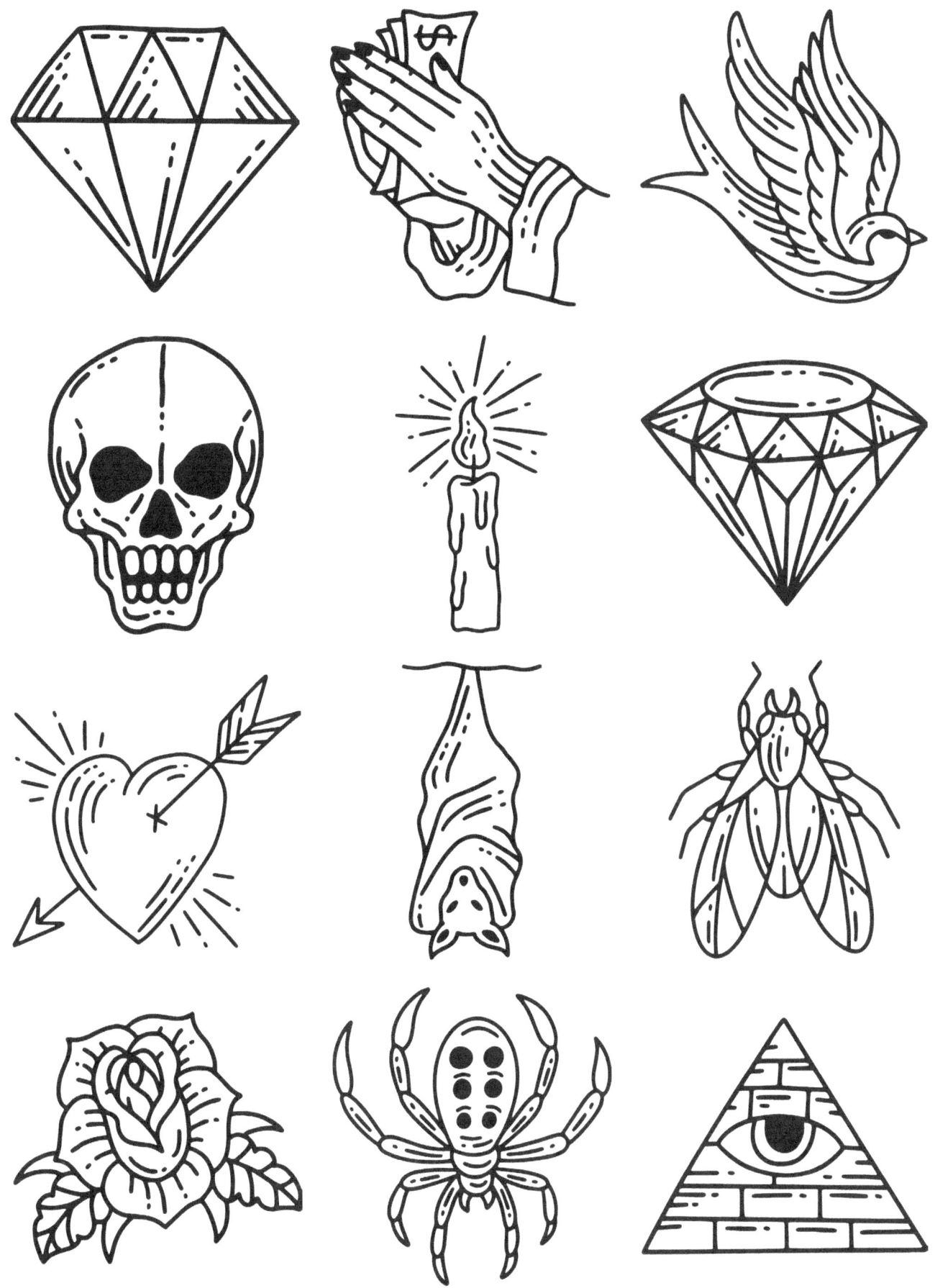

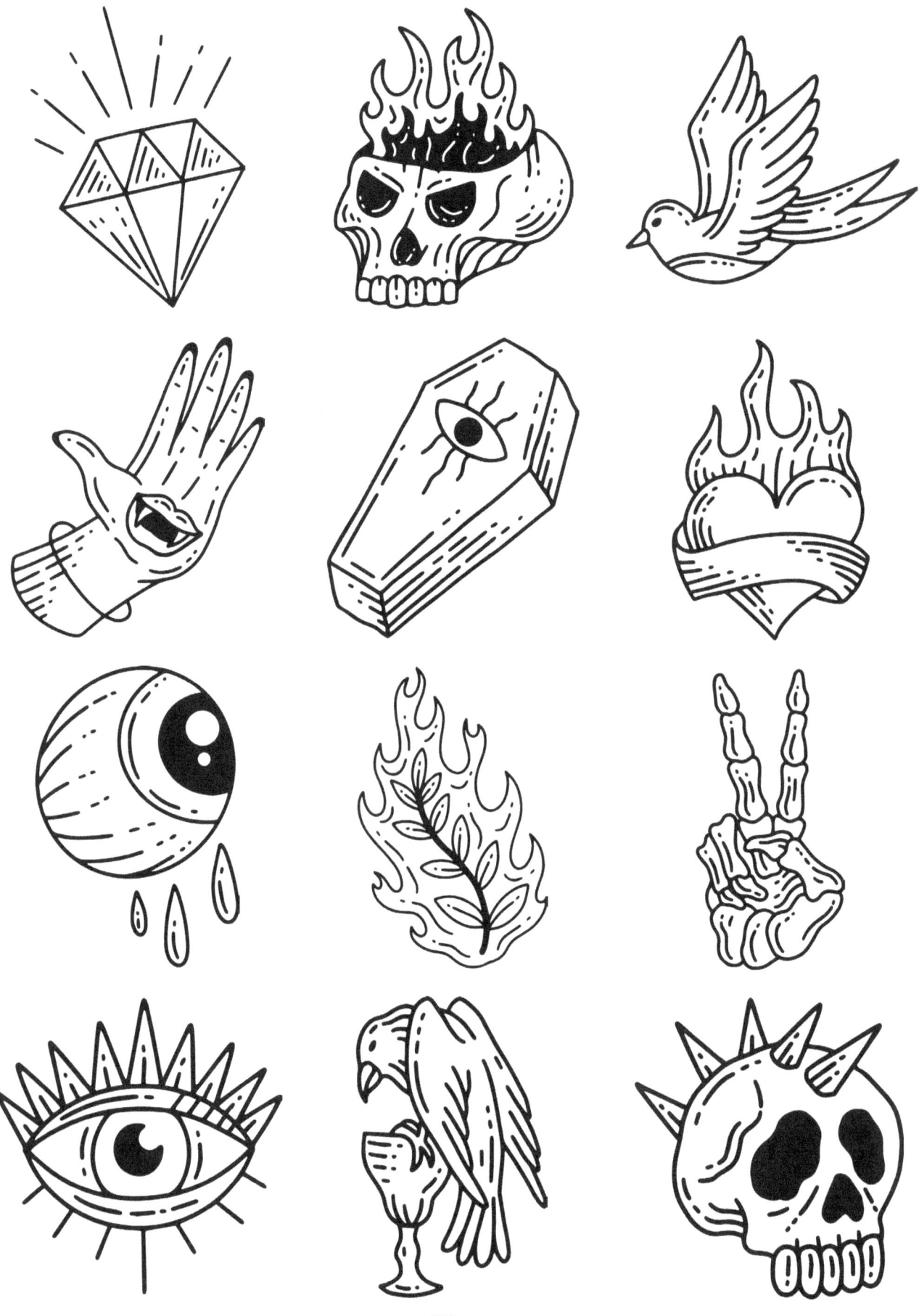

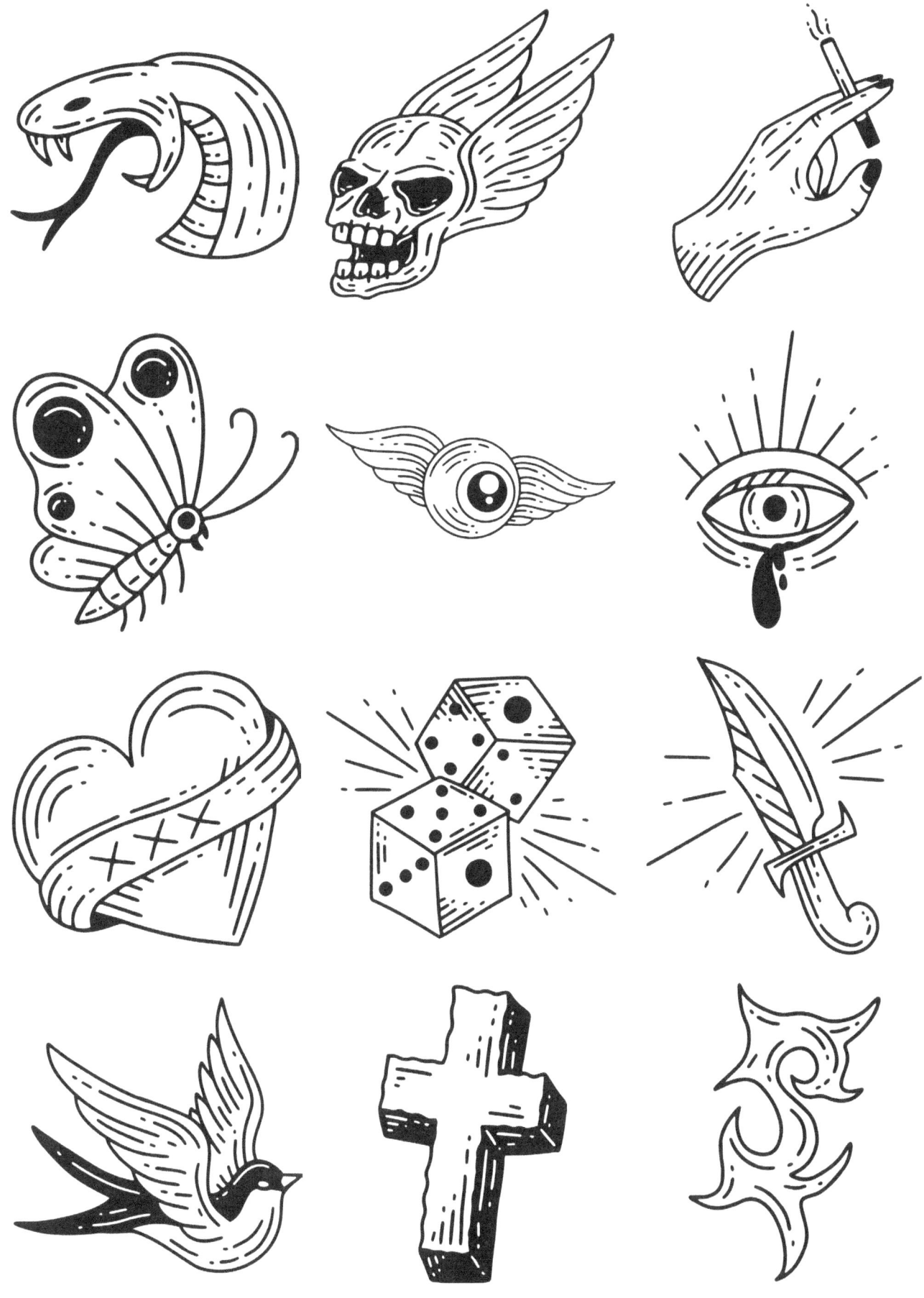

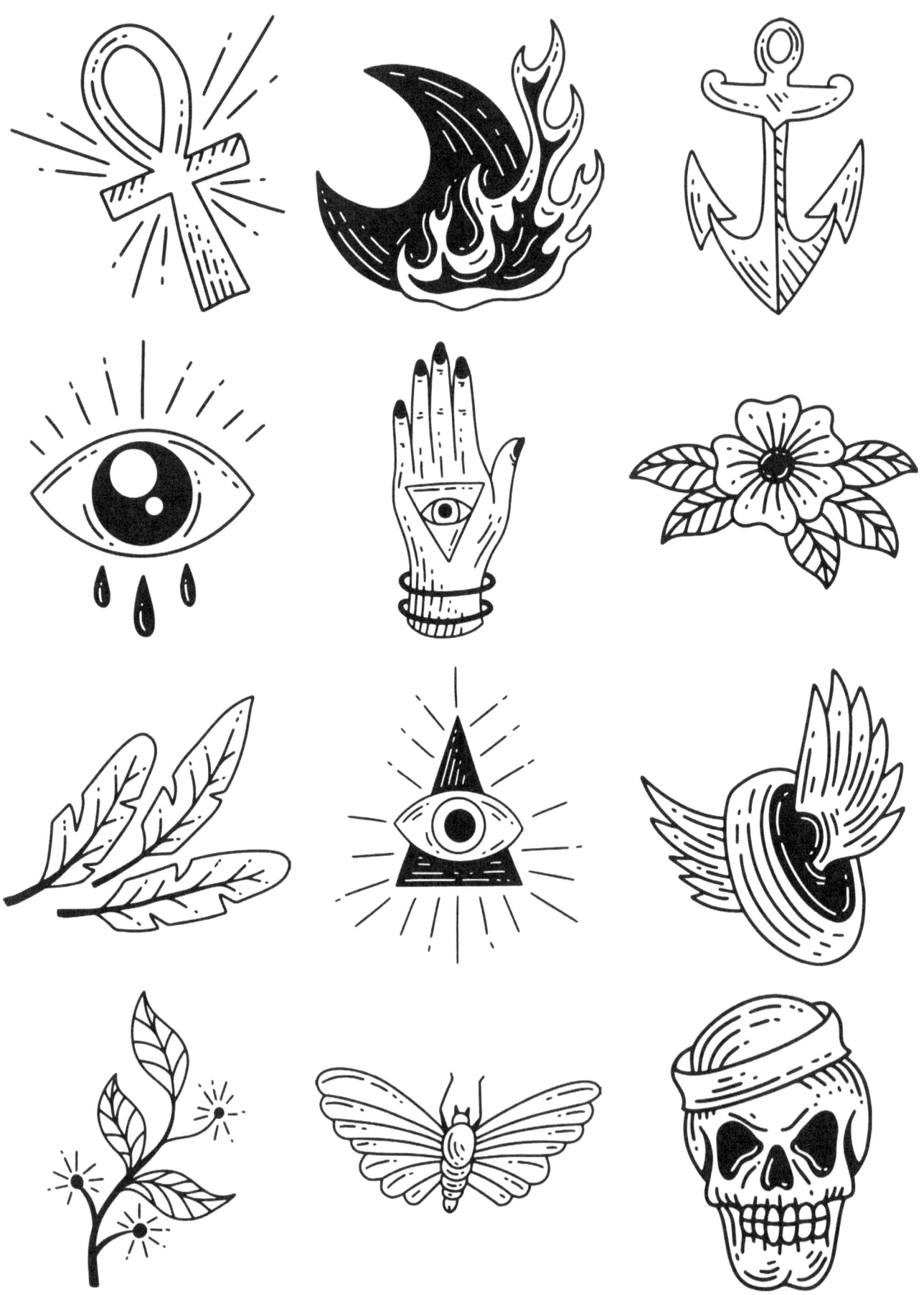

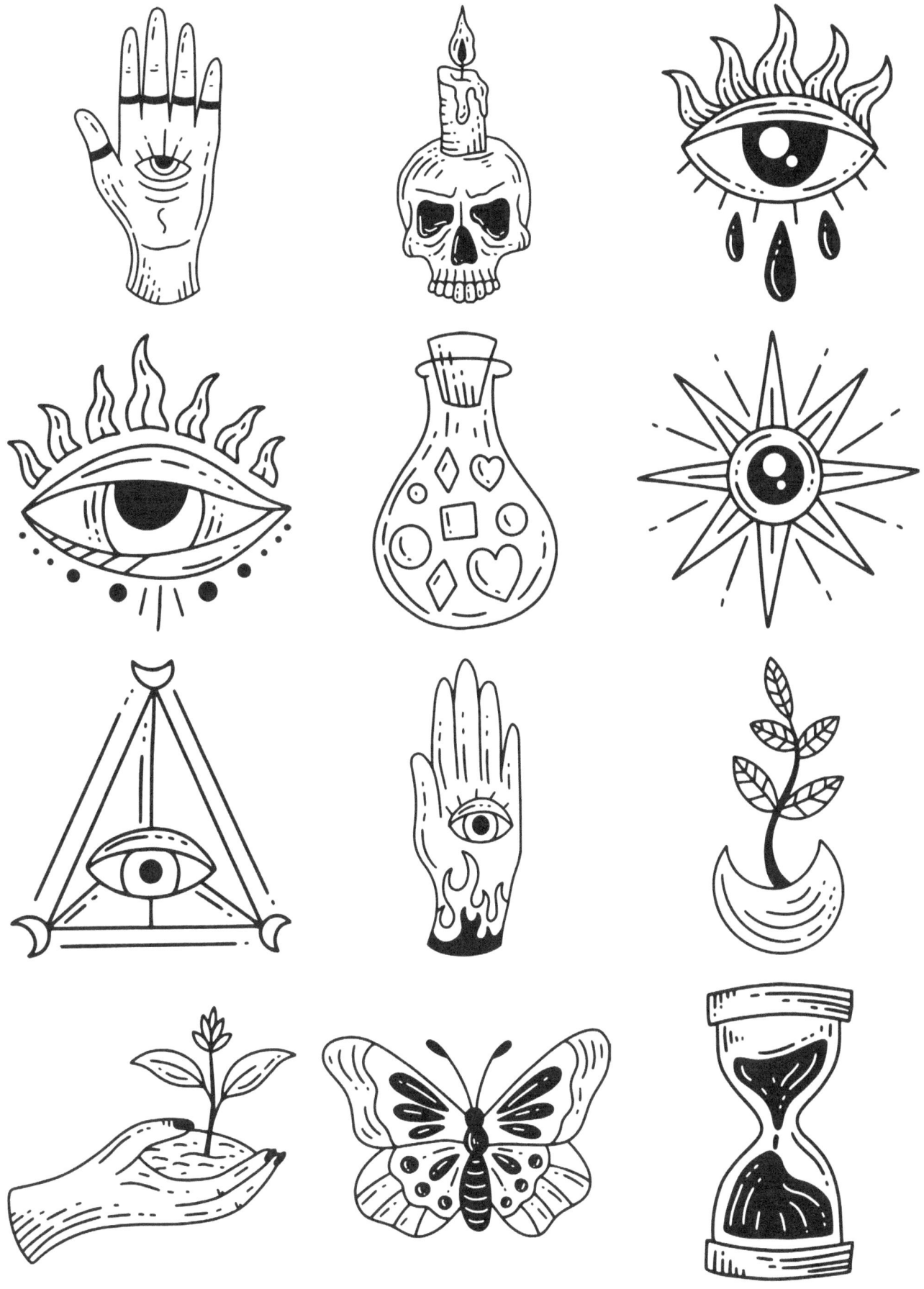

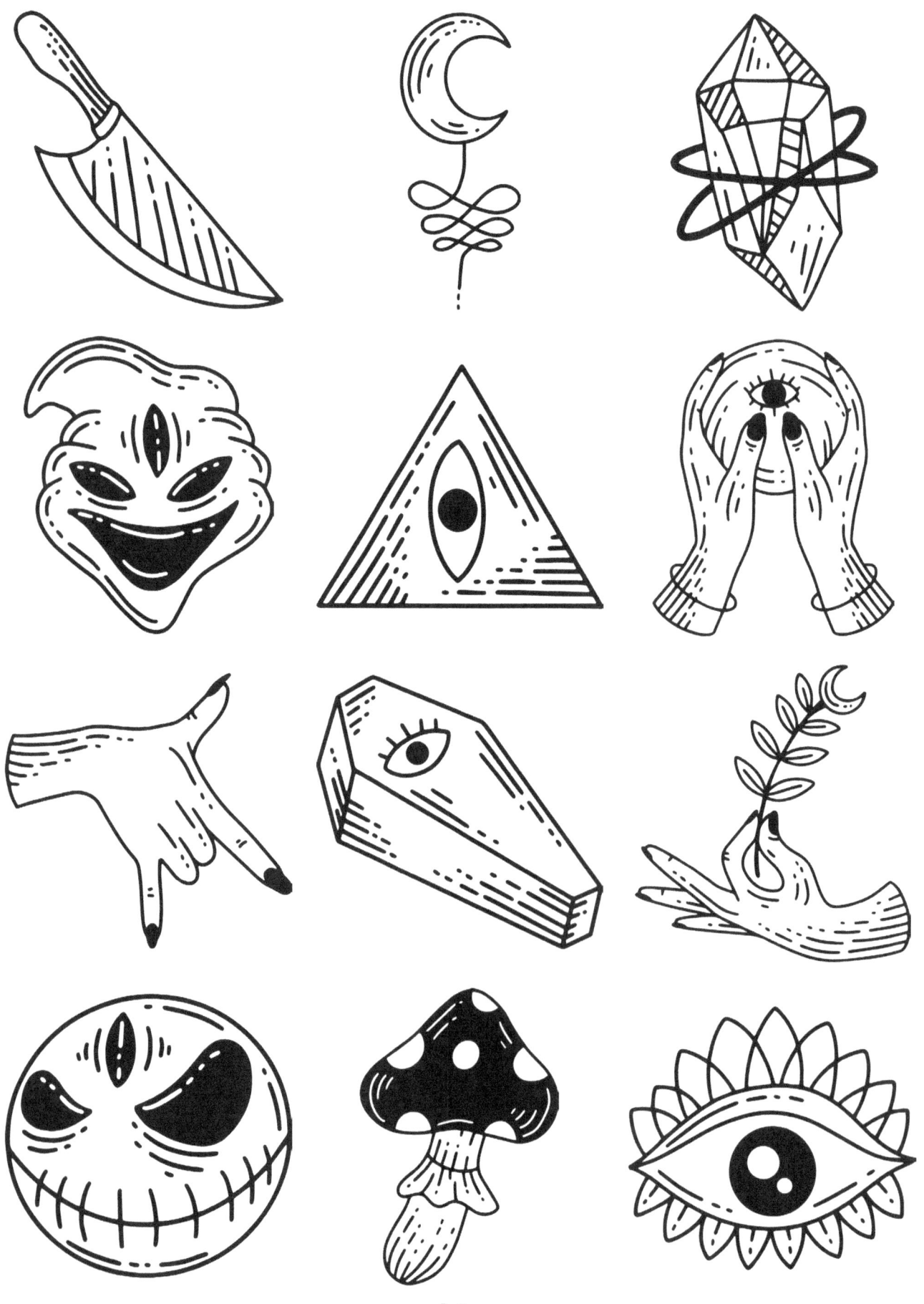

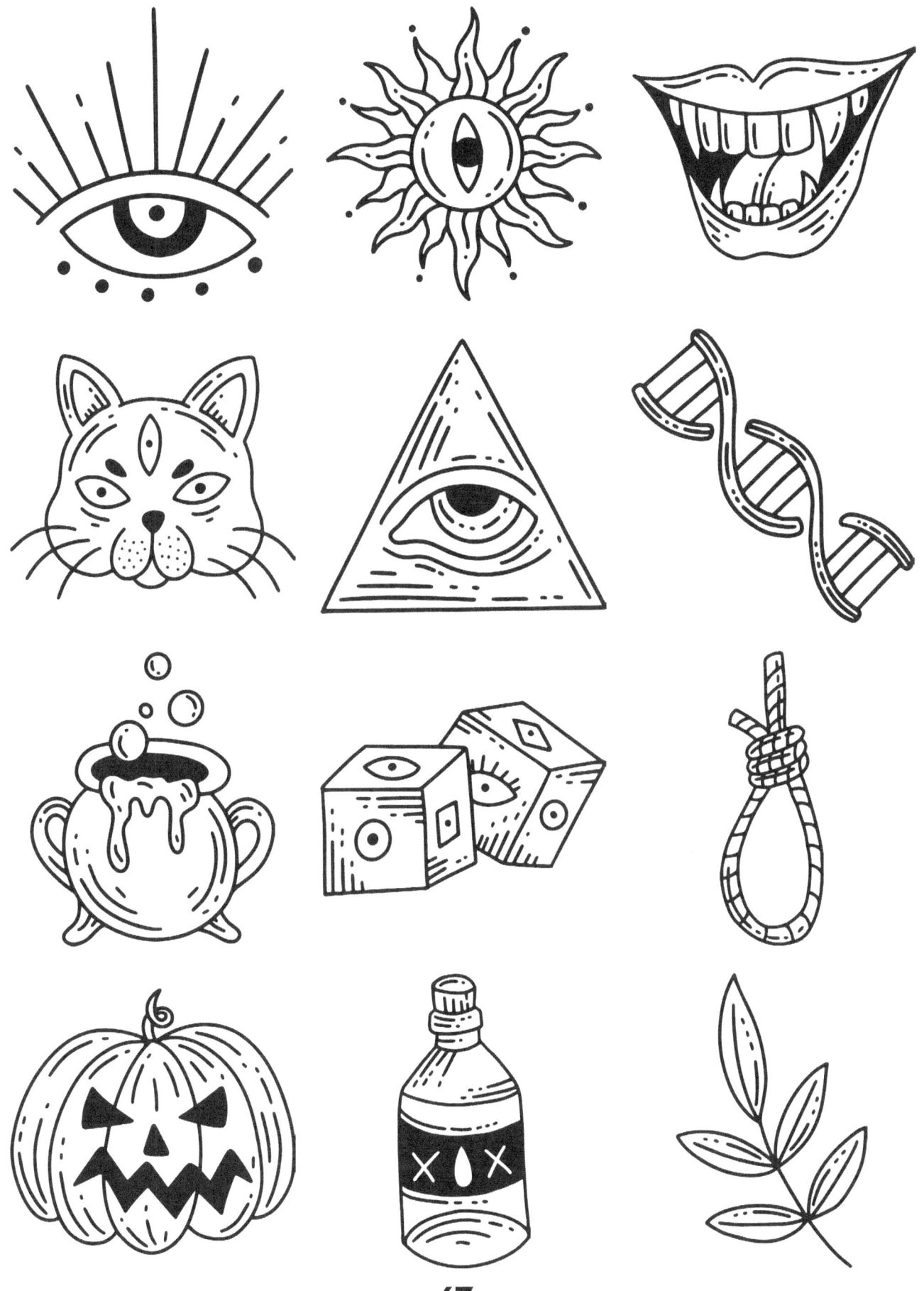

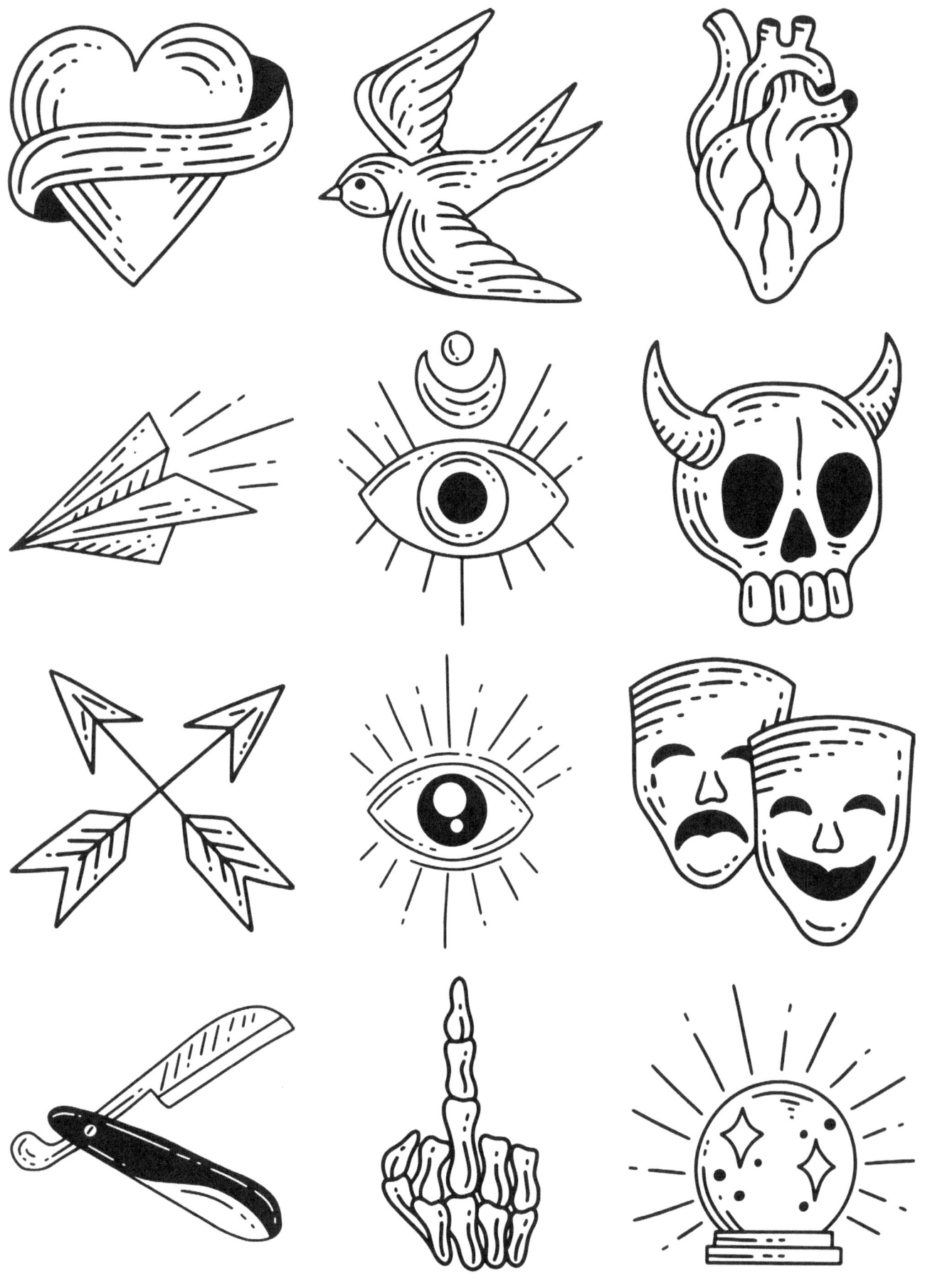

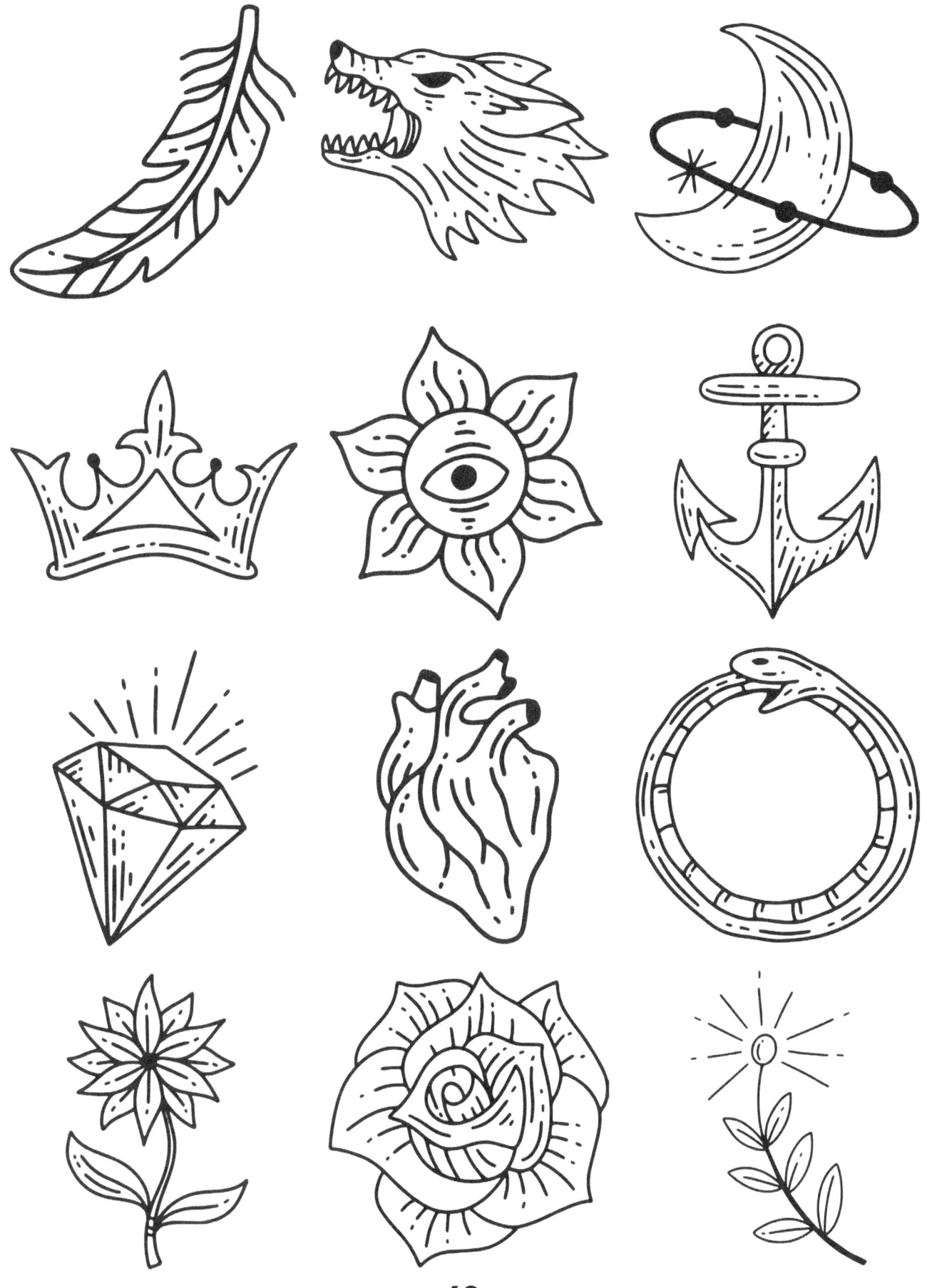

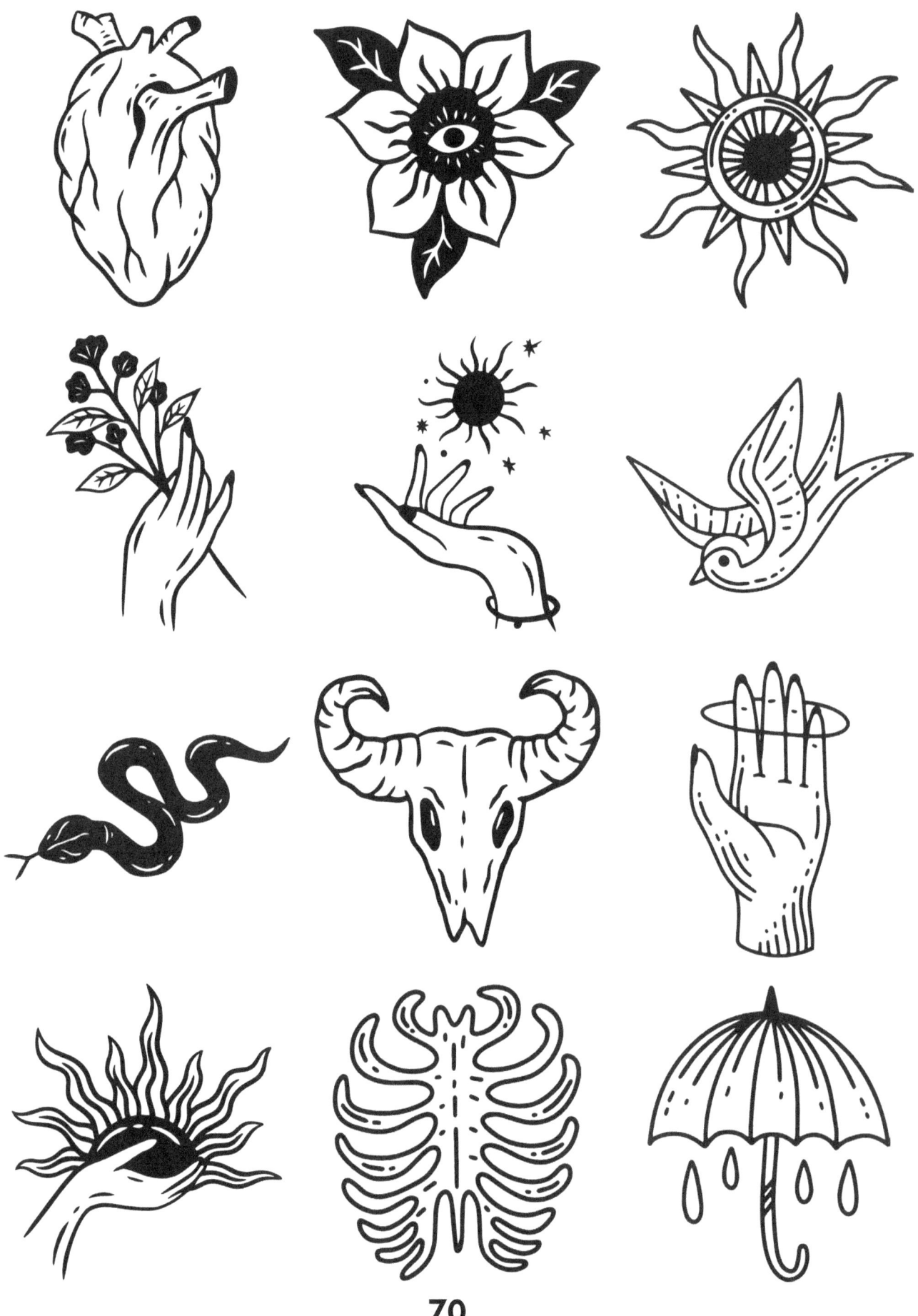

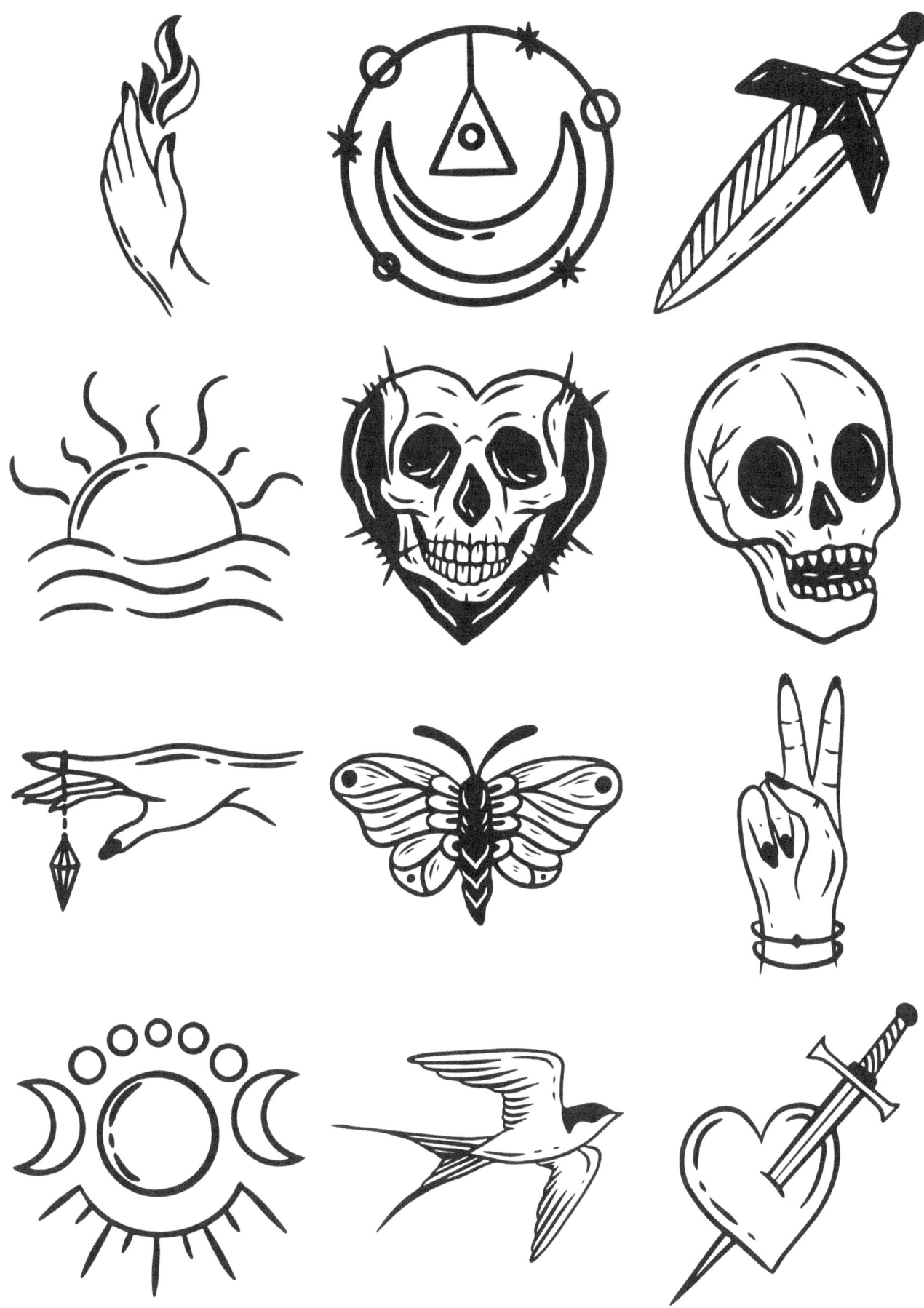

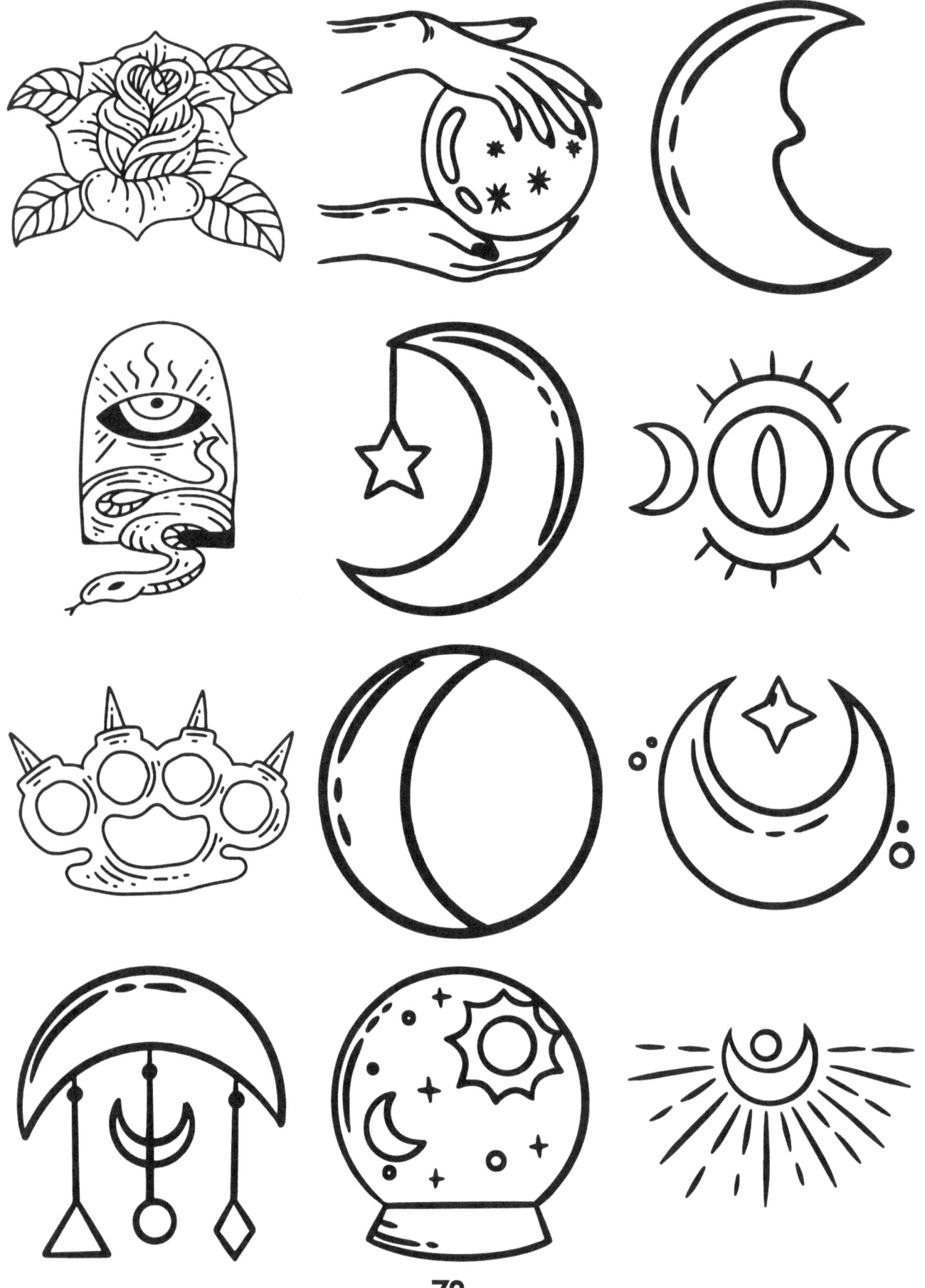

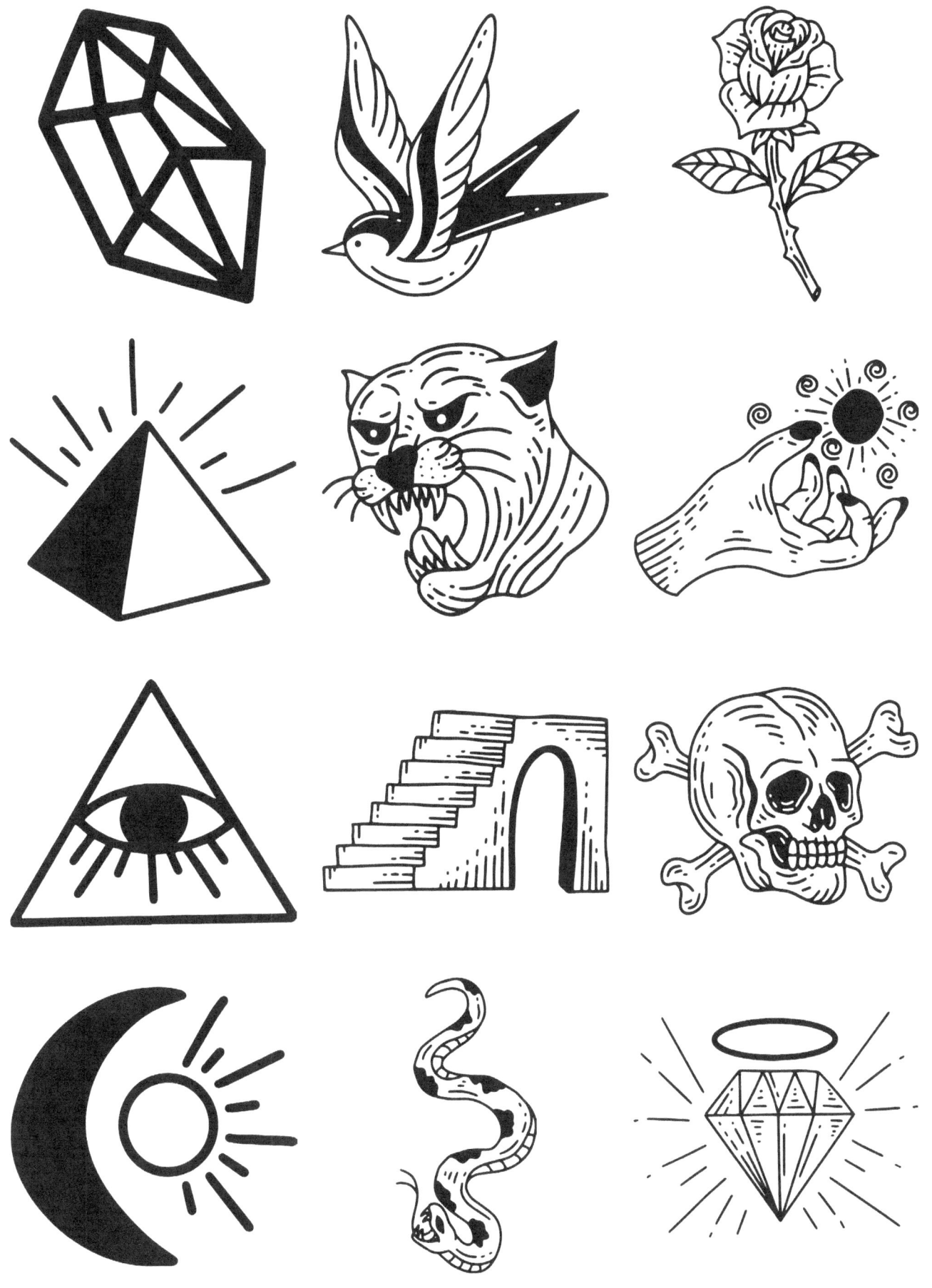

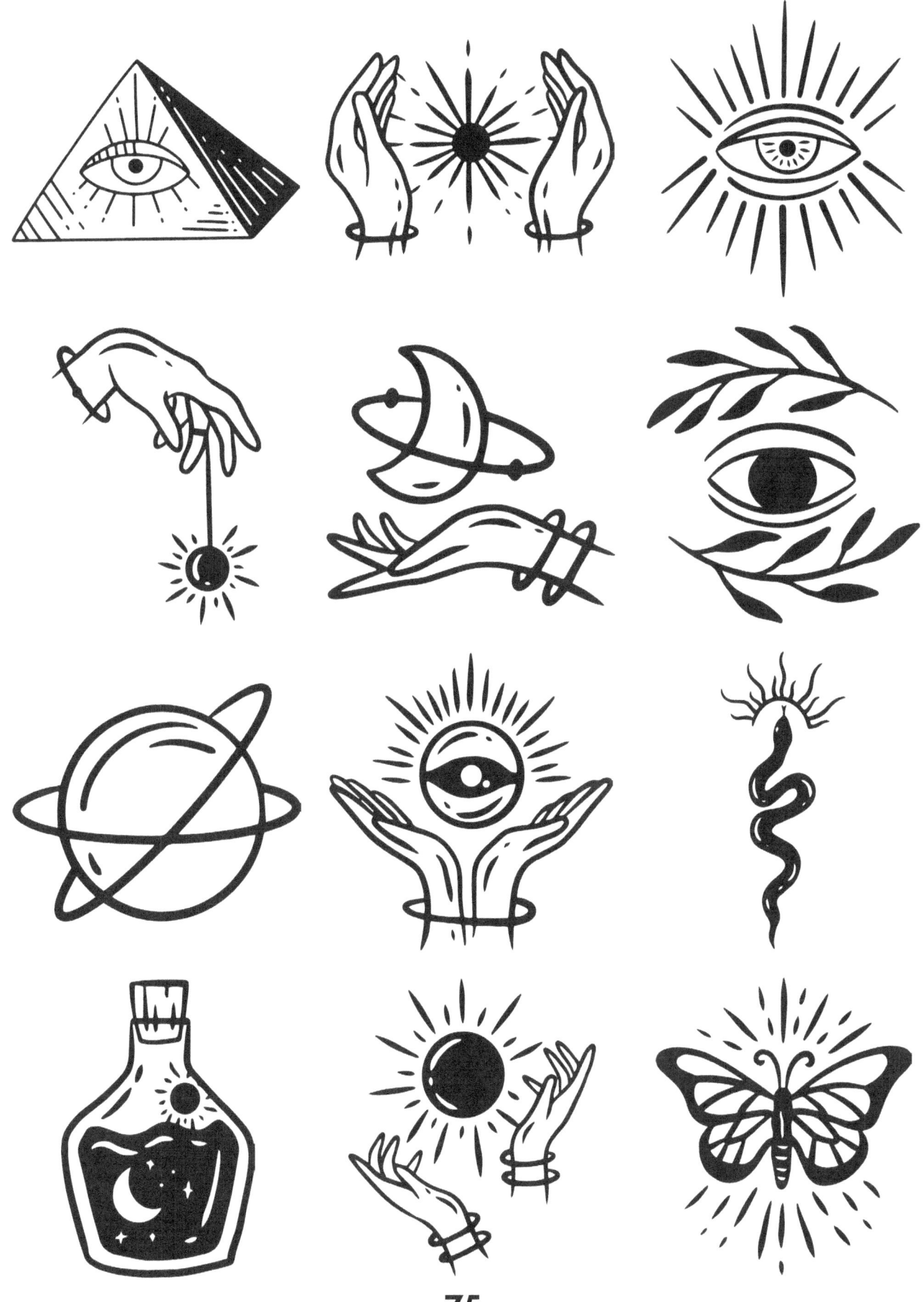

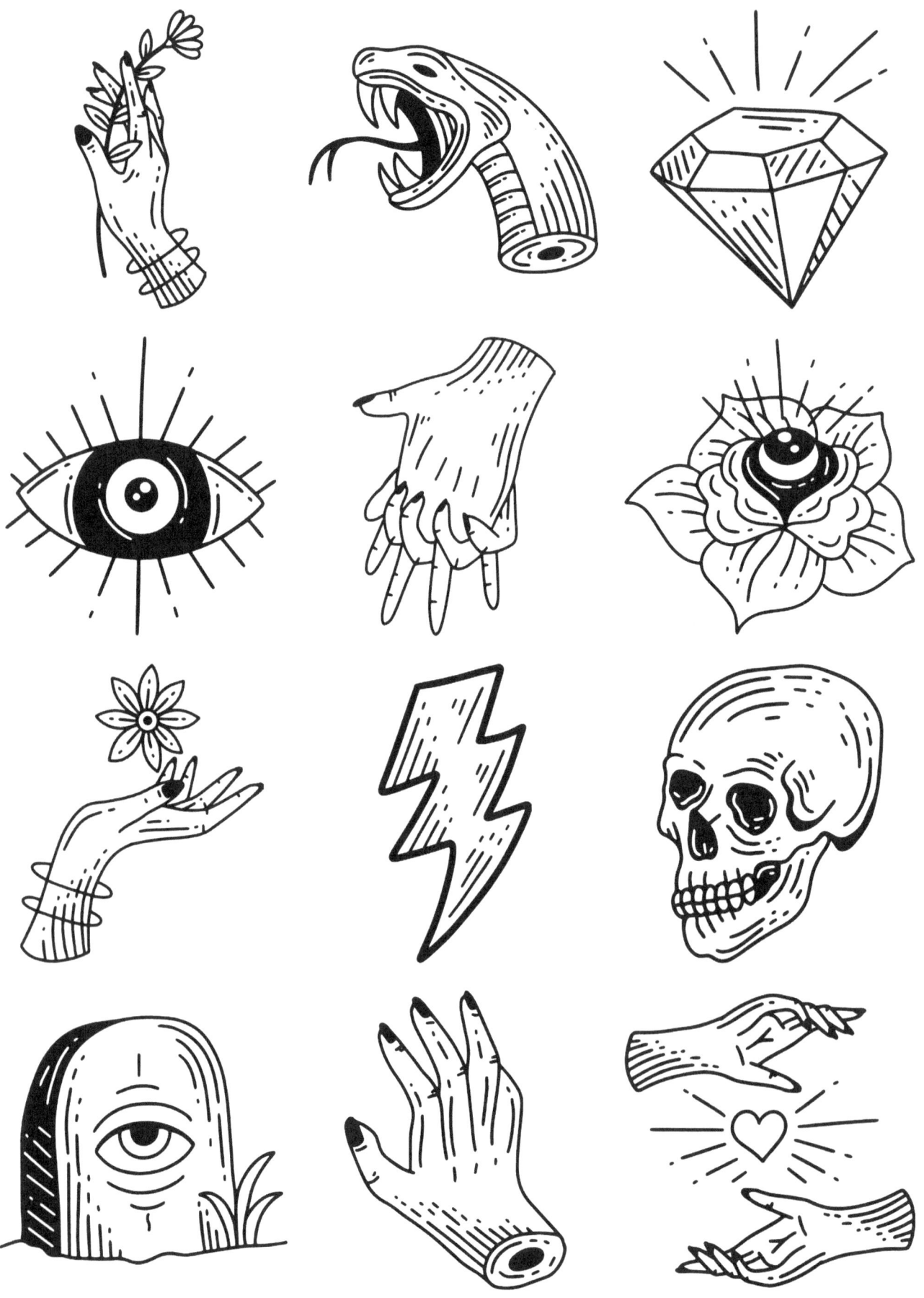

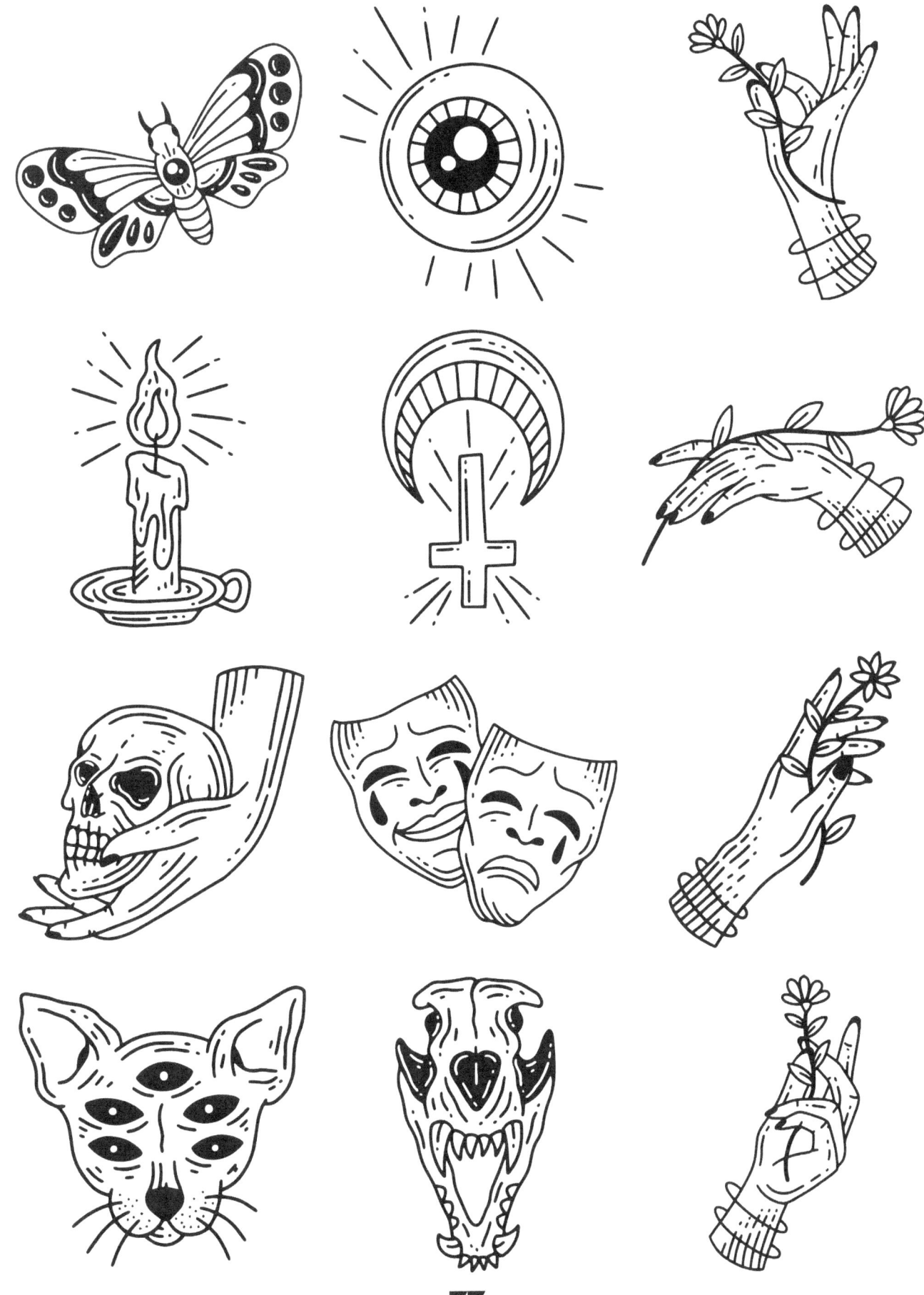

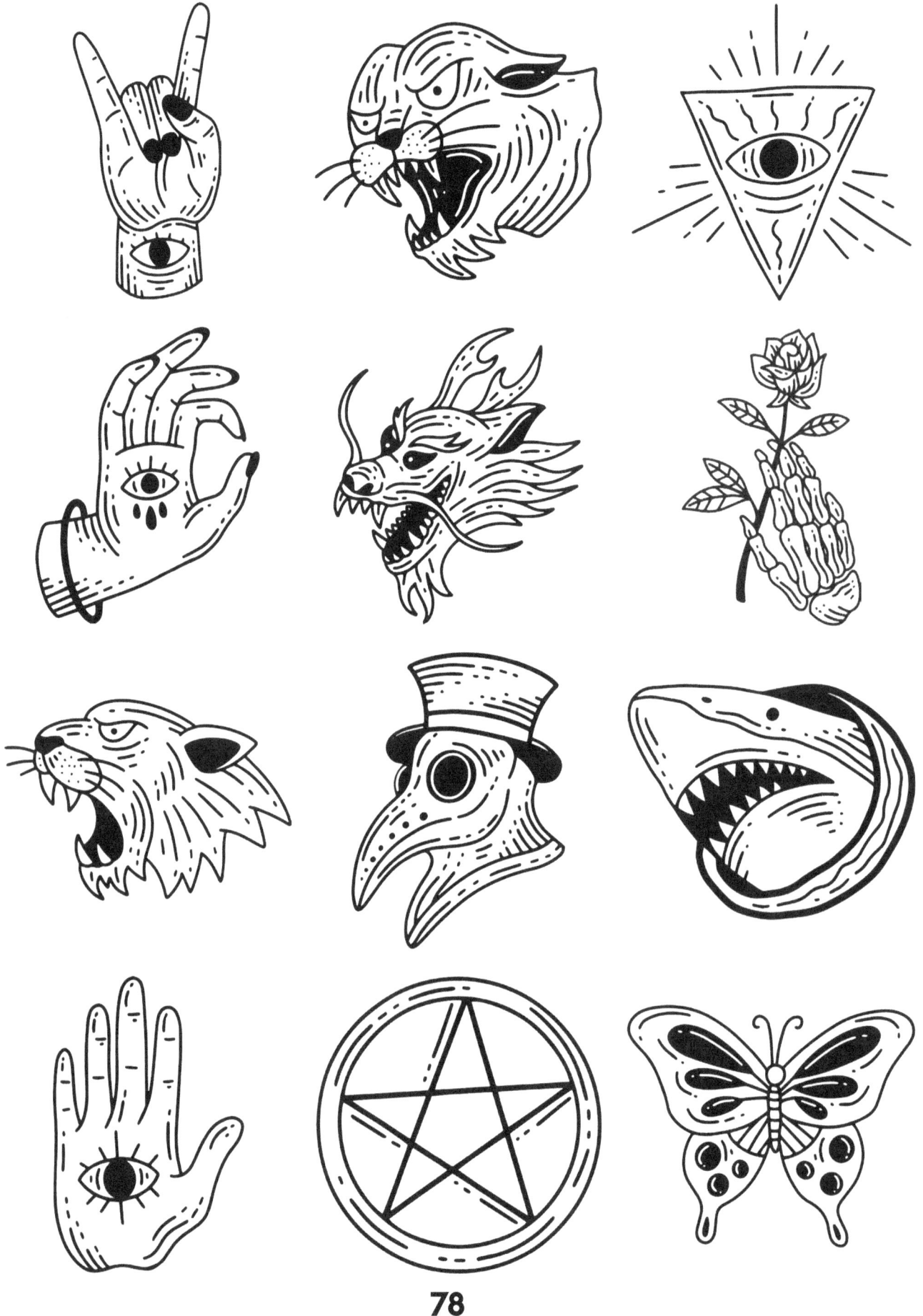

78

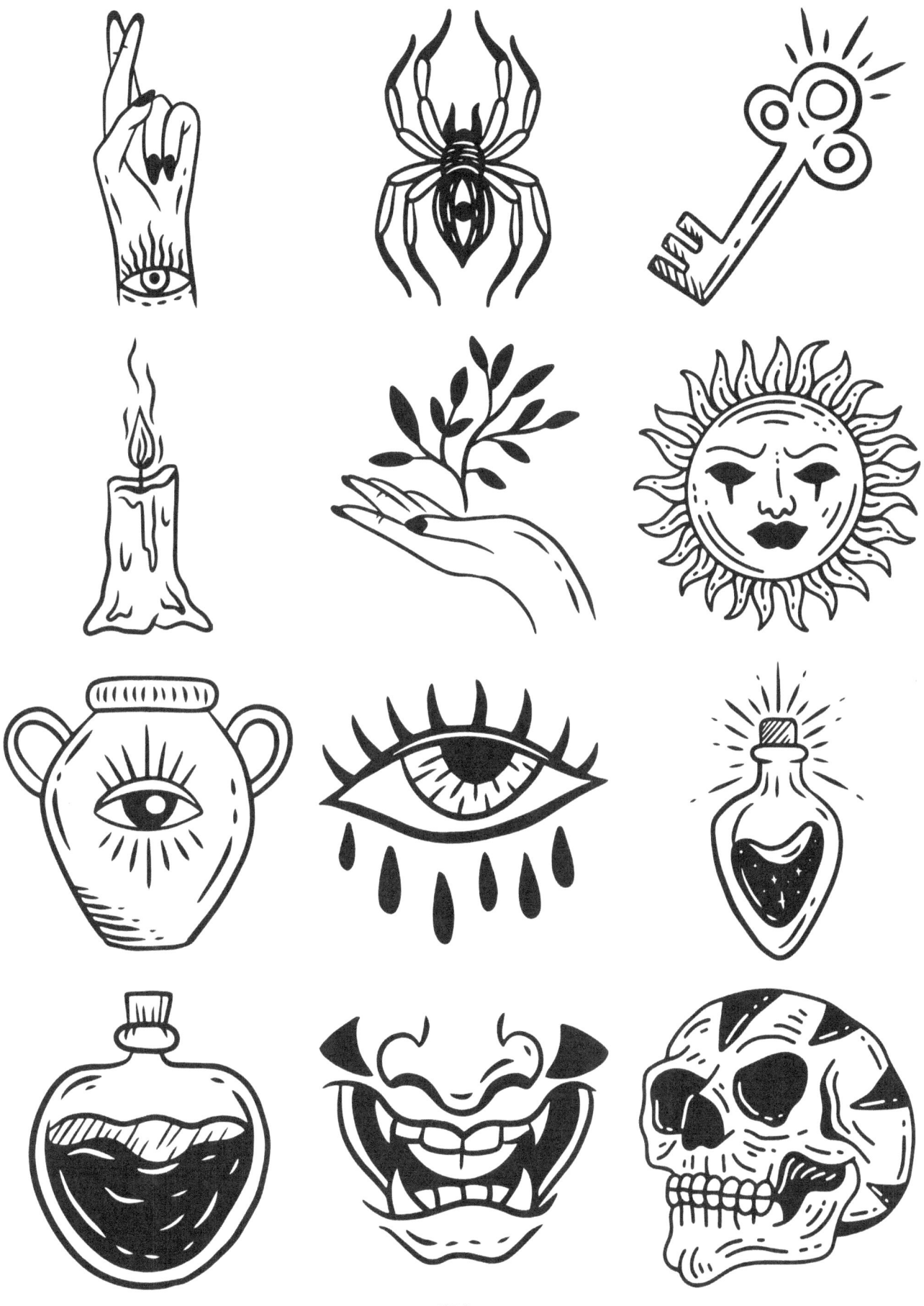

79

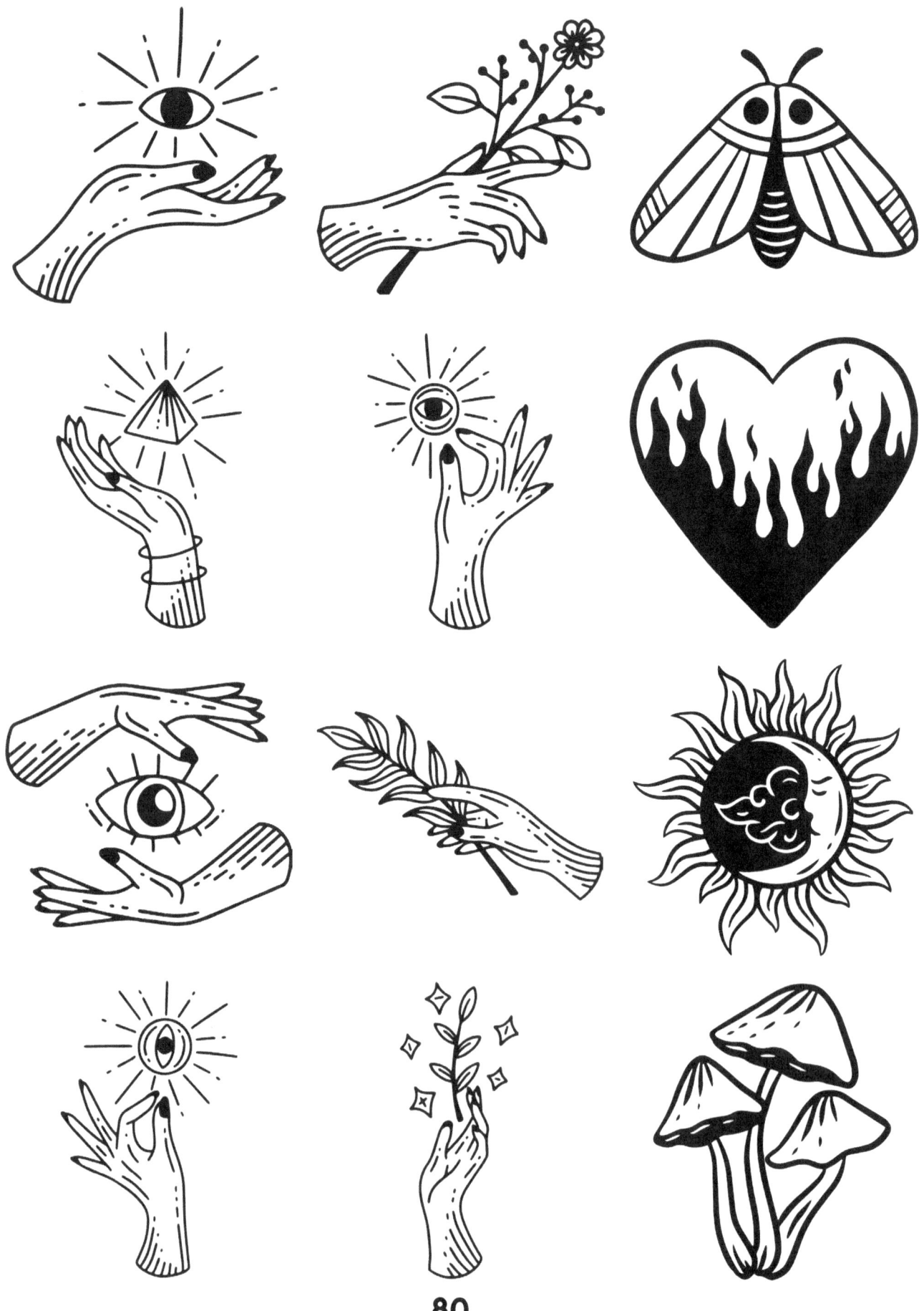

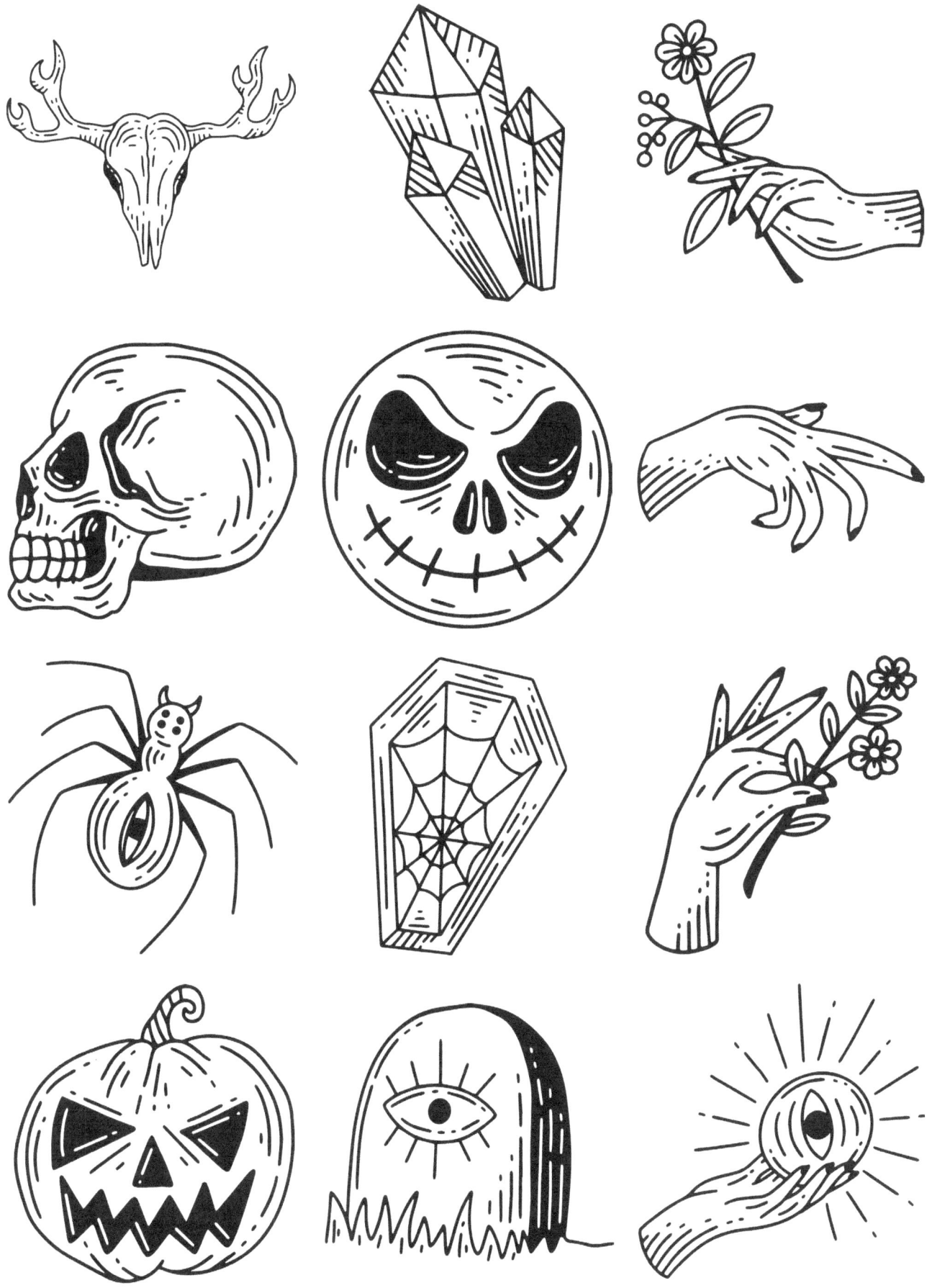

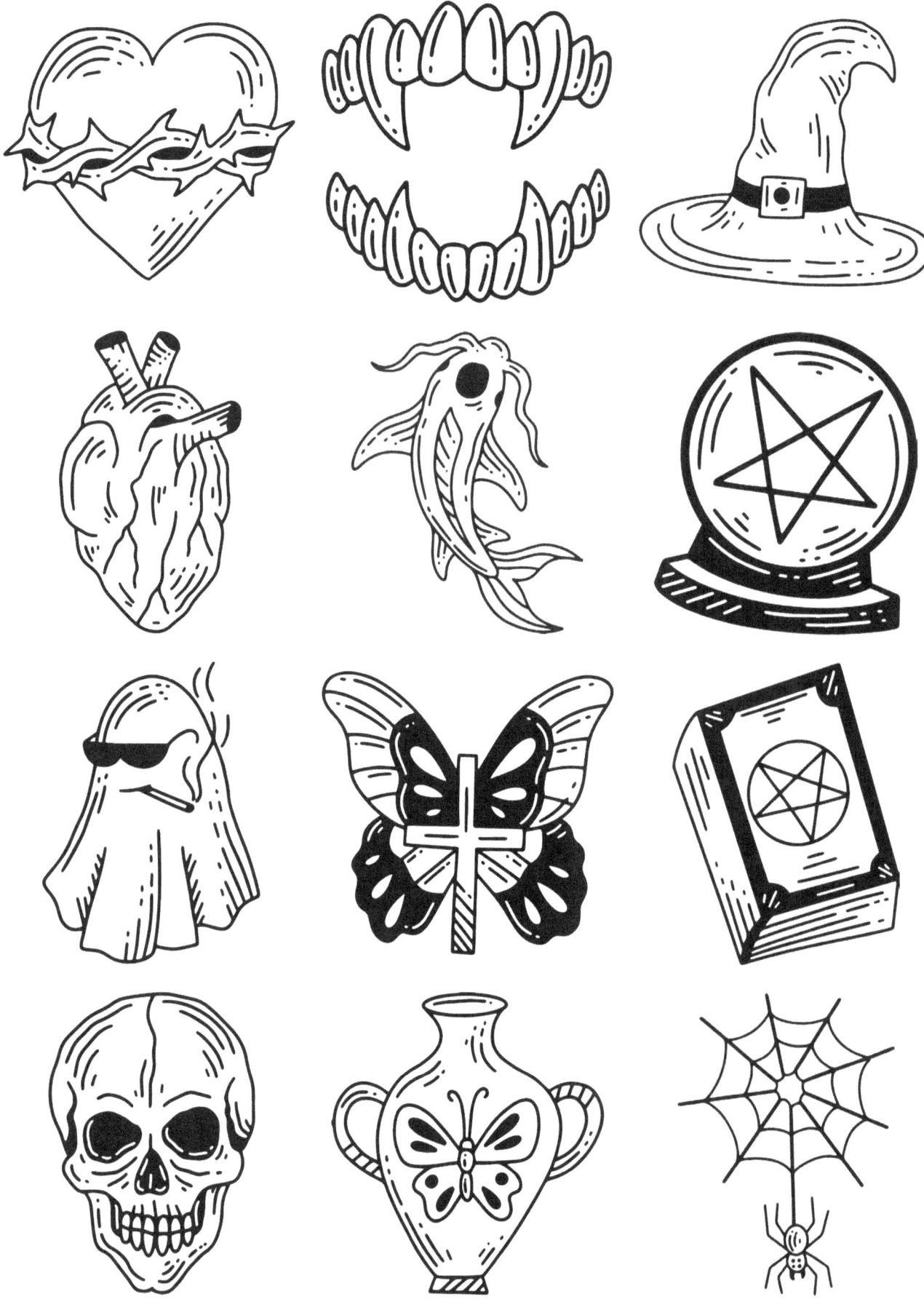

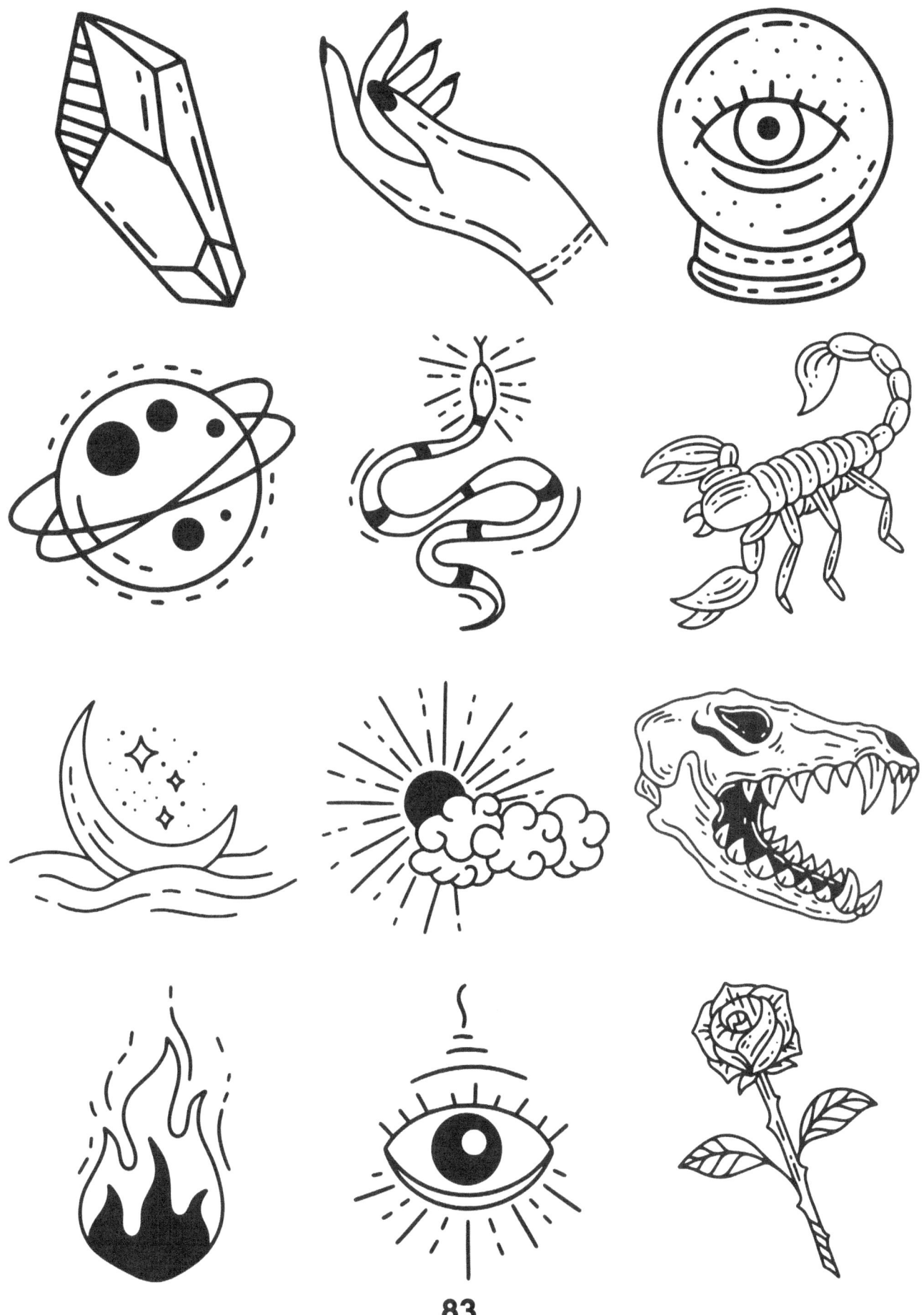

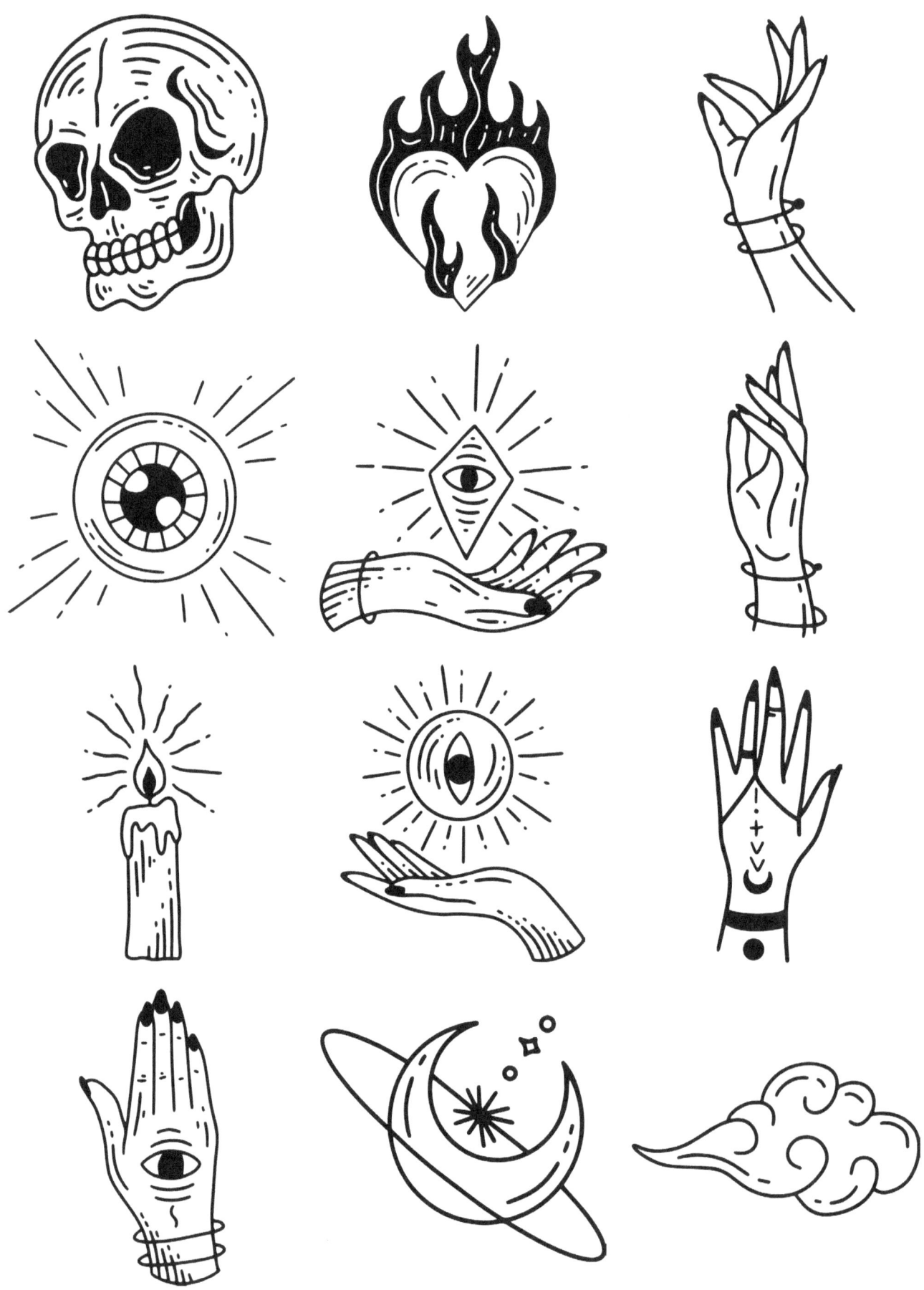

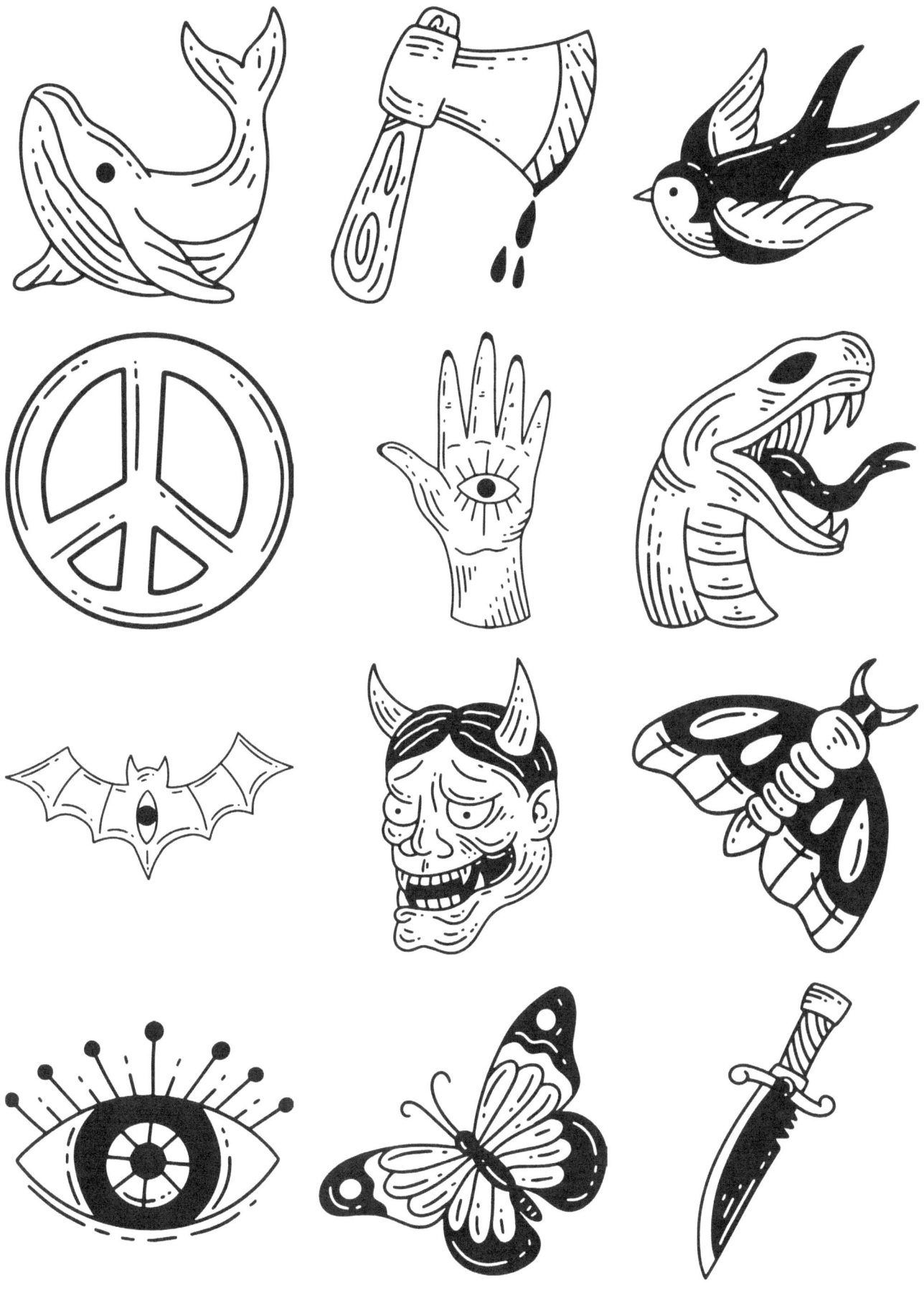

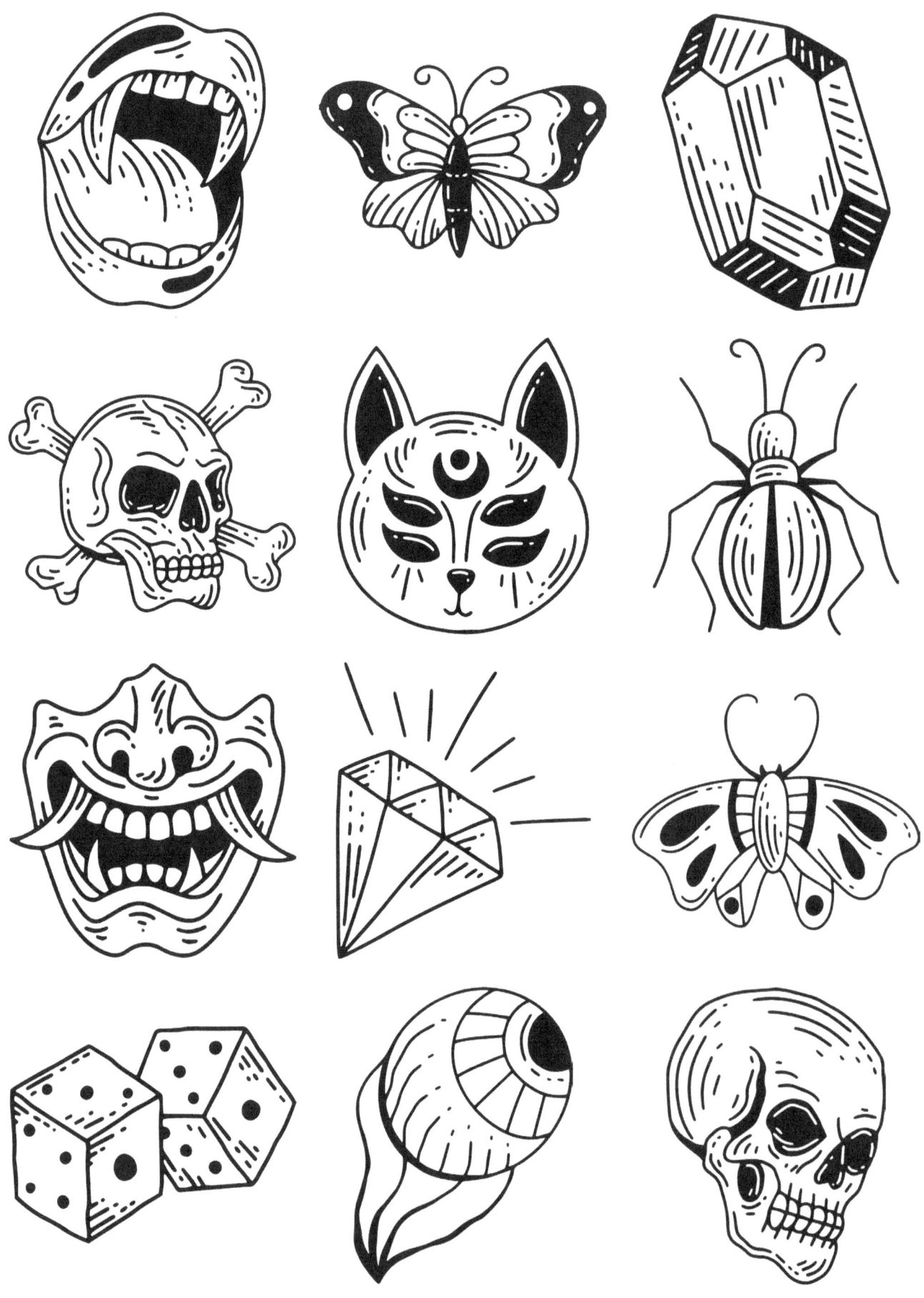

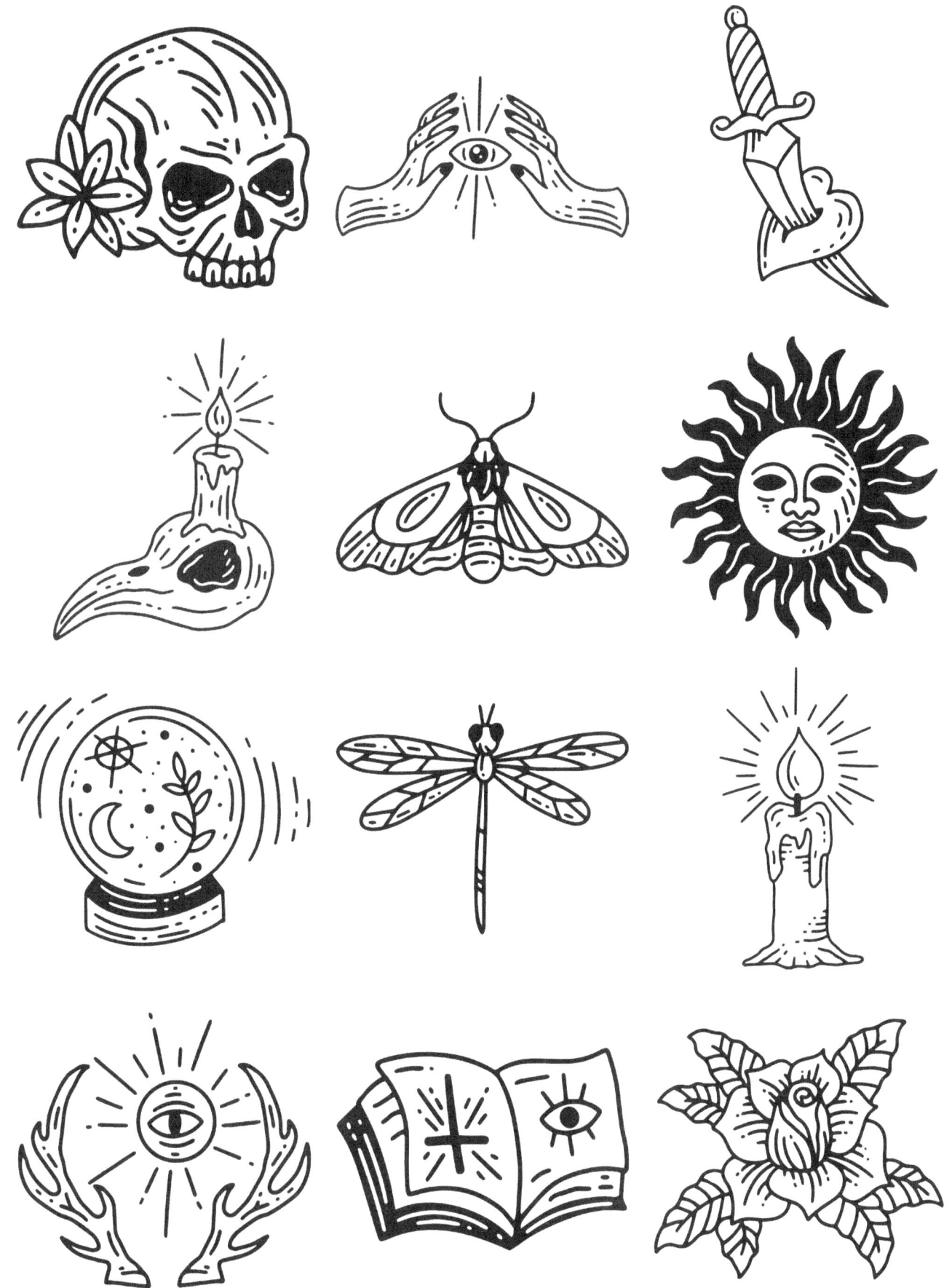

87

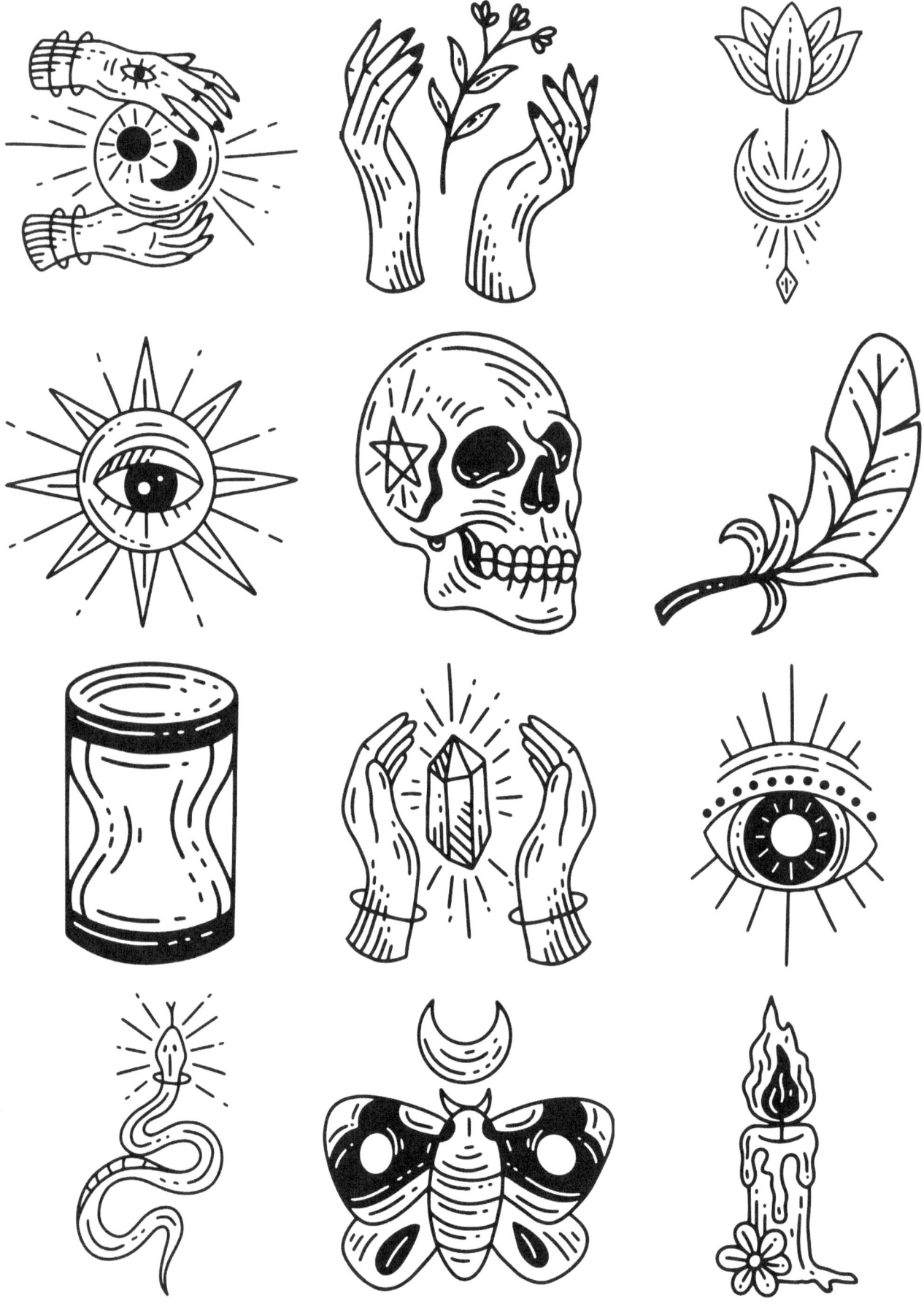

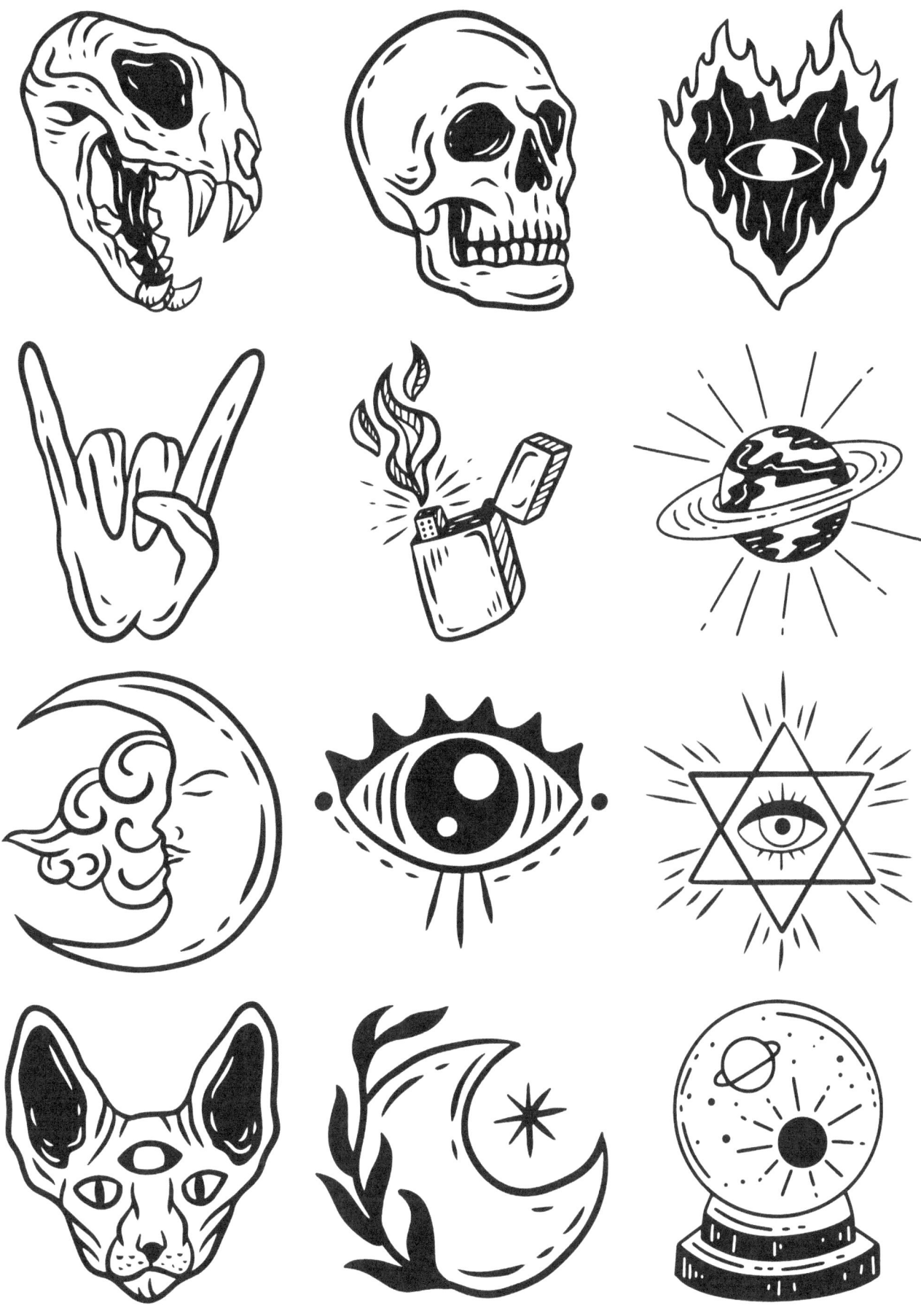

89

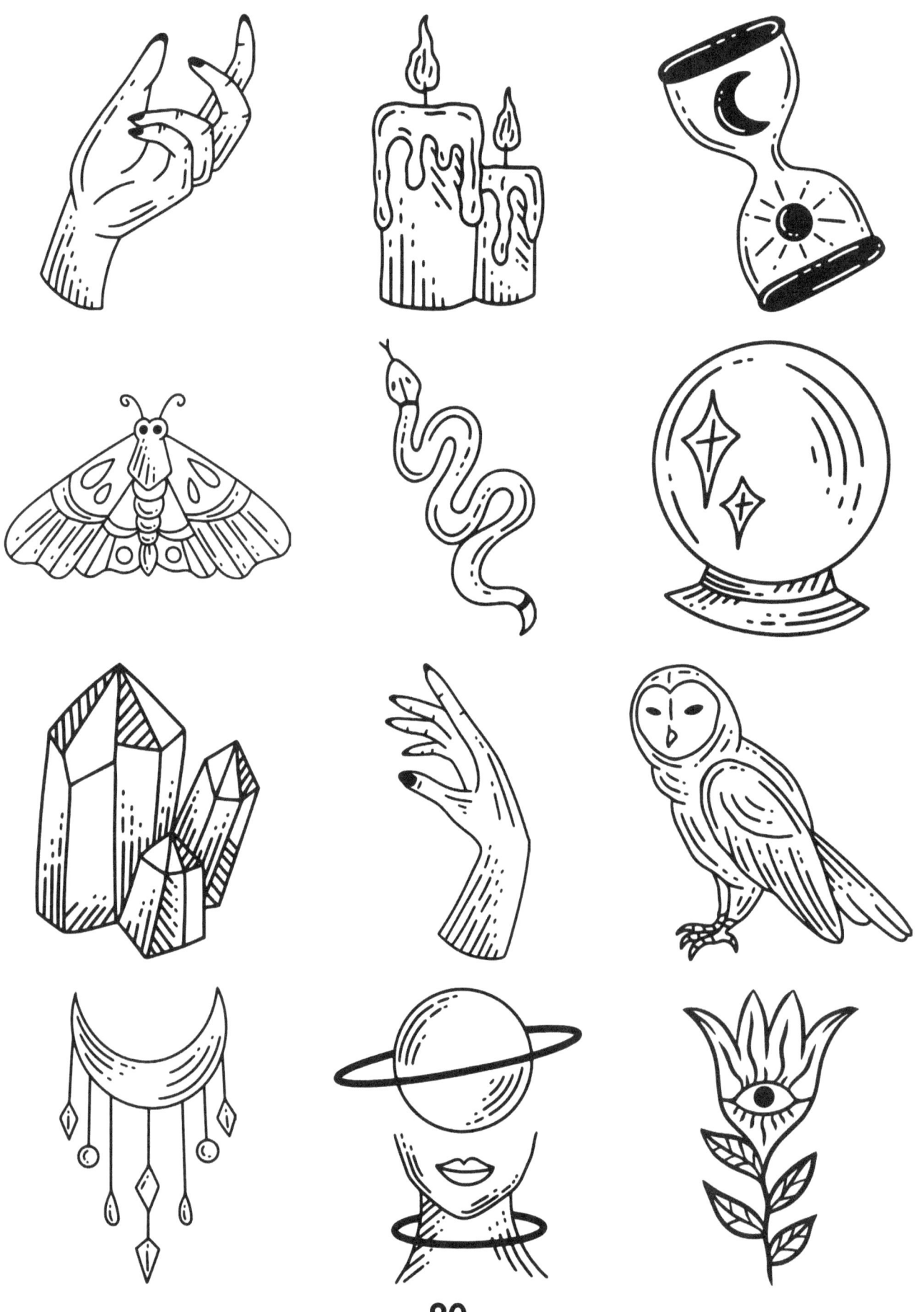

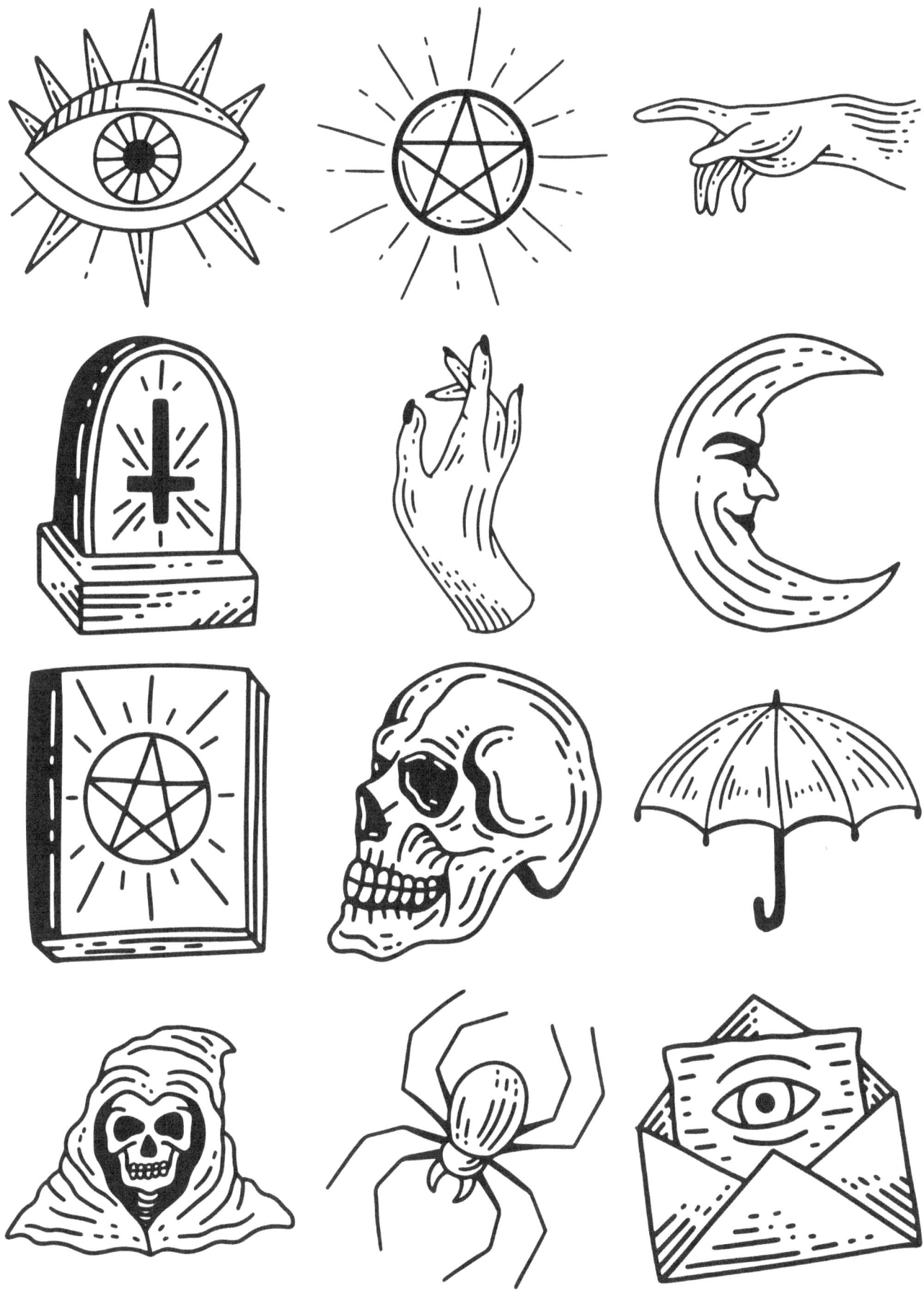

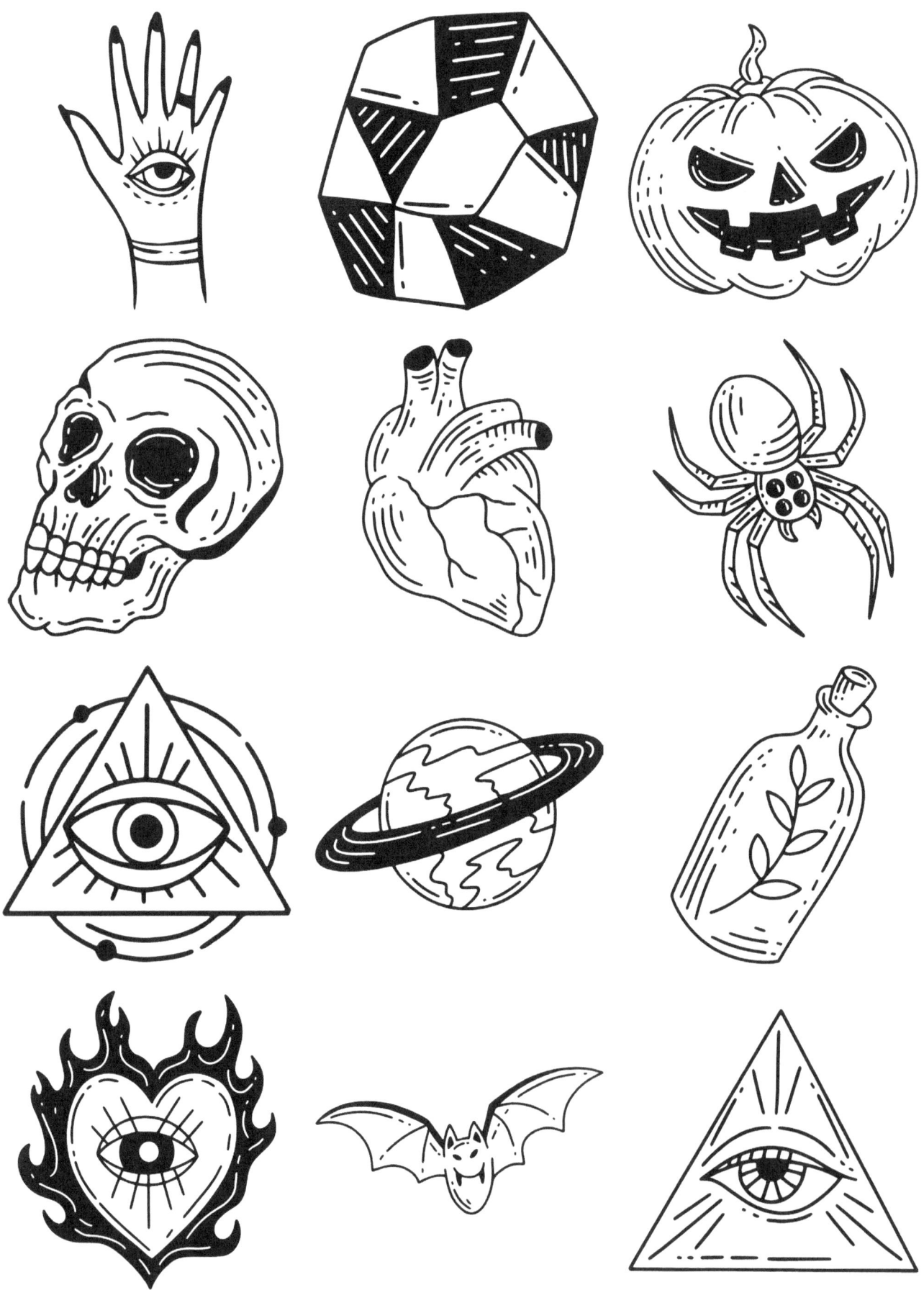

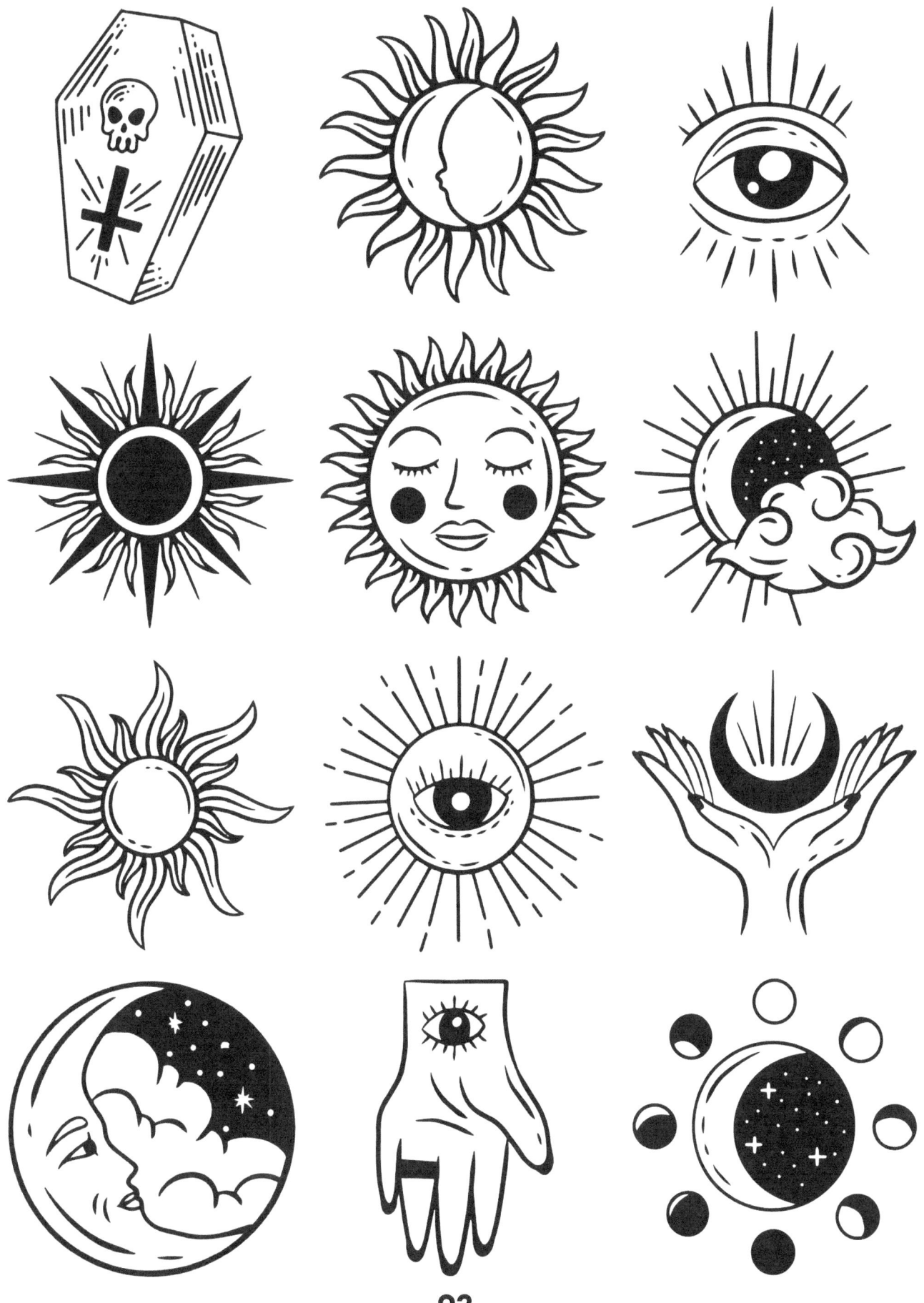

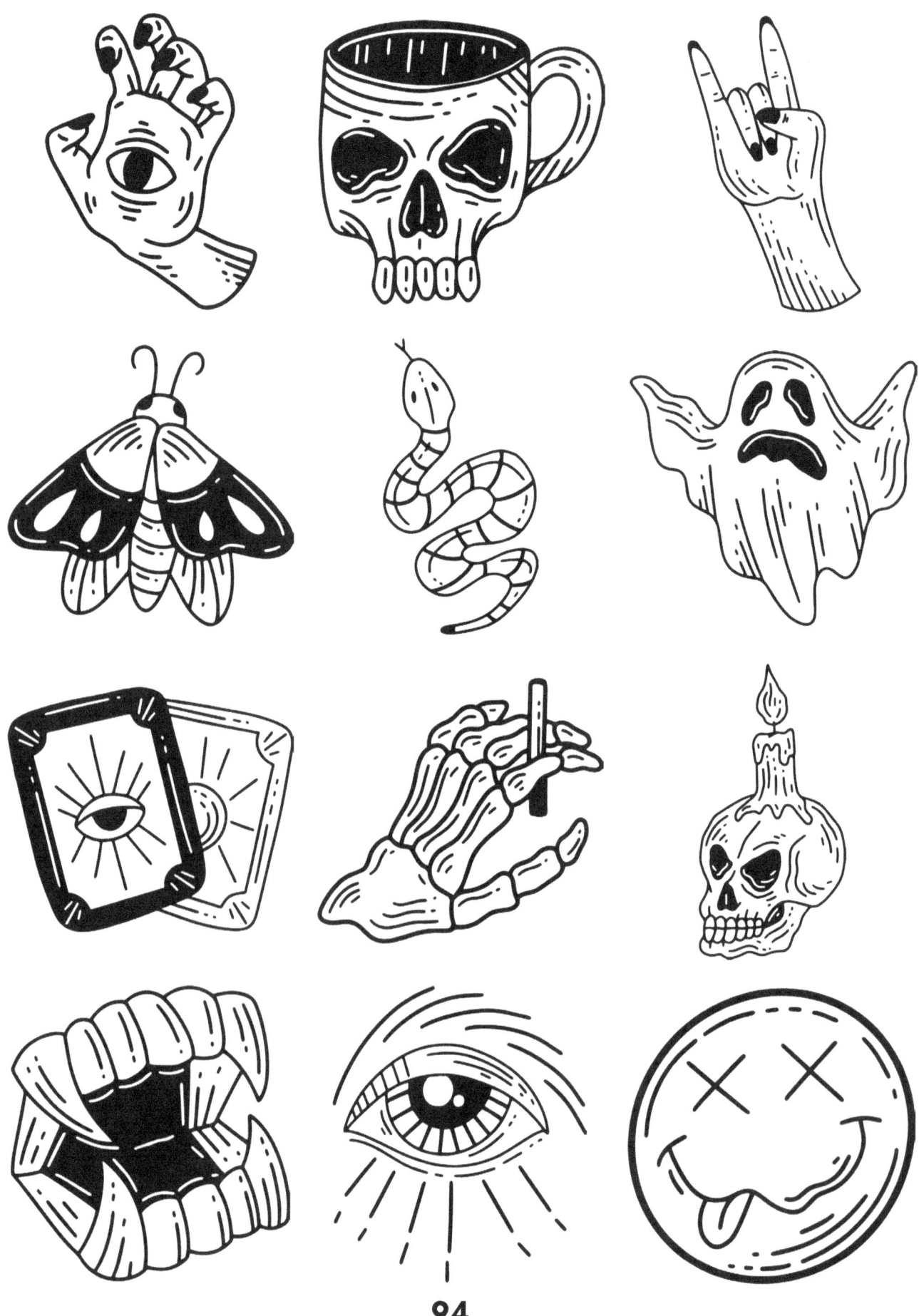

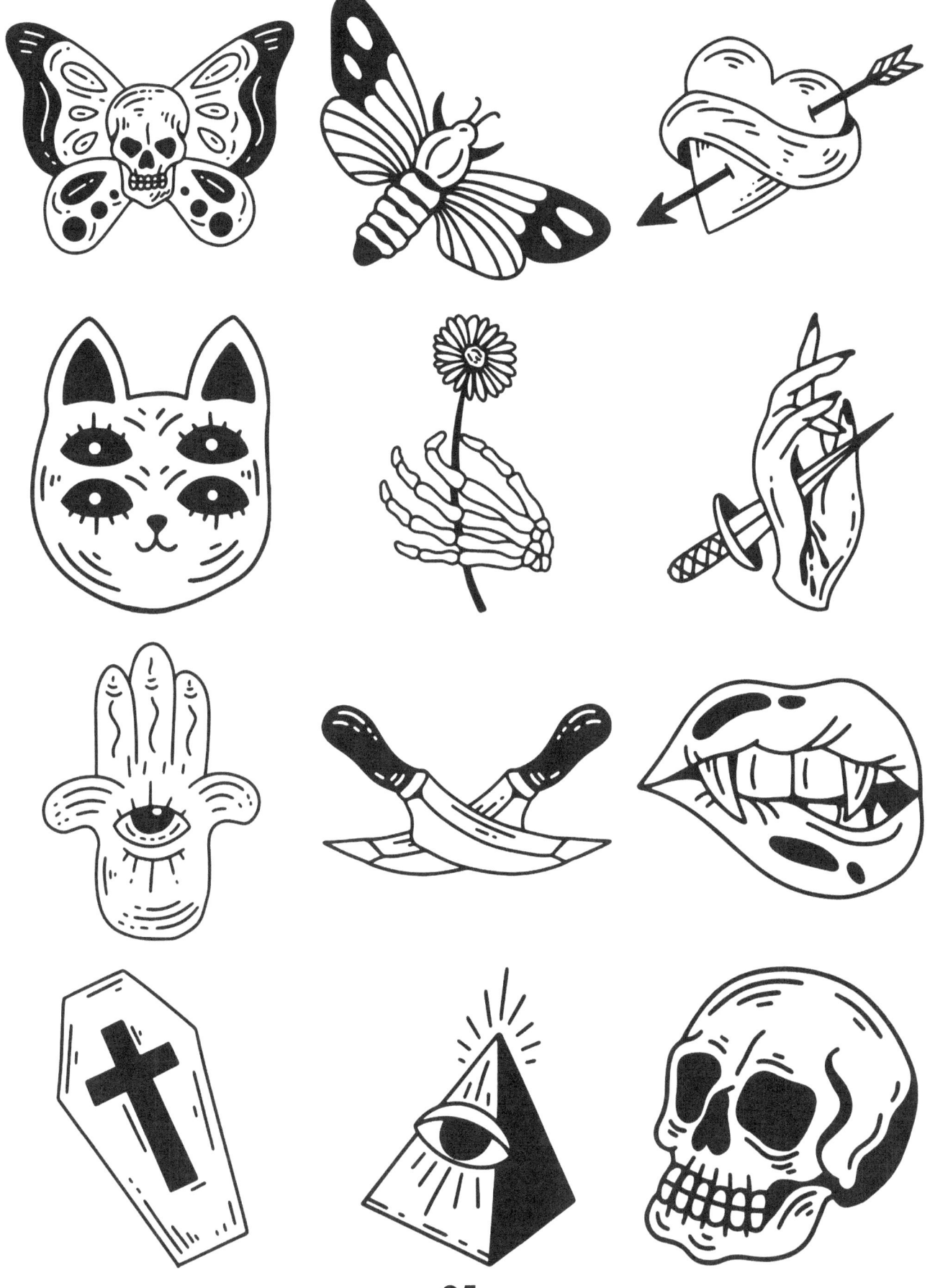

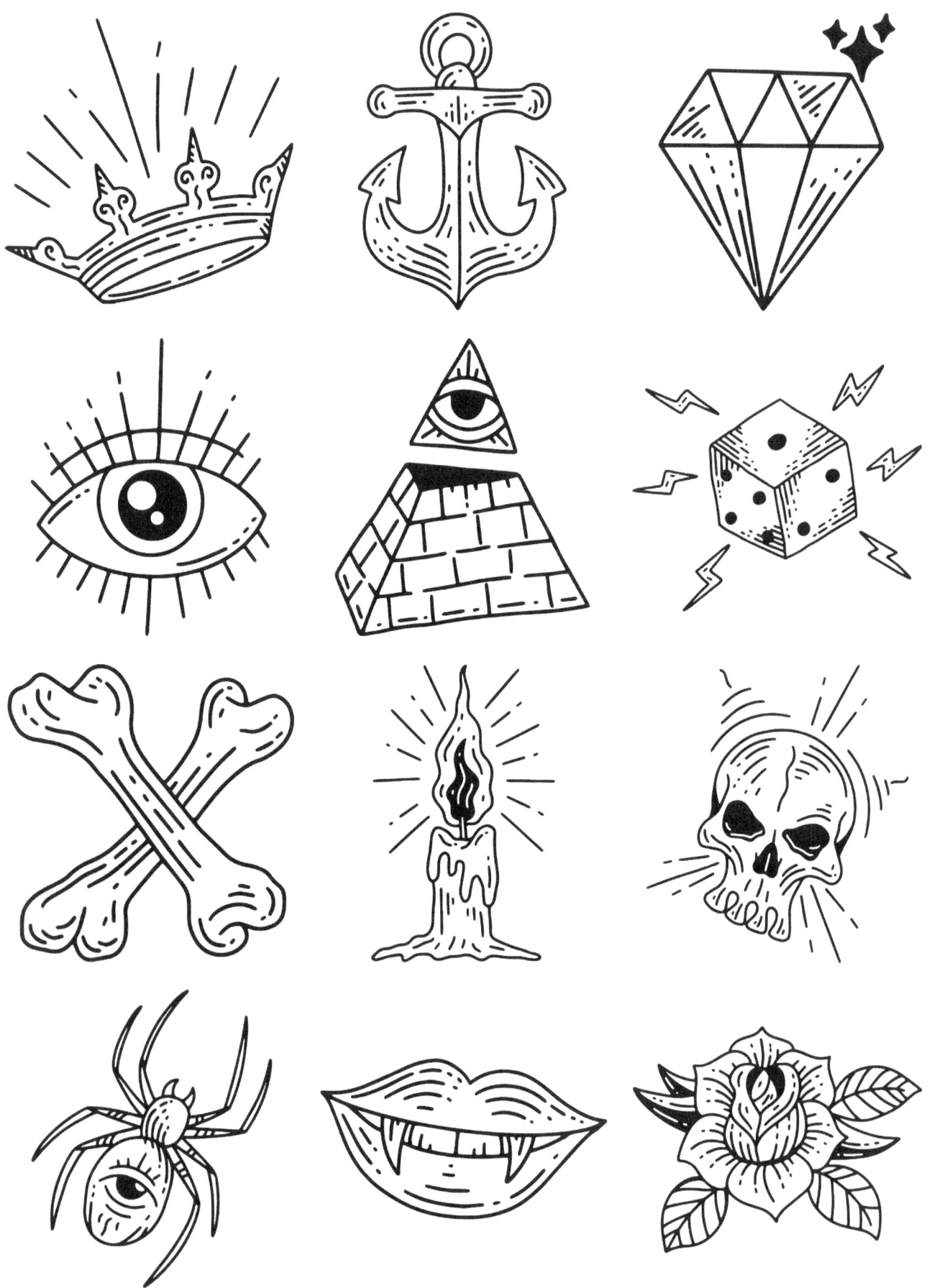

96

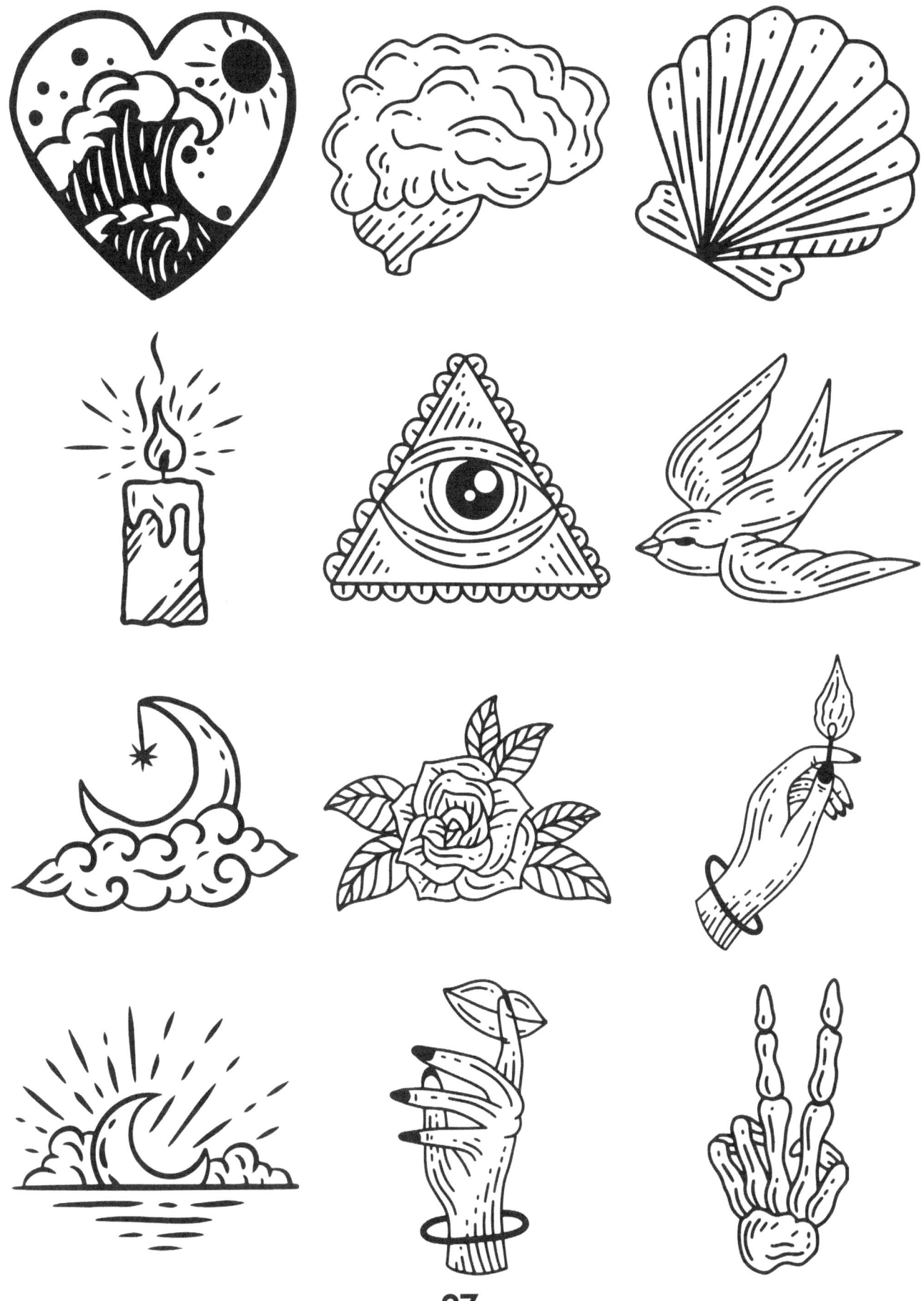

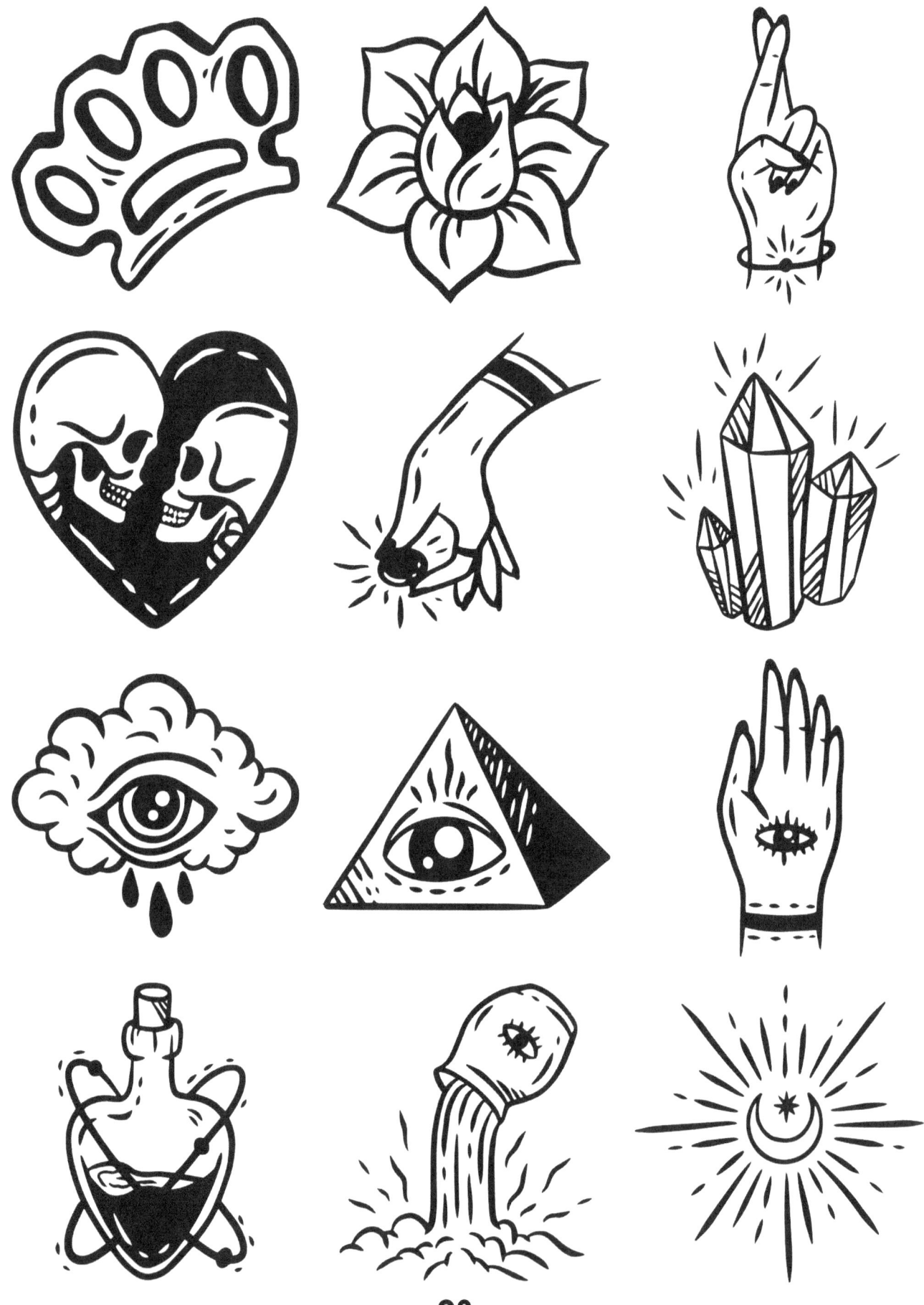

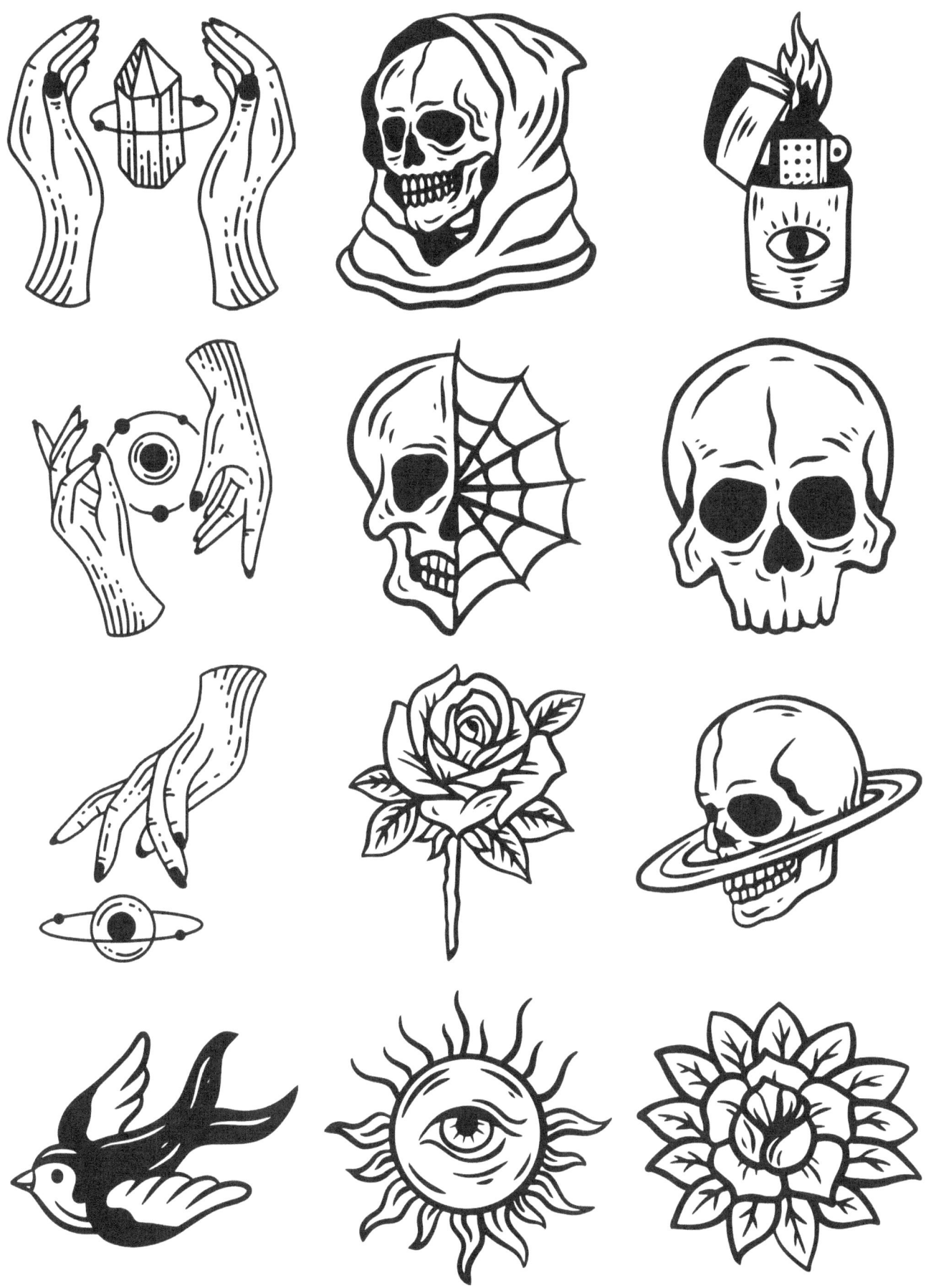

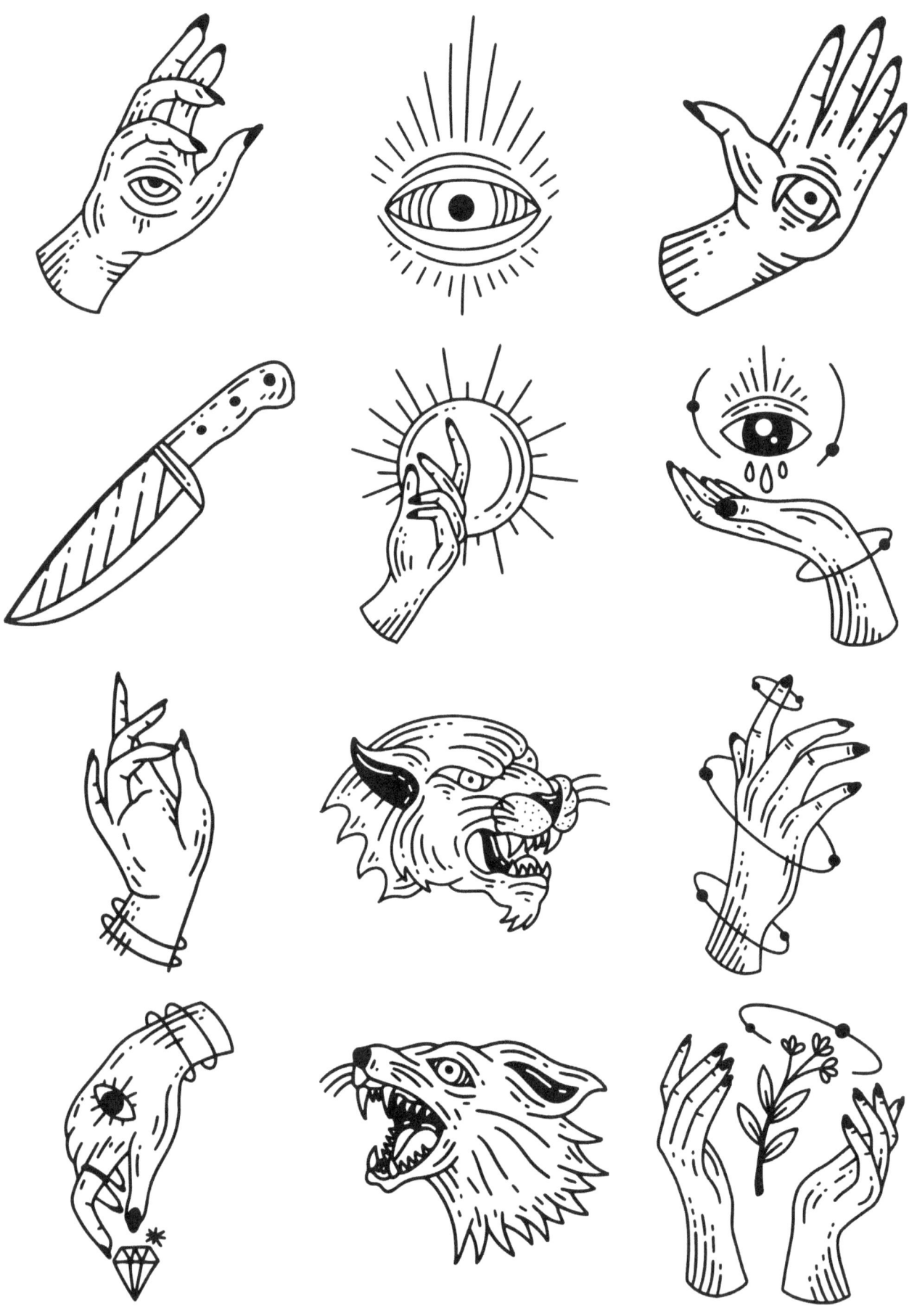

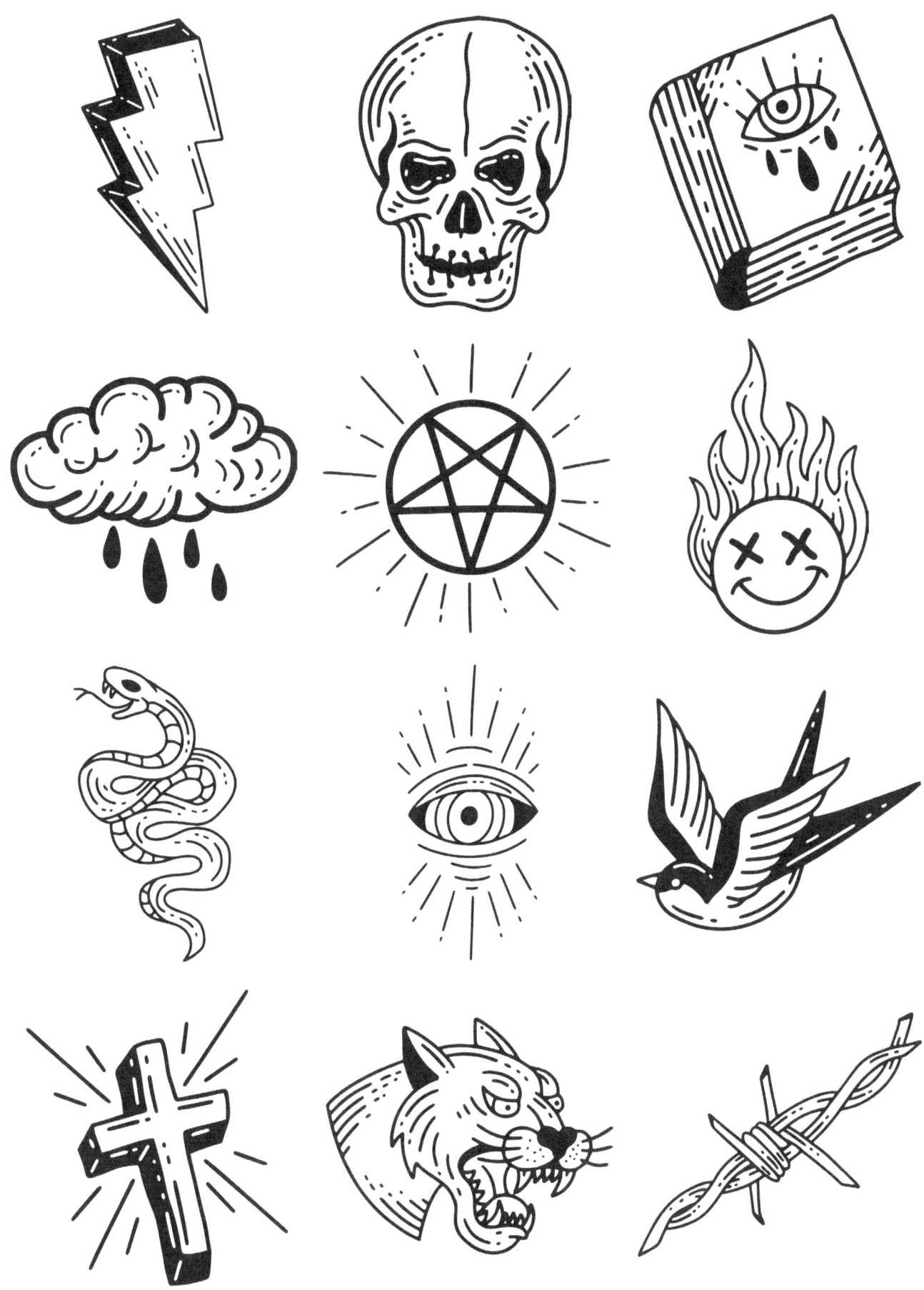

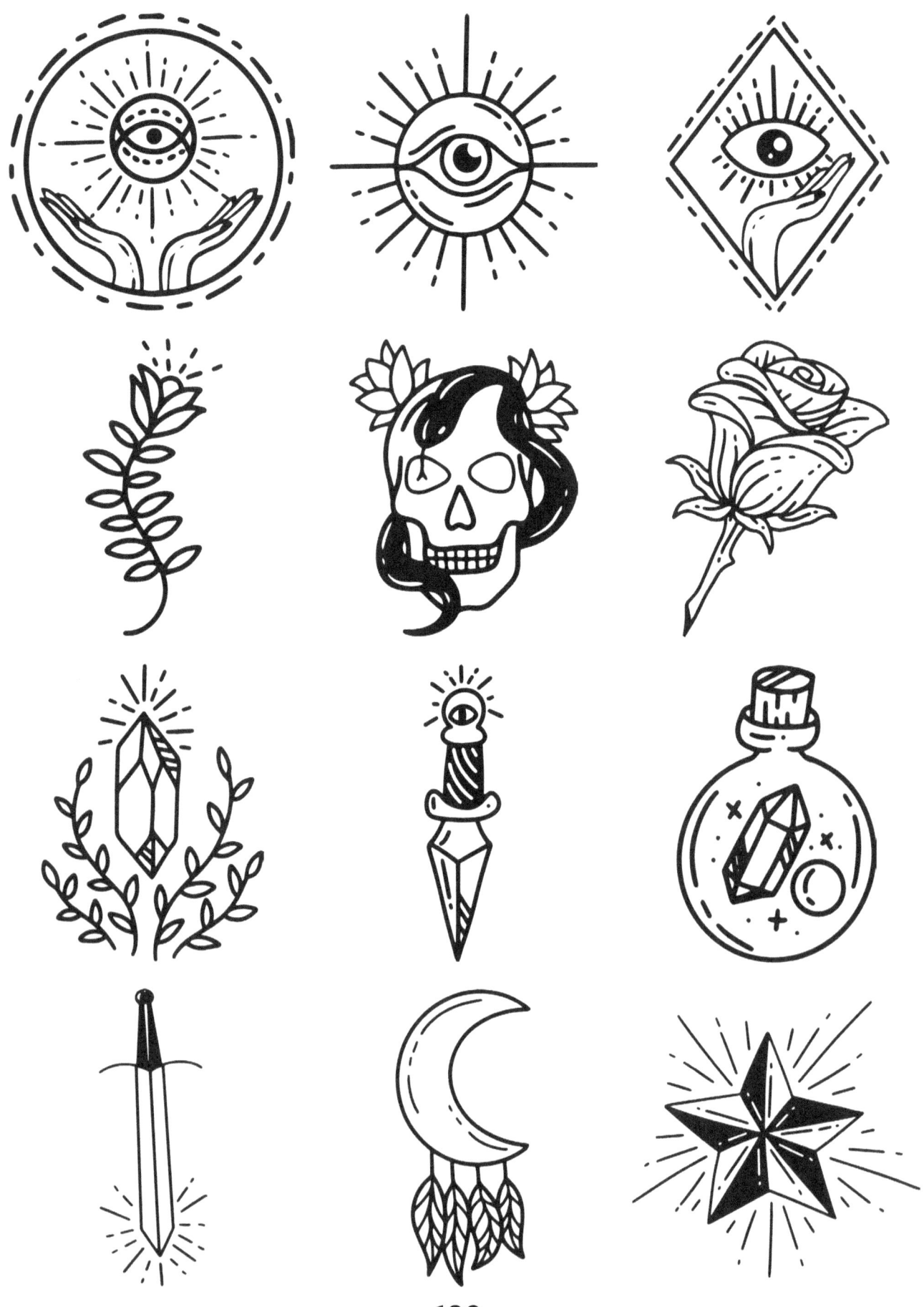

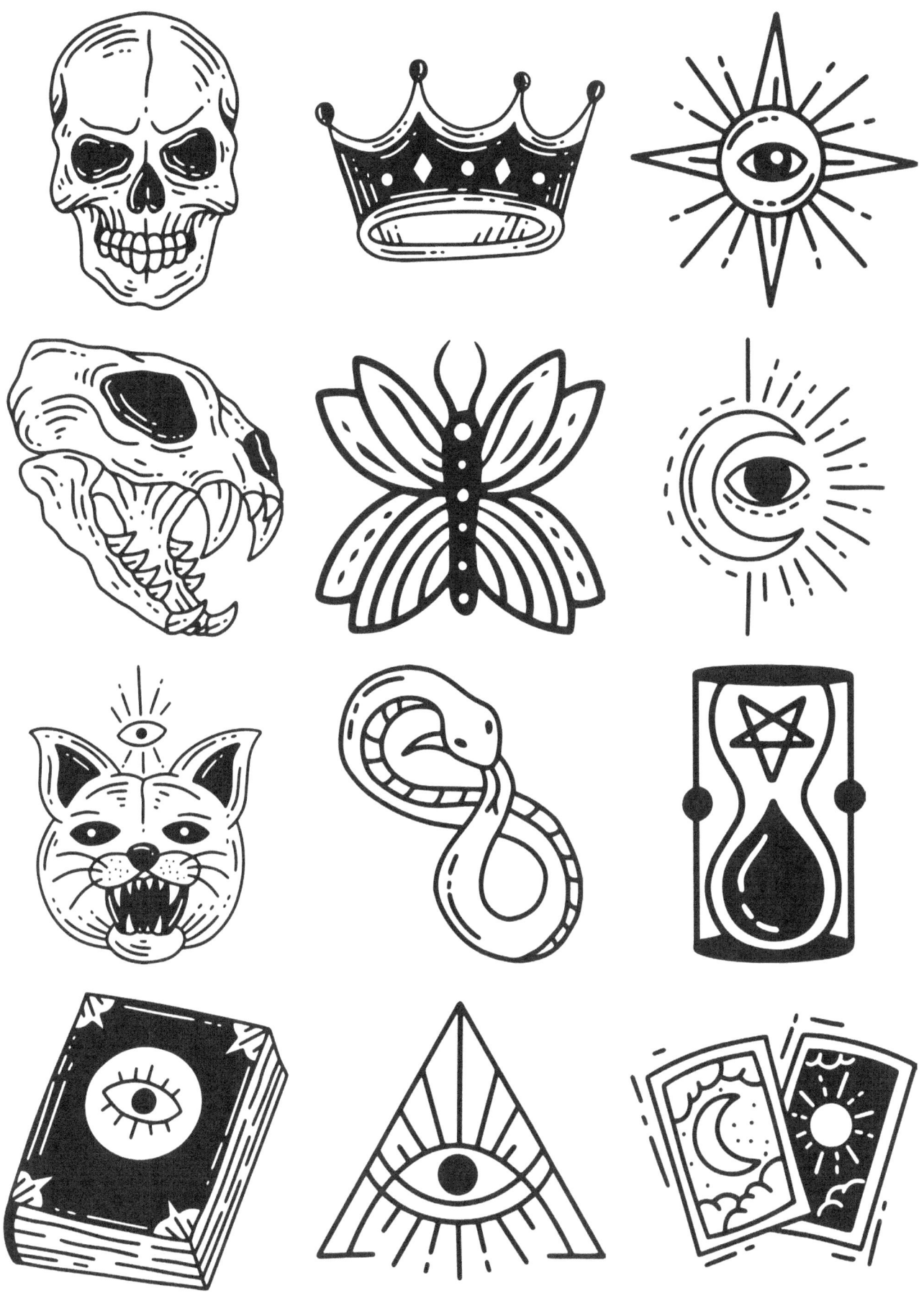

103

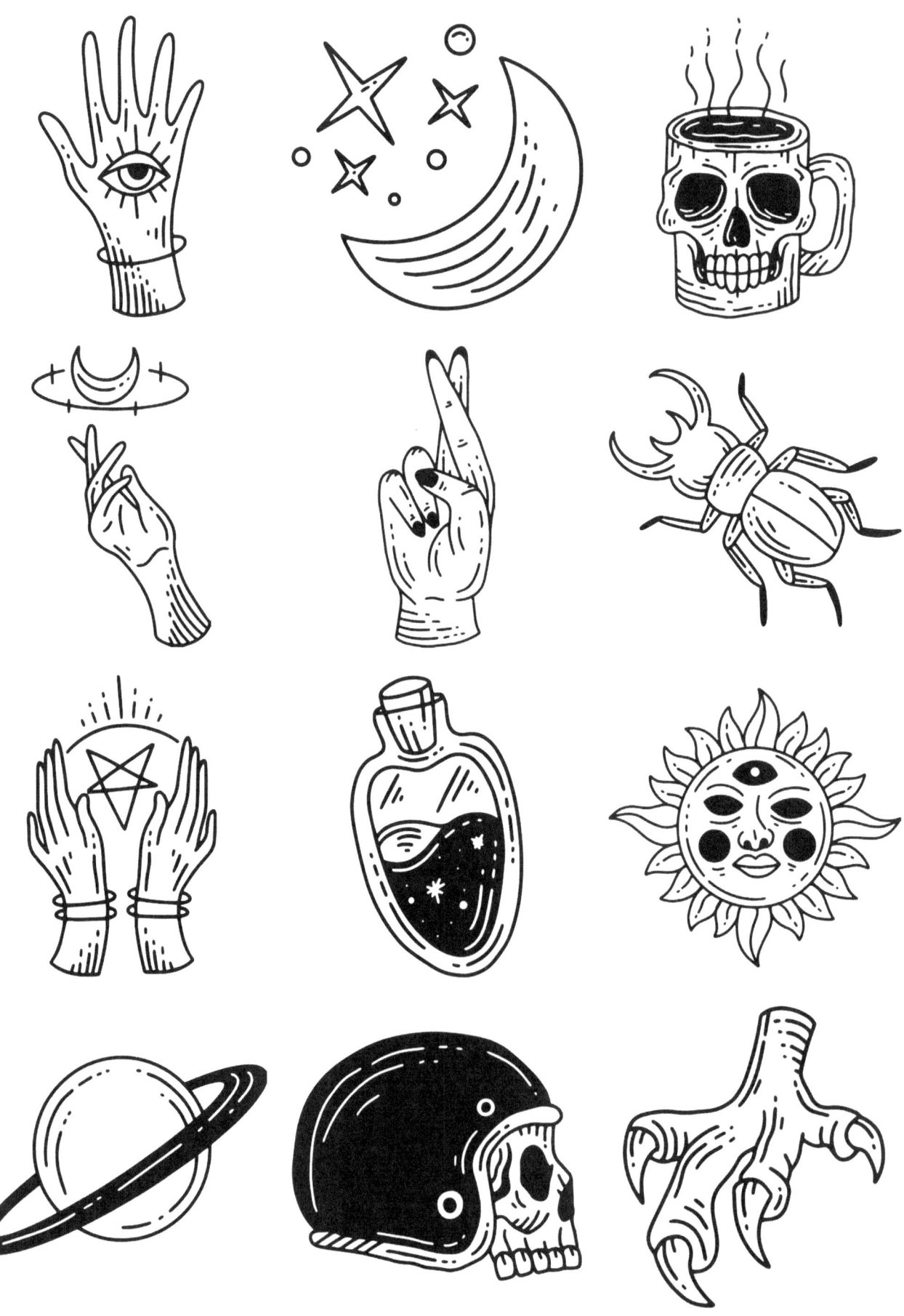

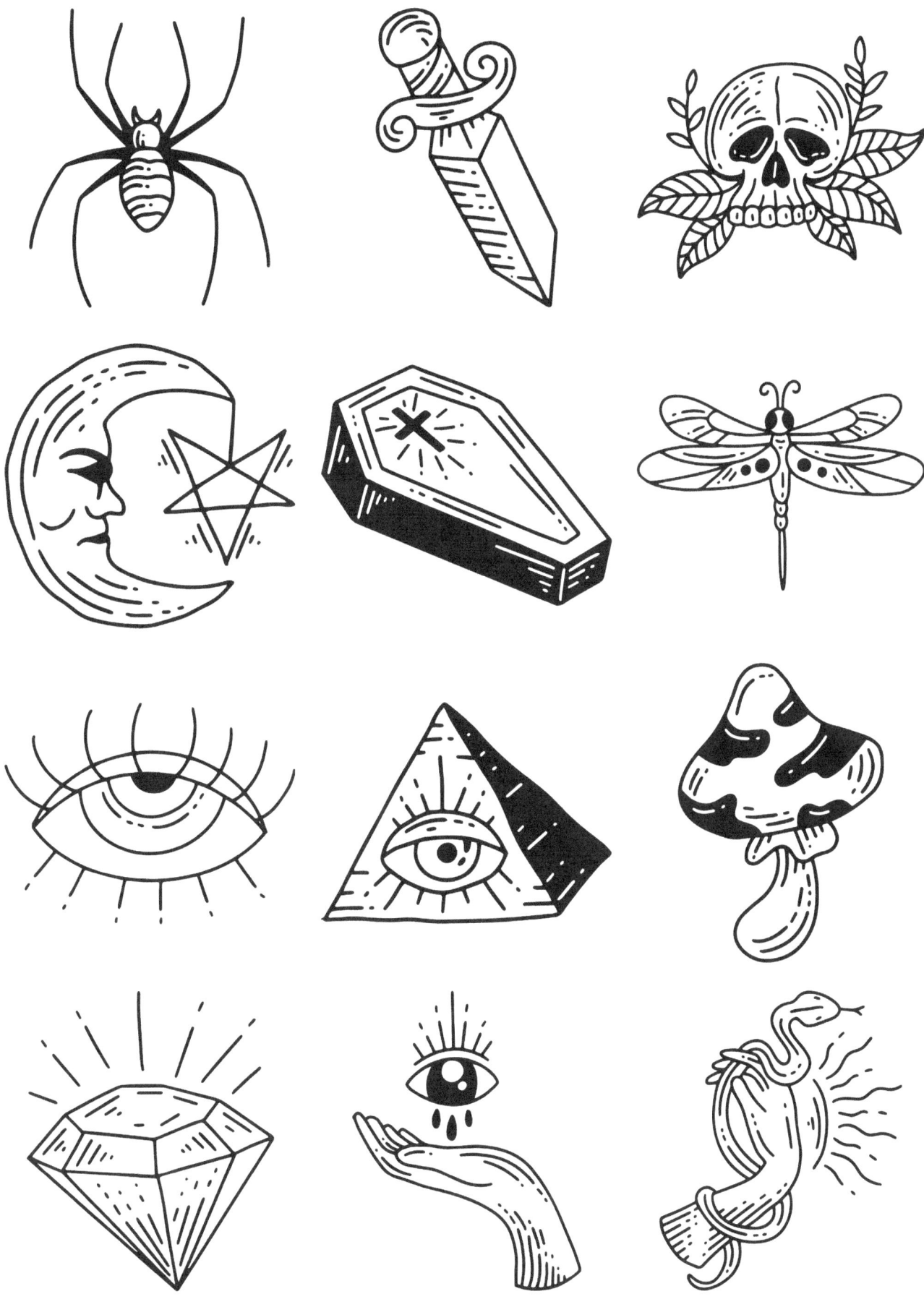

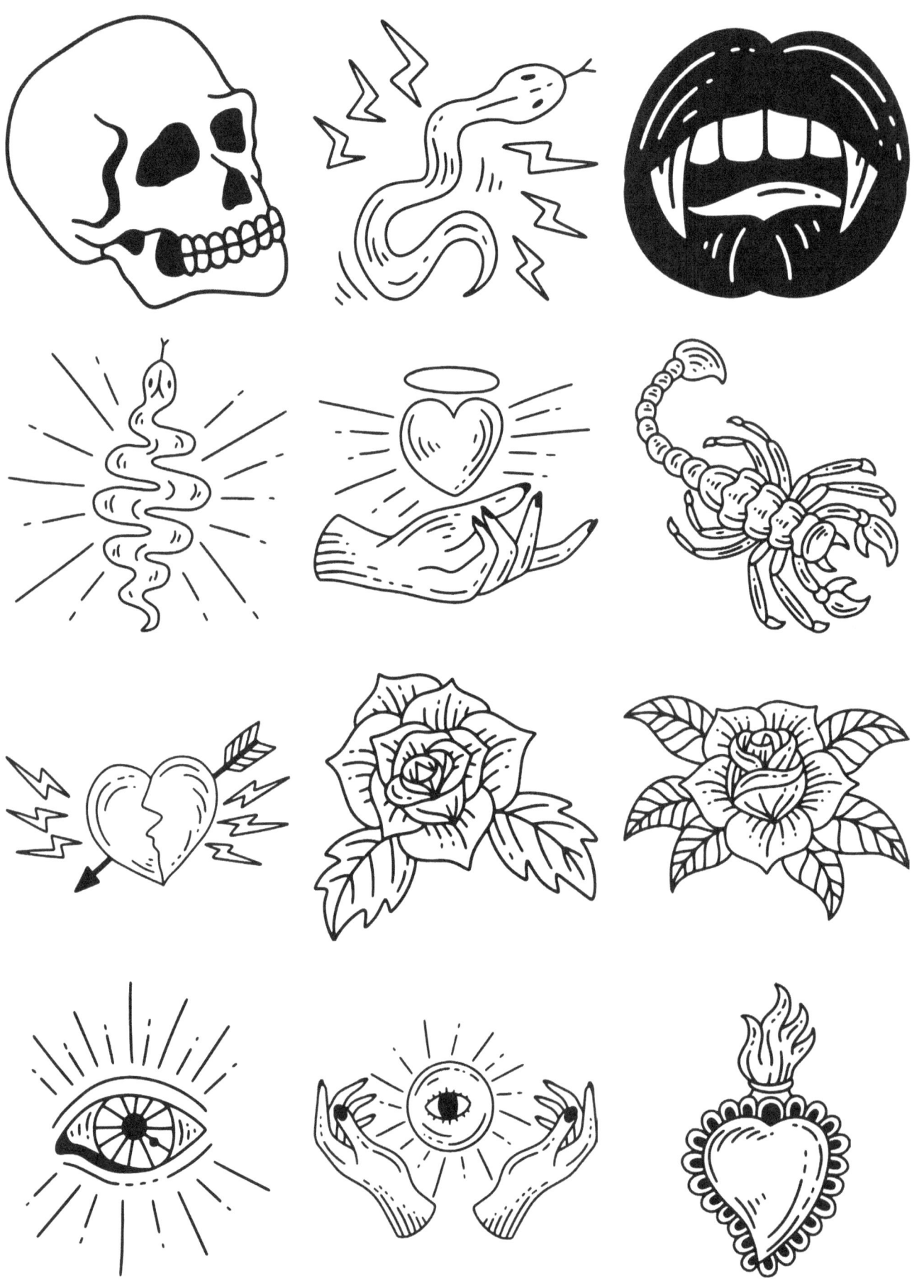

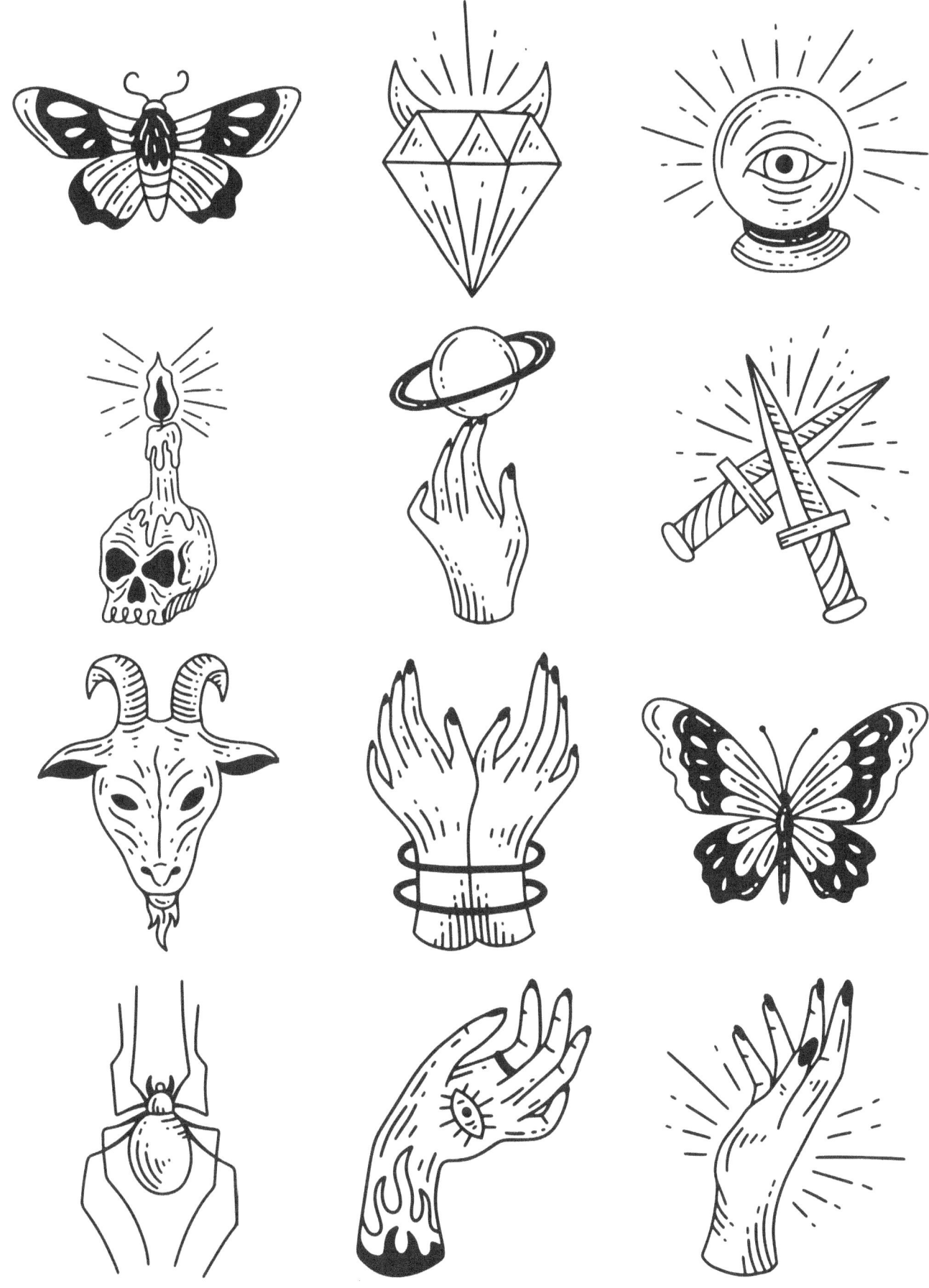

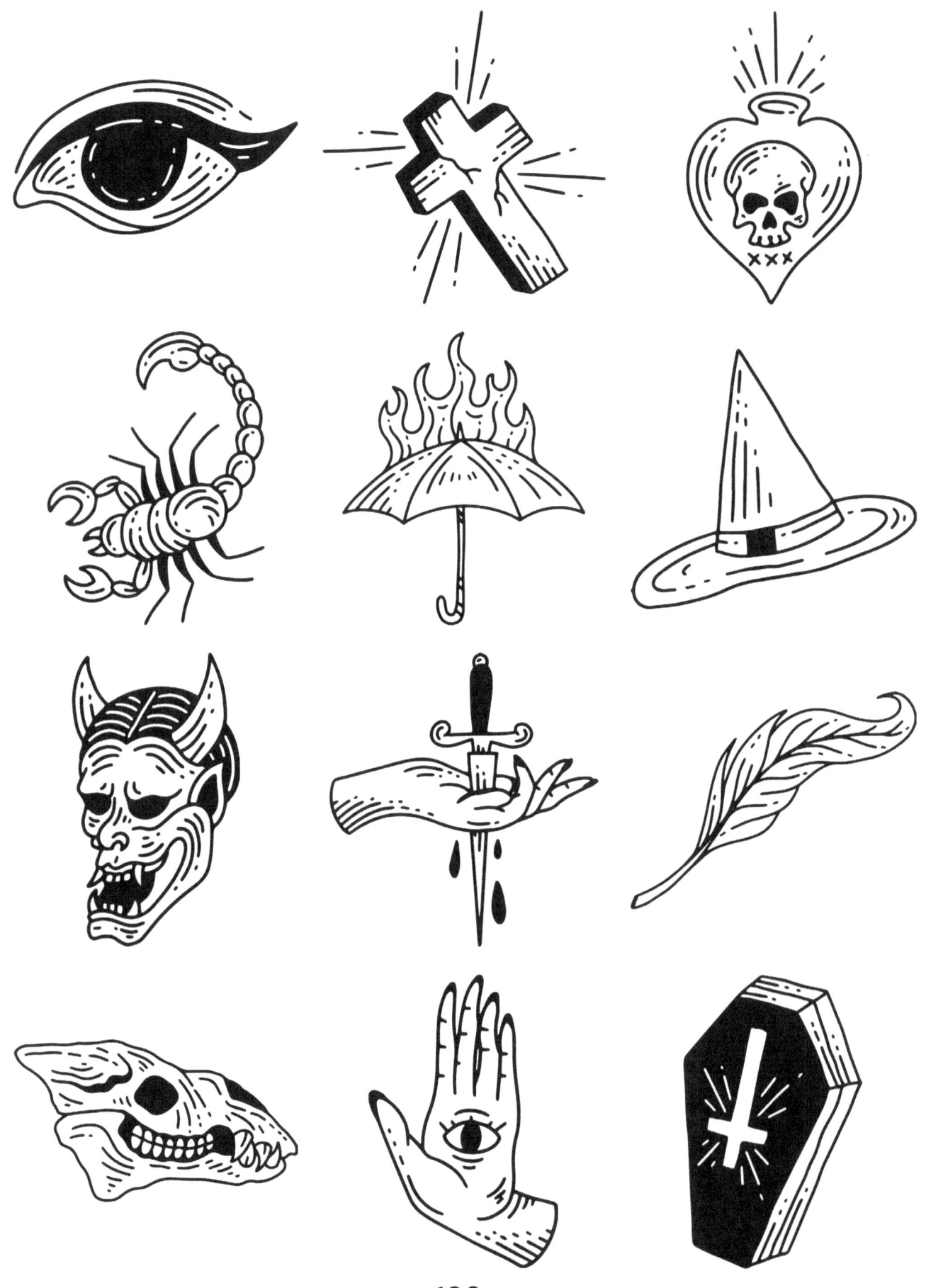

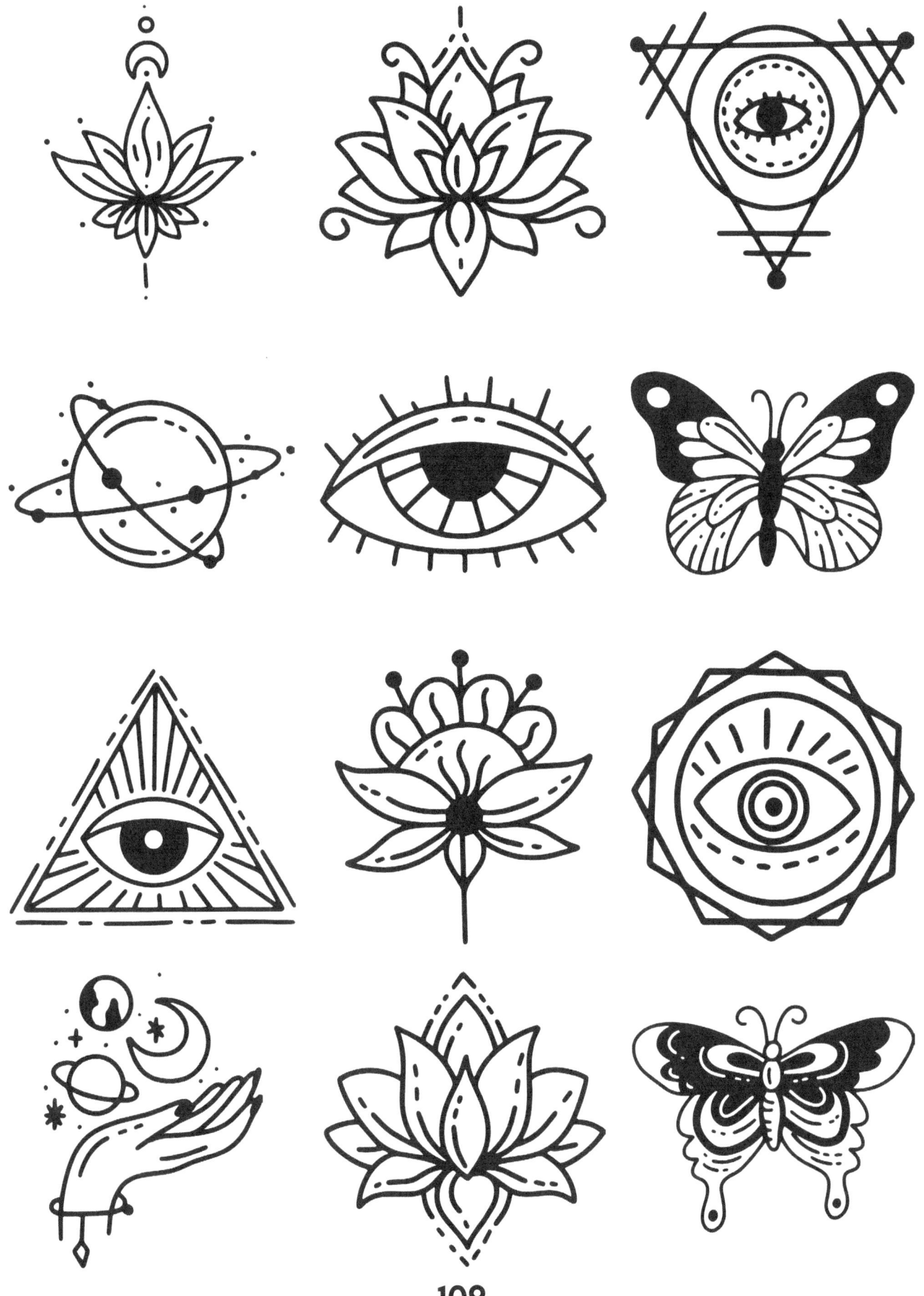

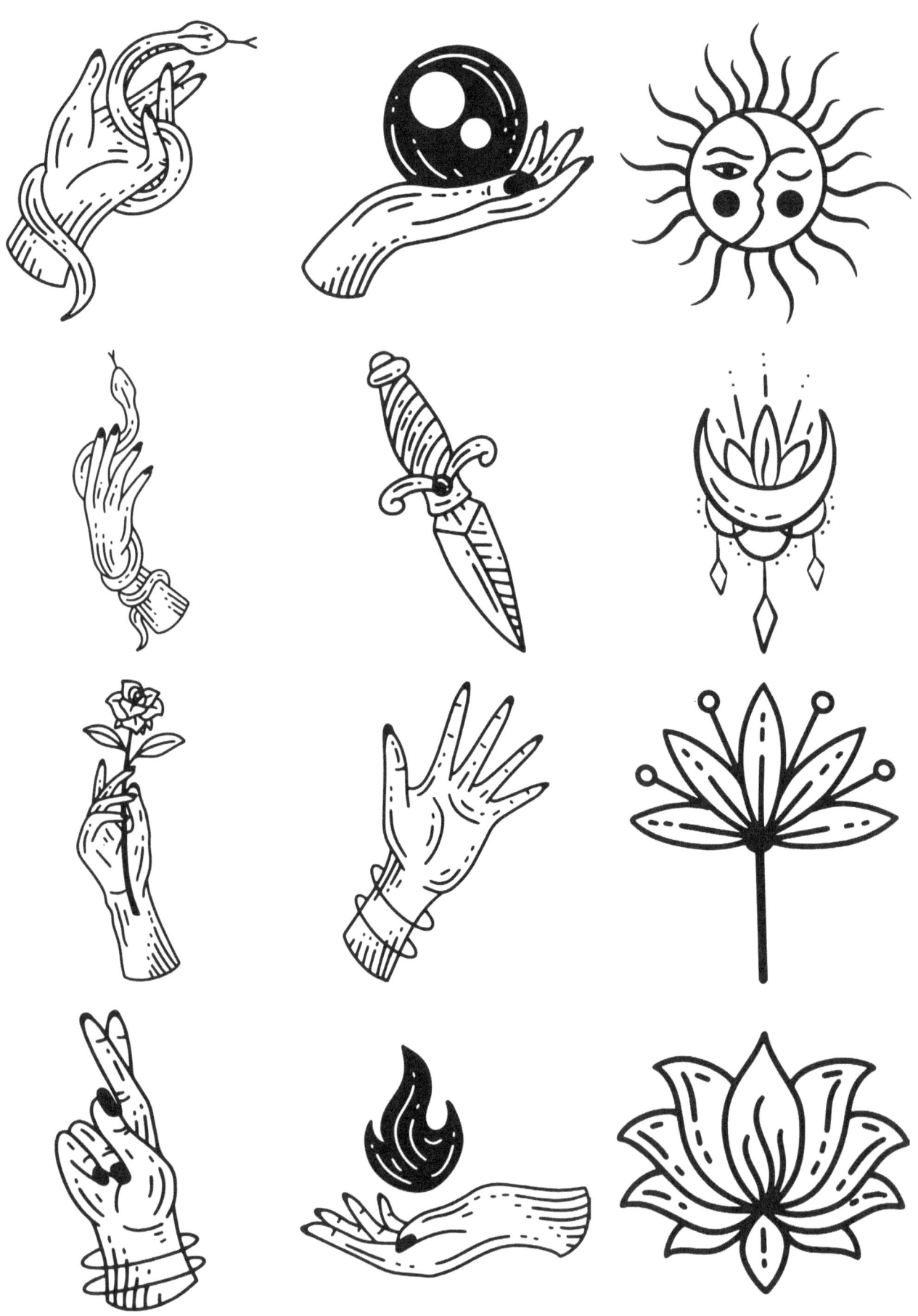

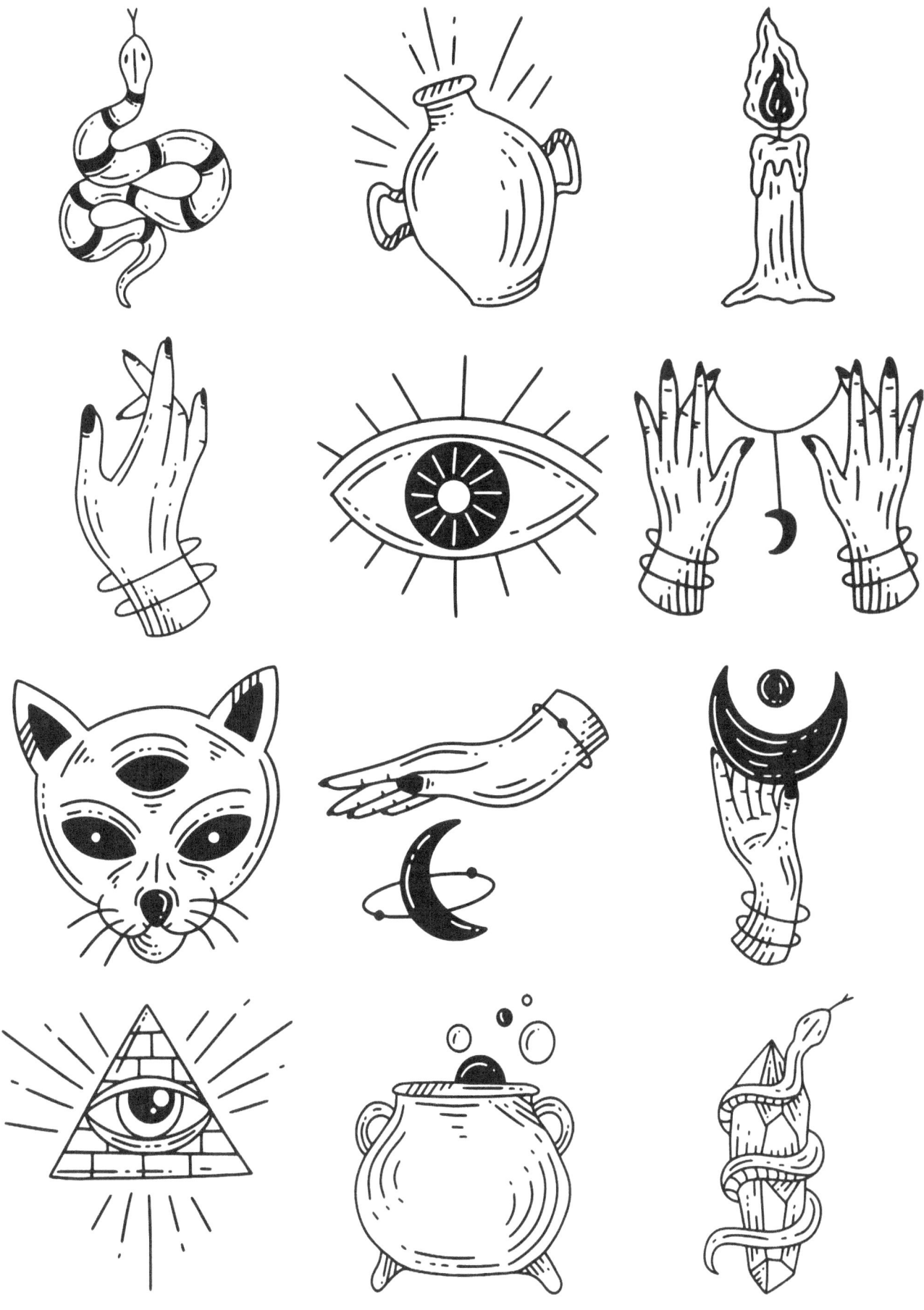

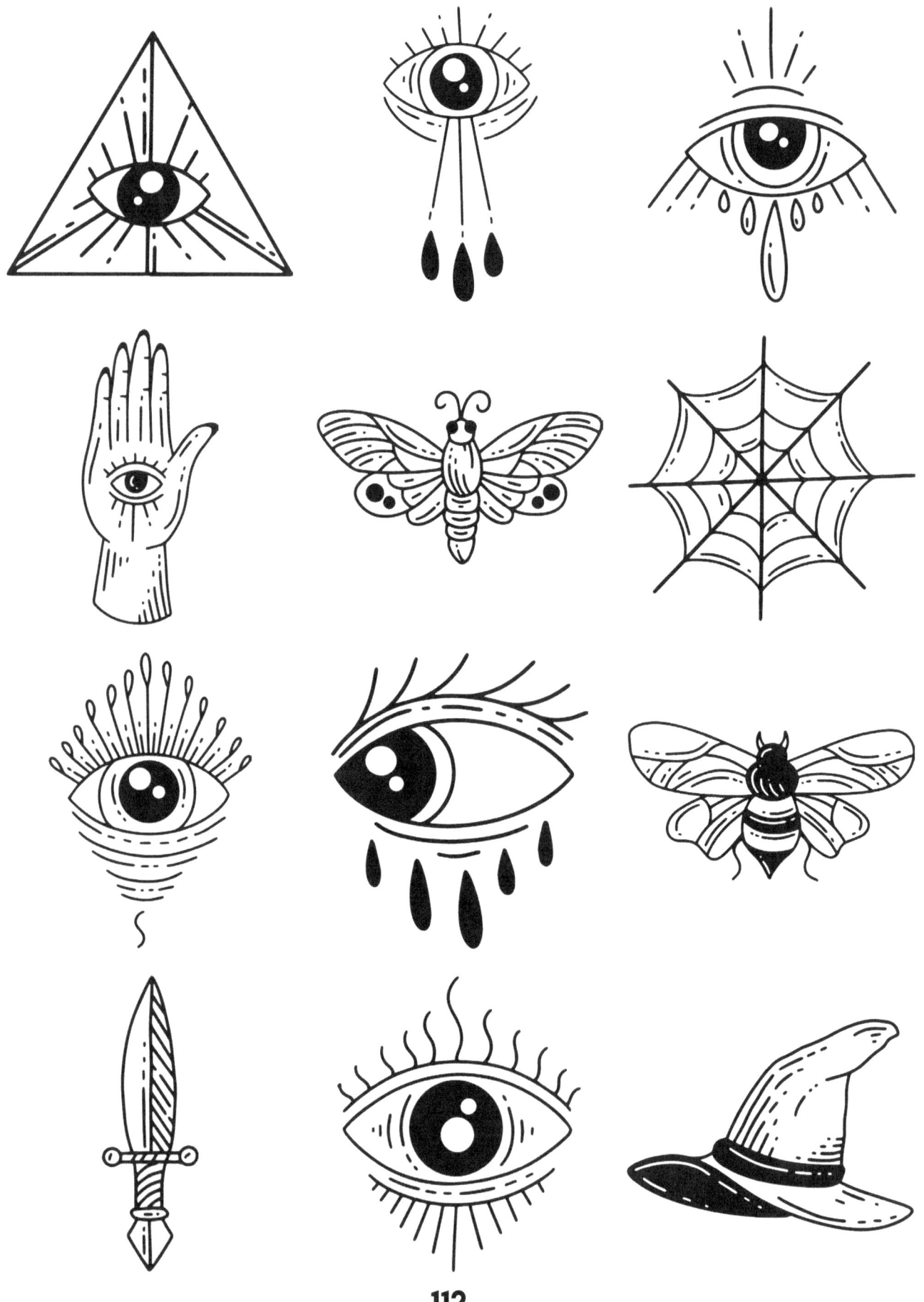

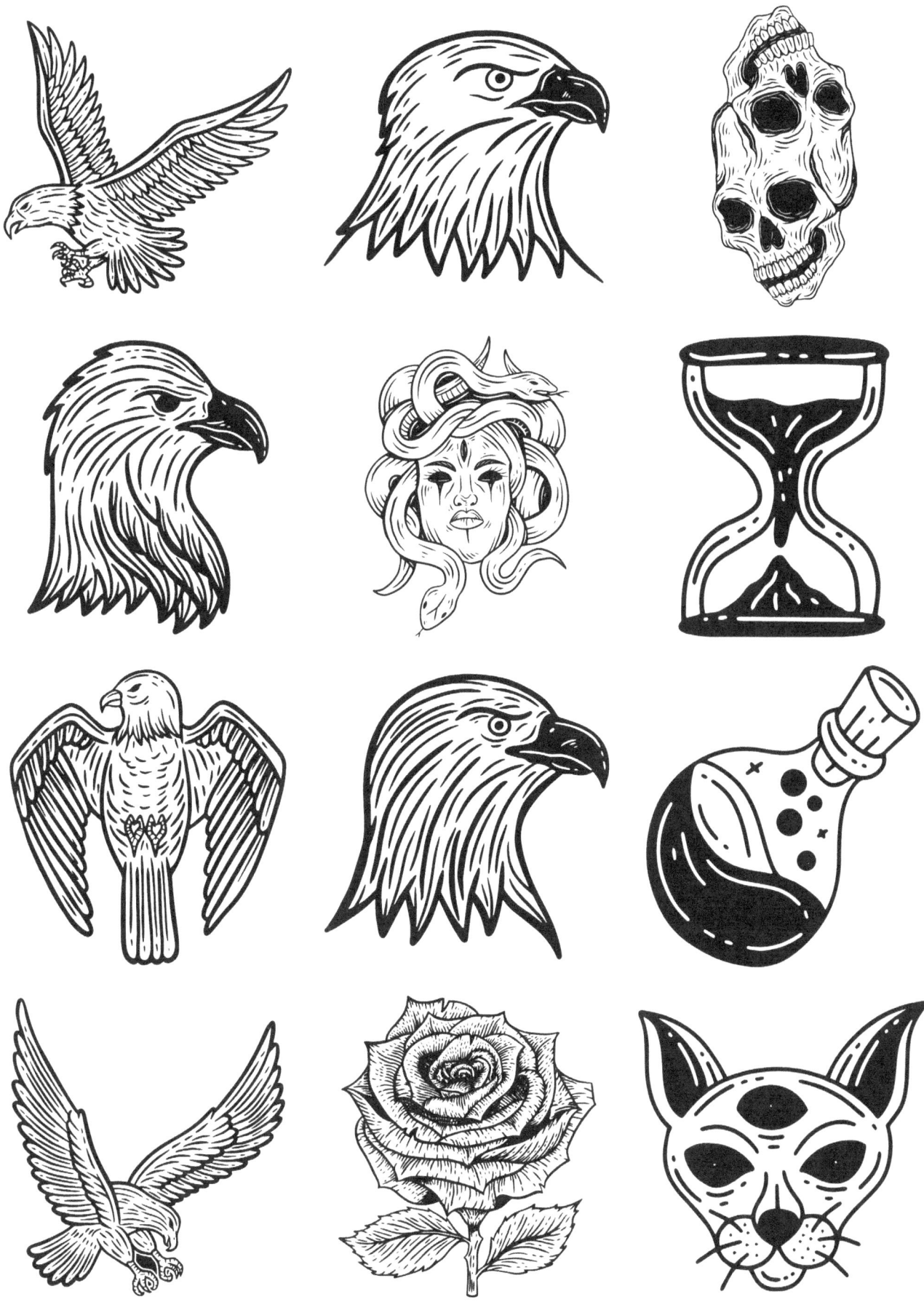

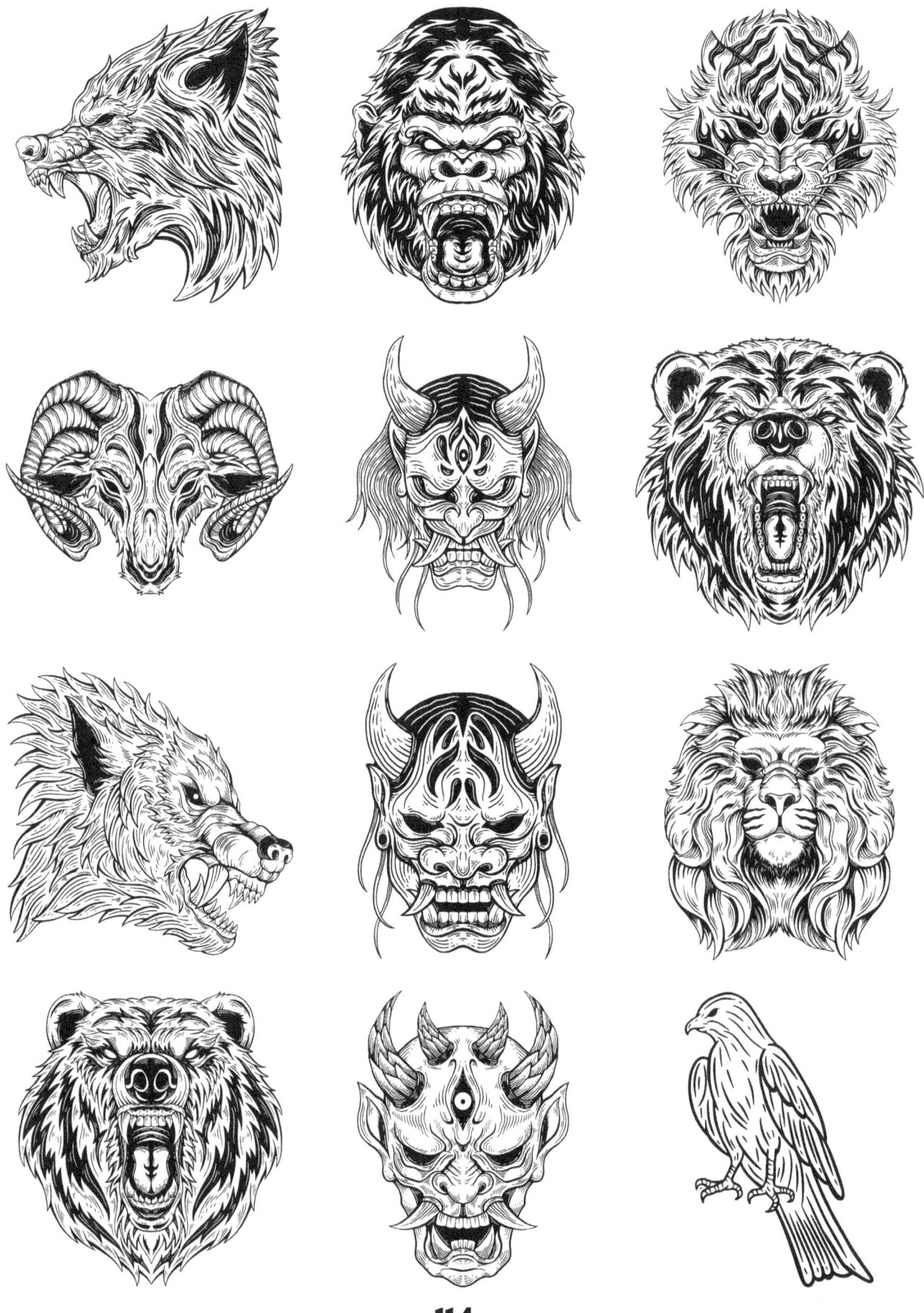

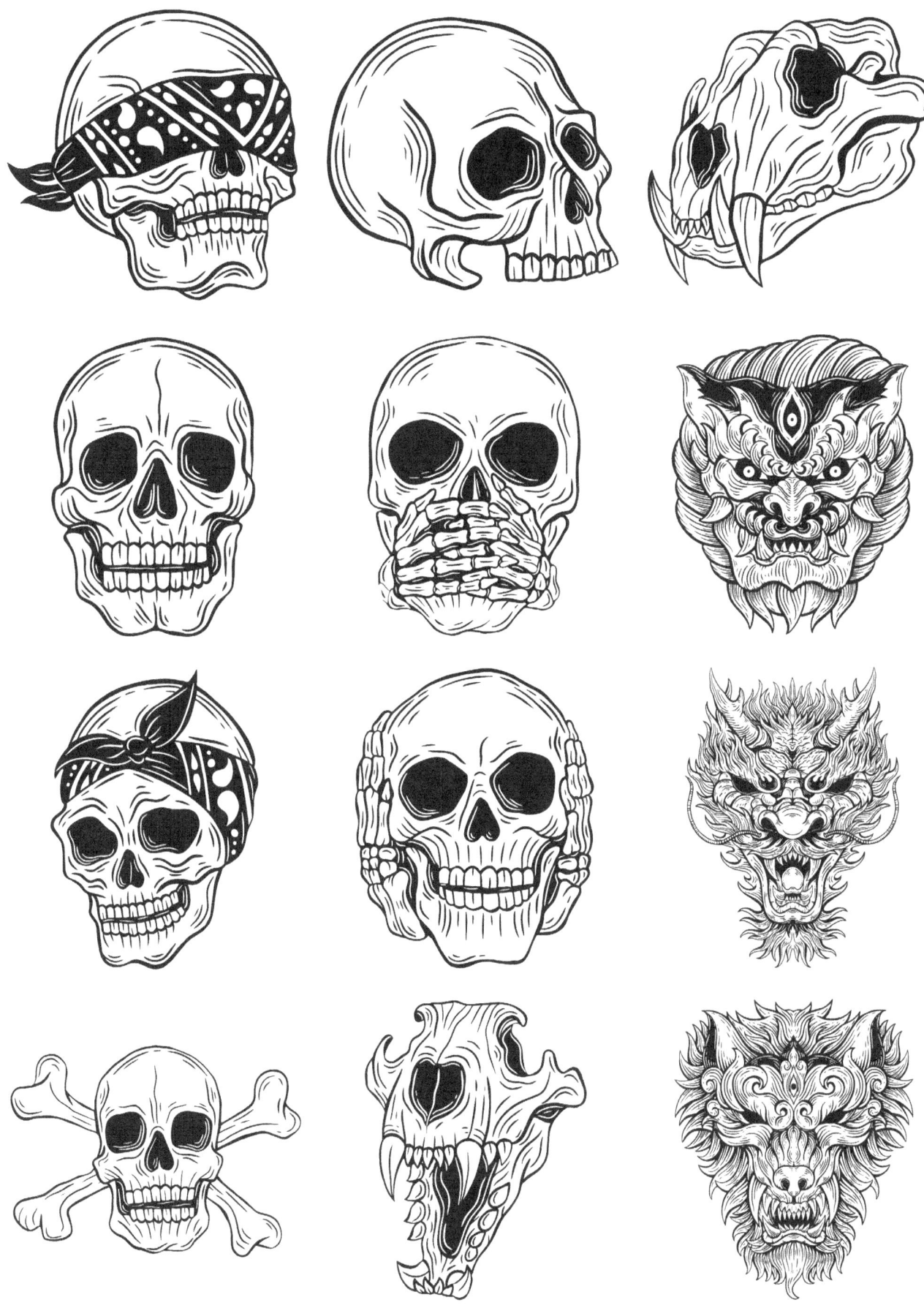

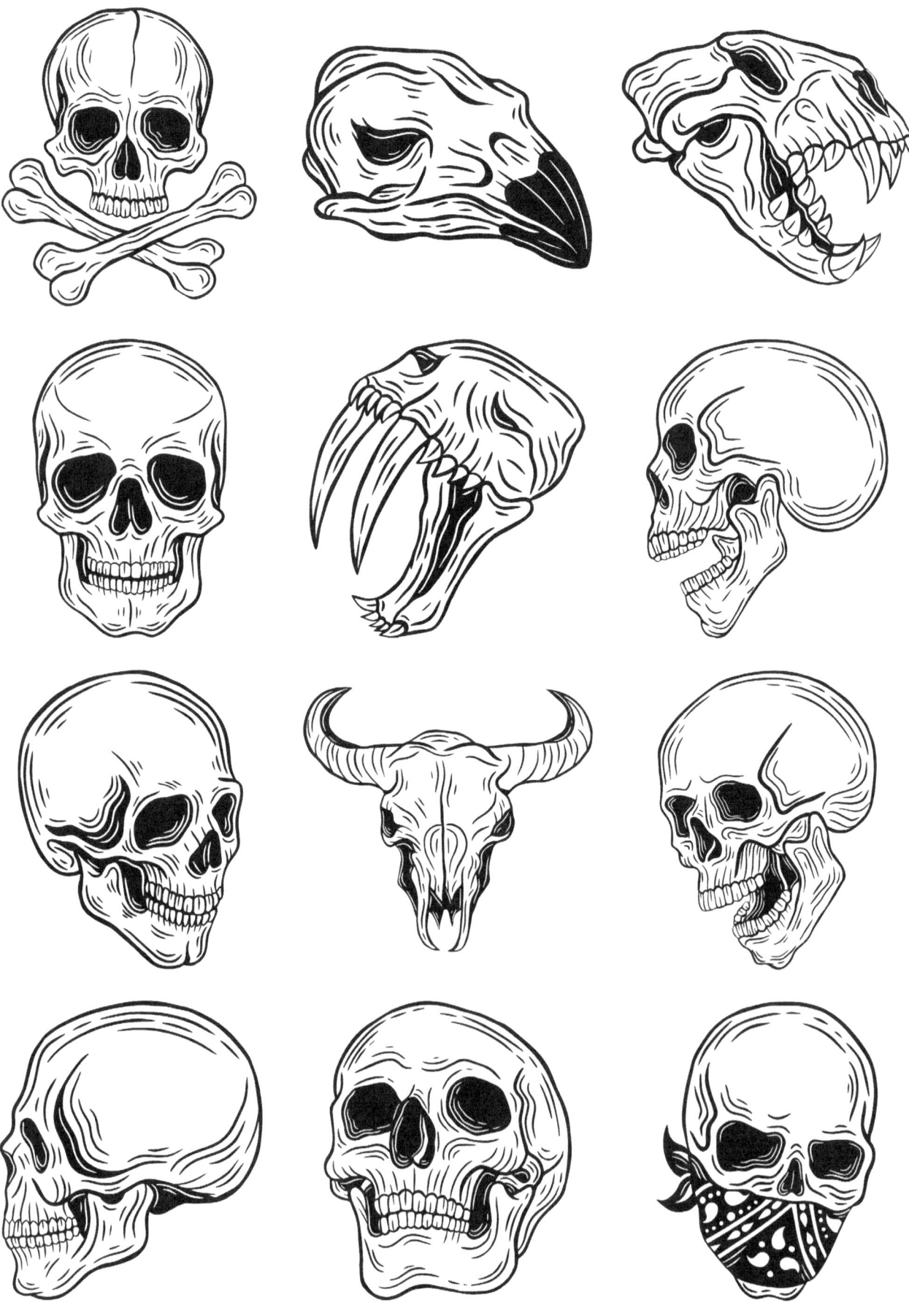

116

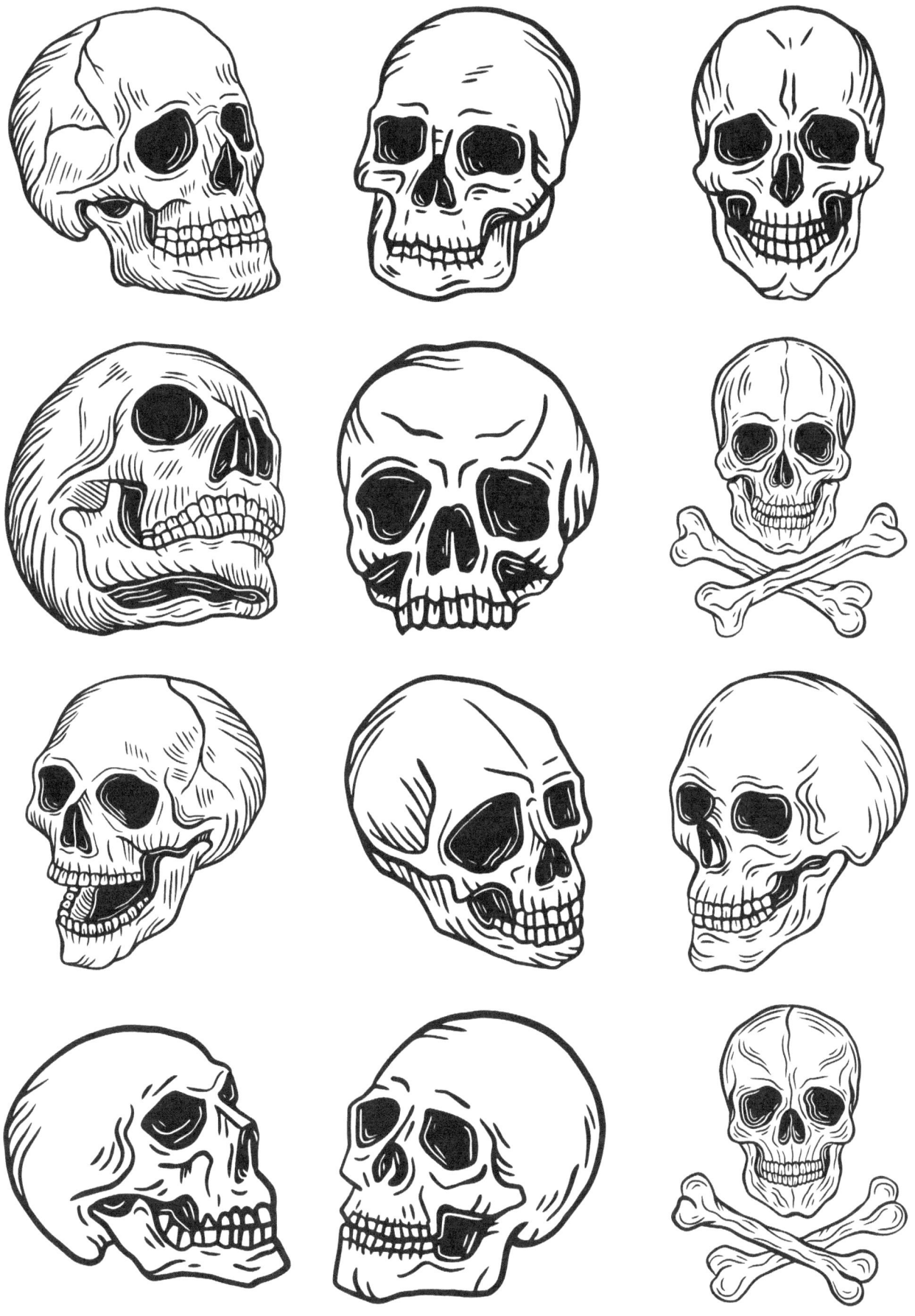

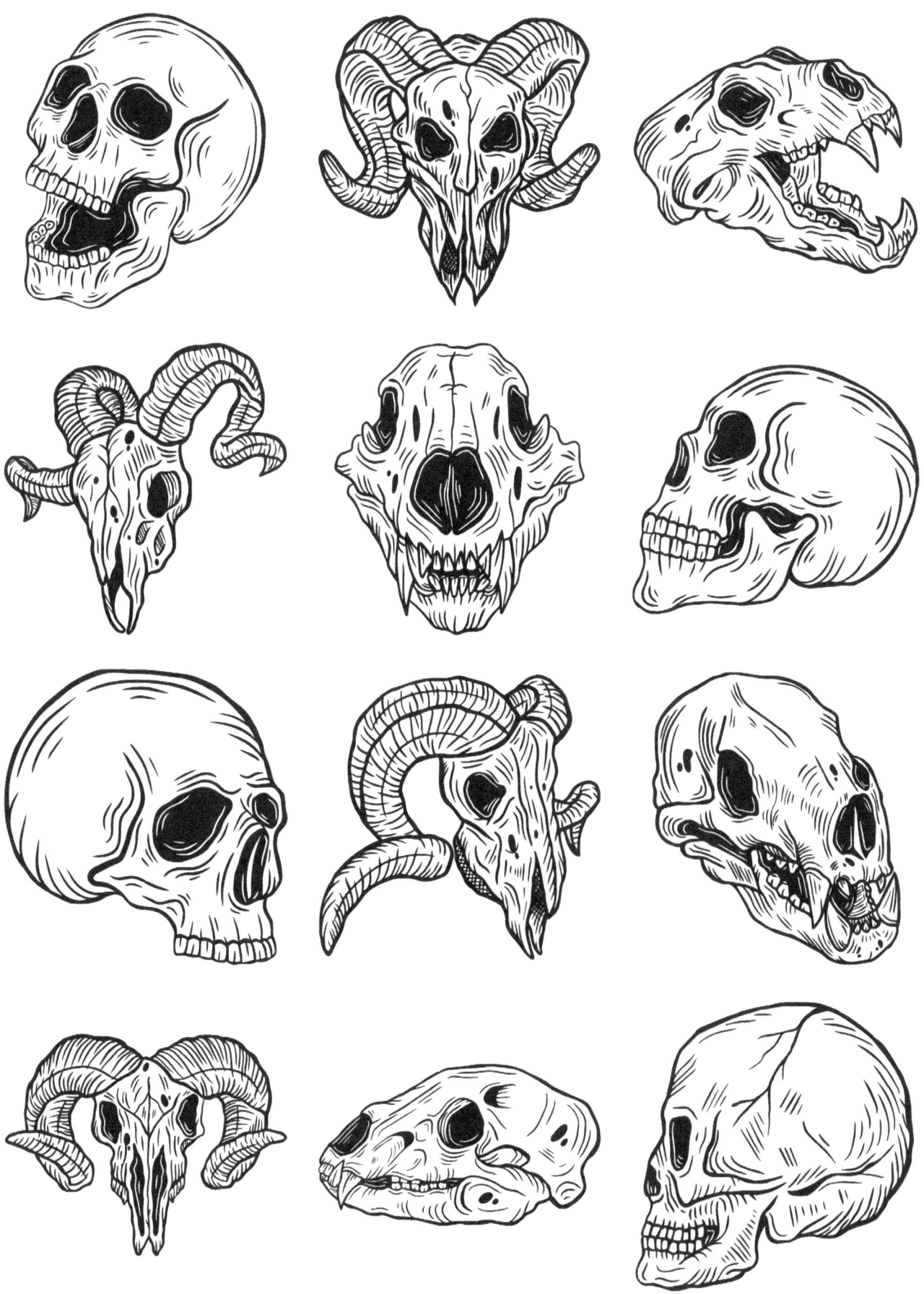

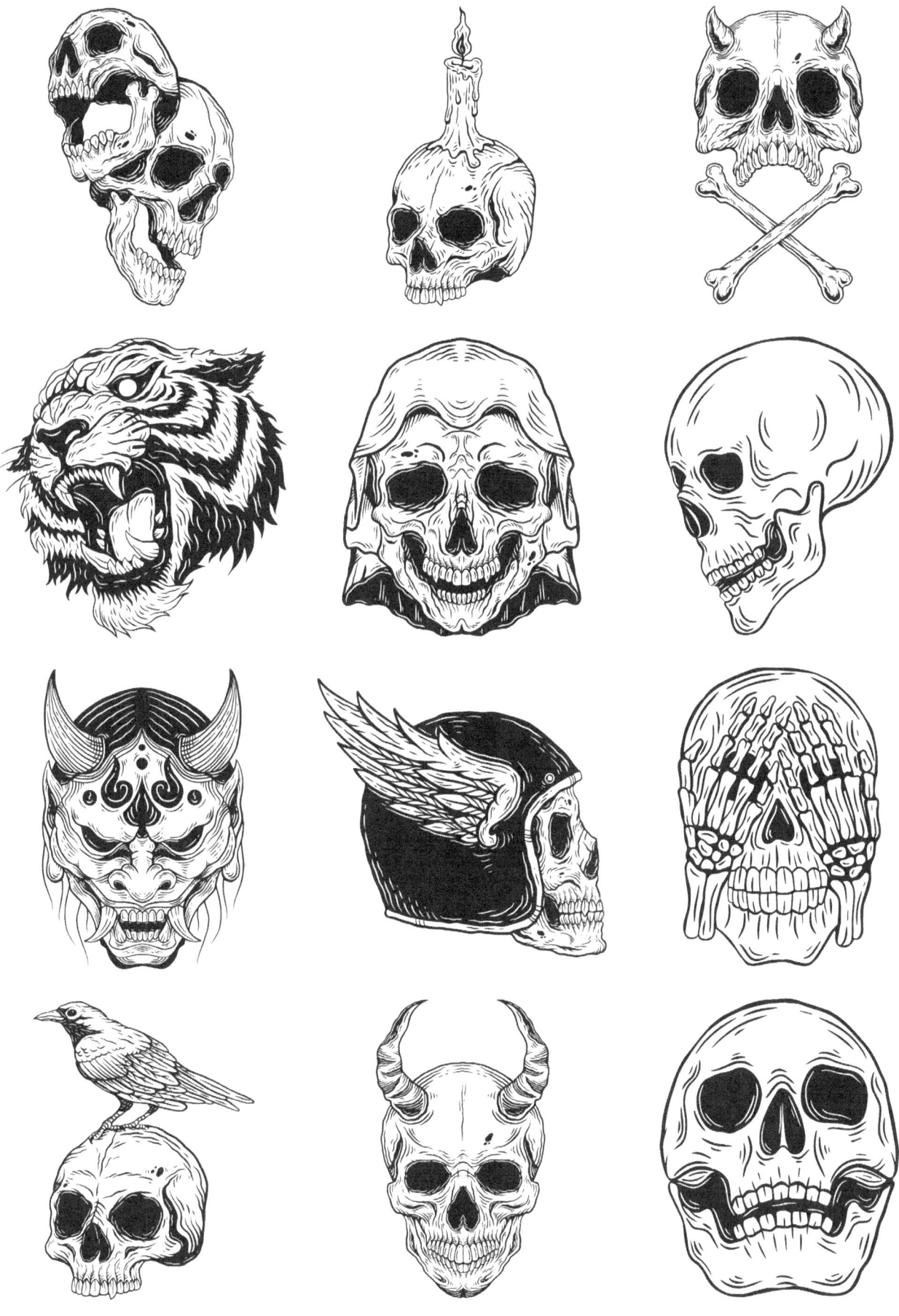

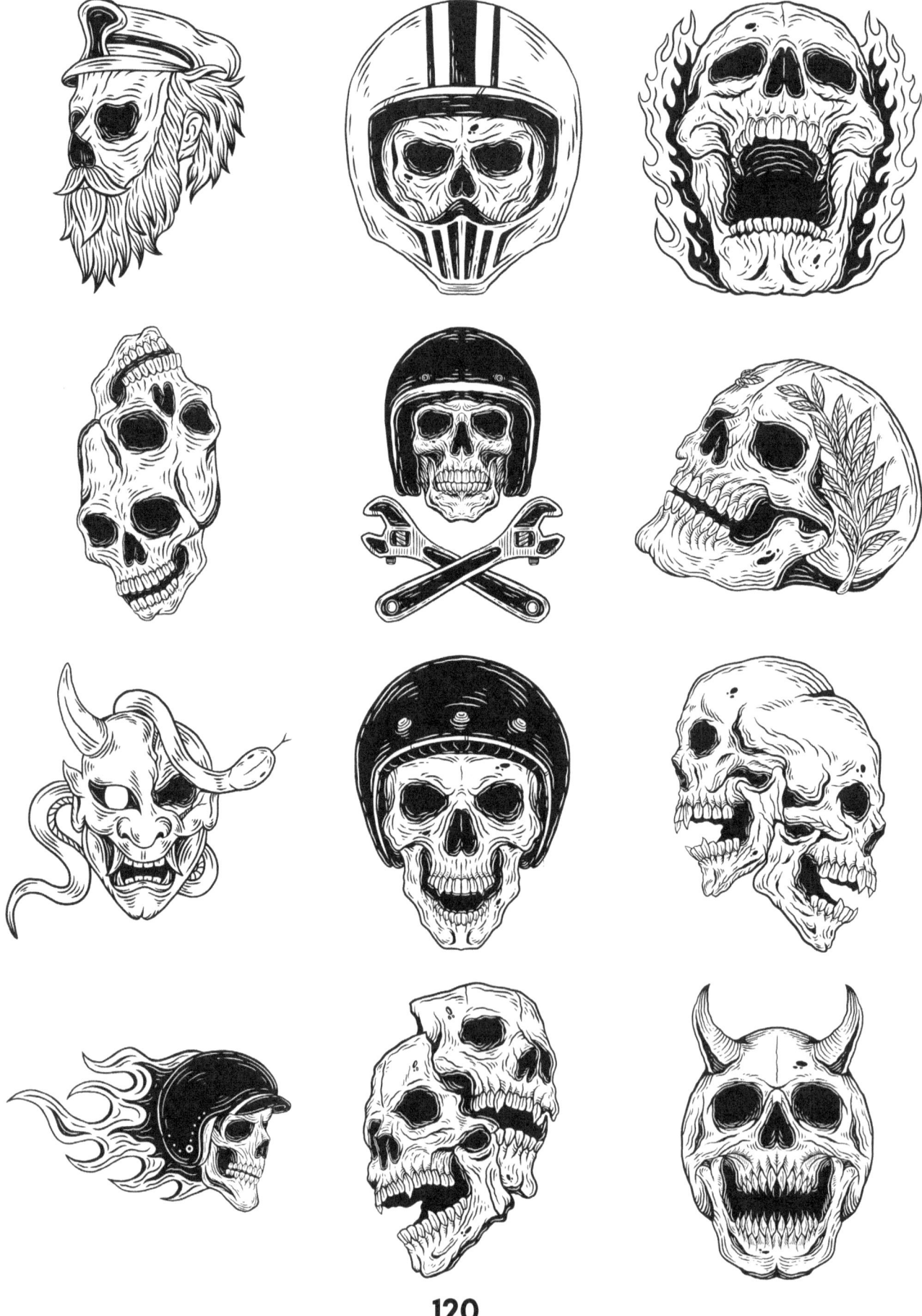

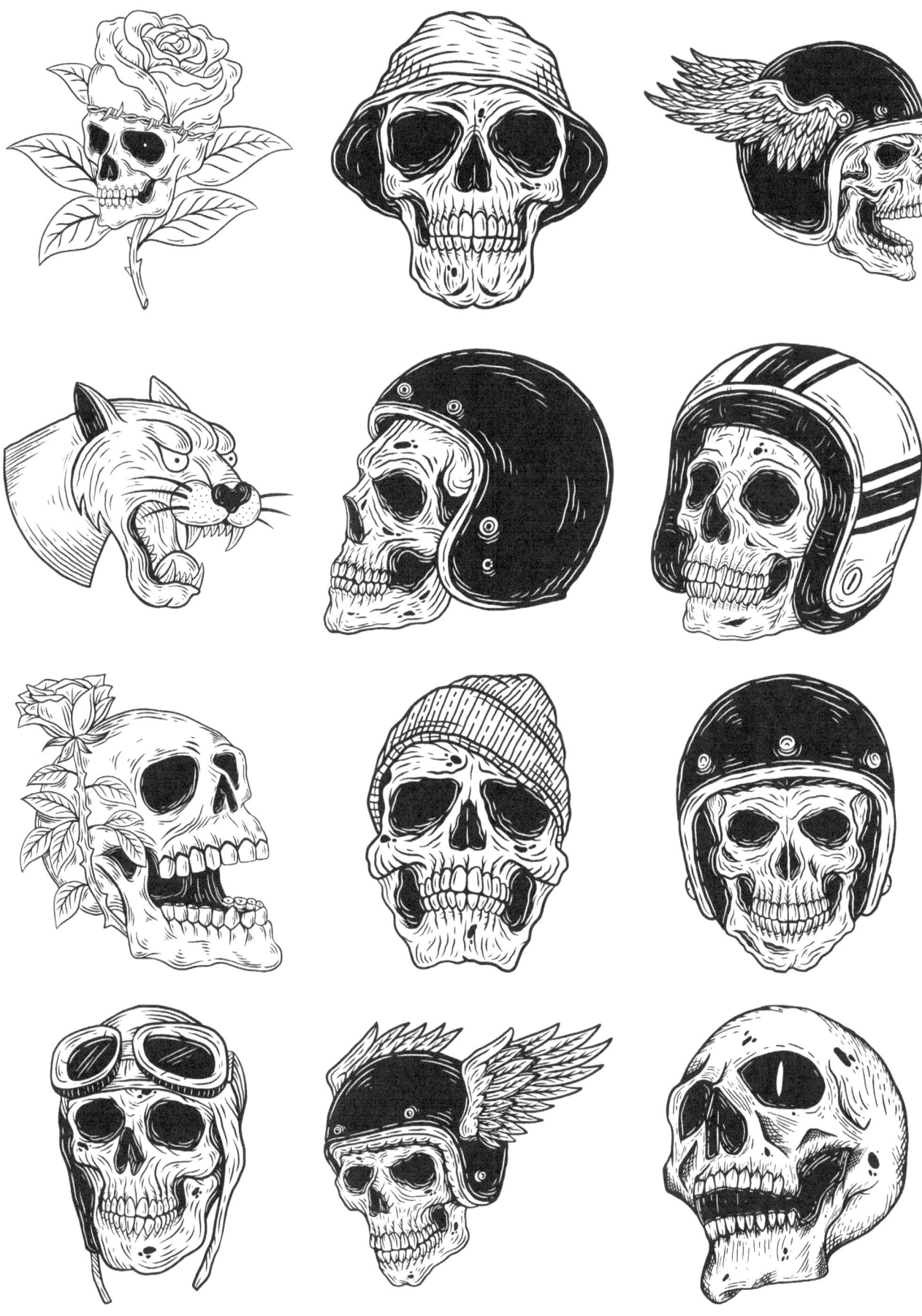

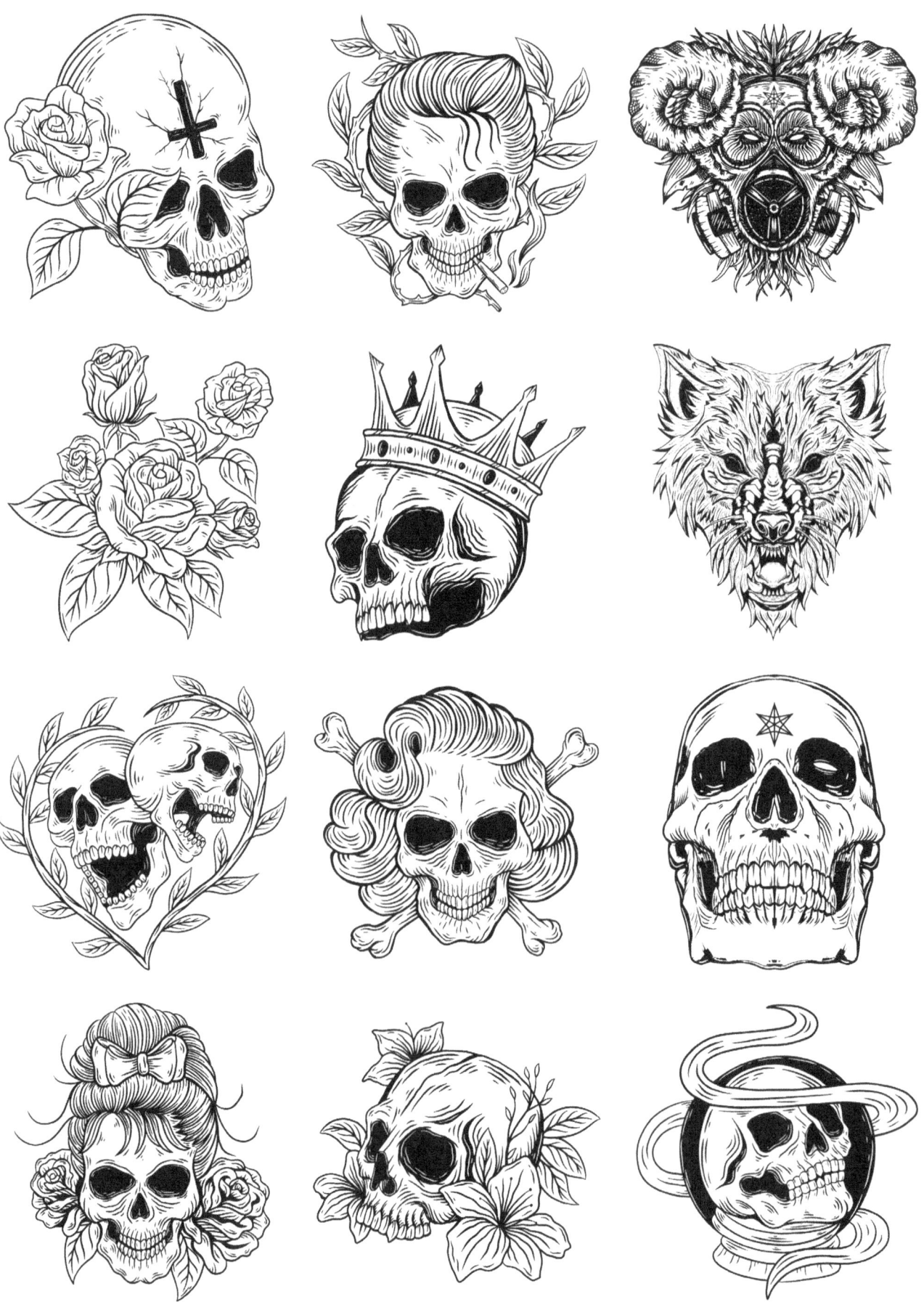

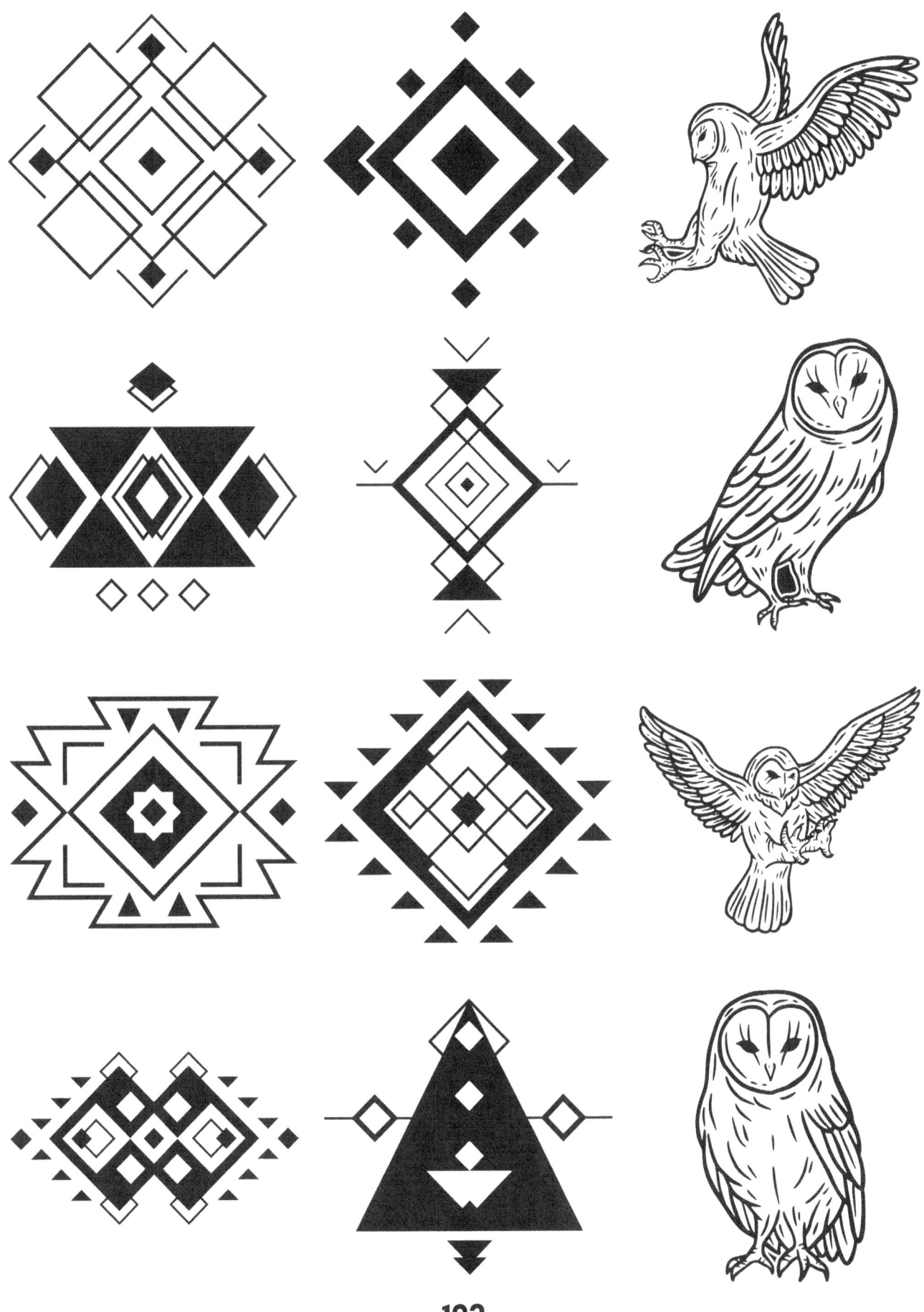

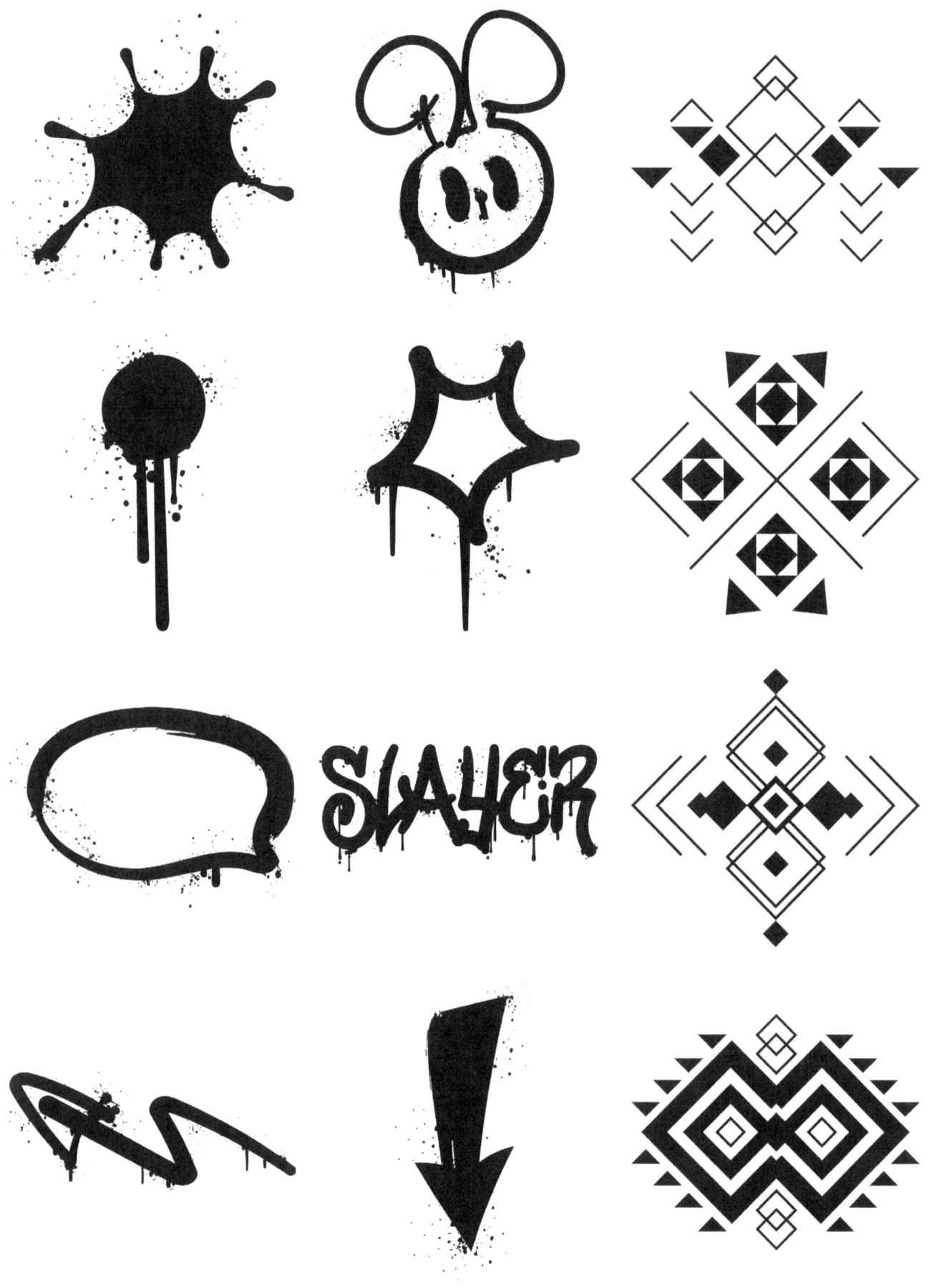

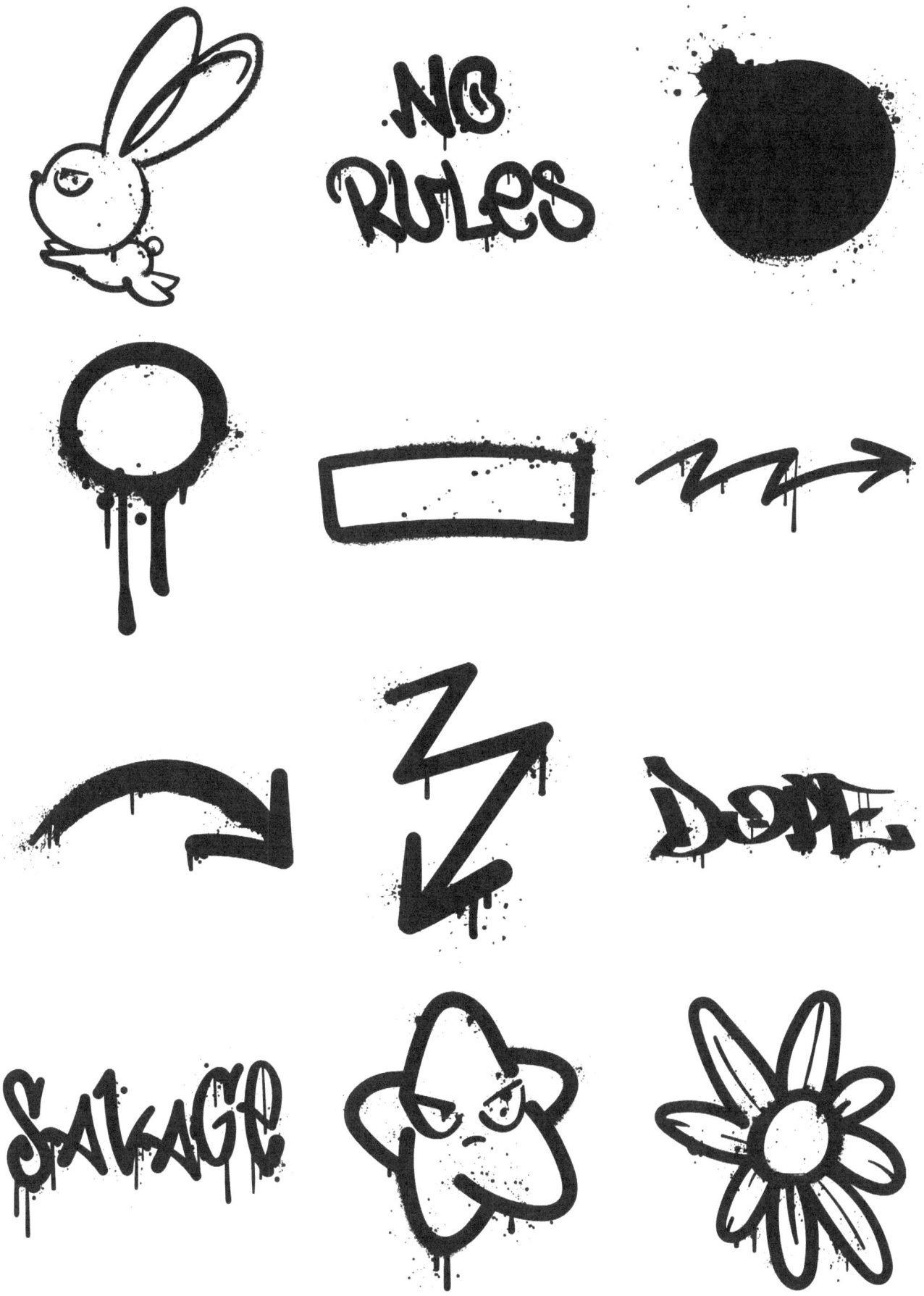

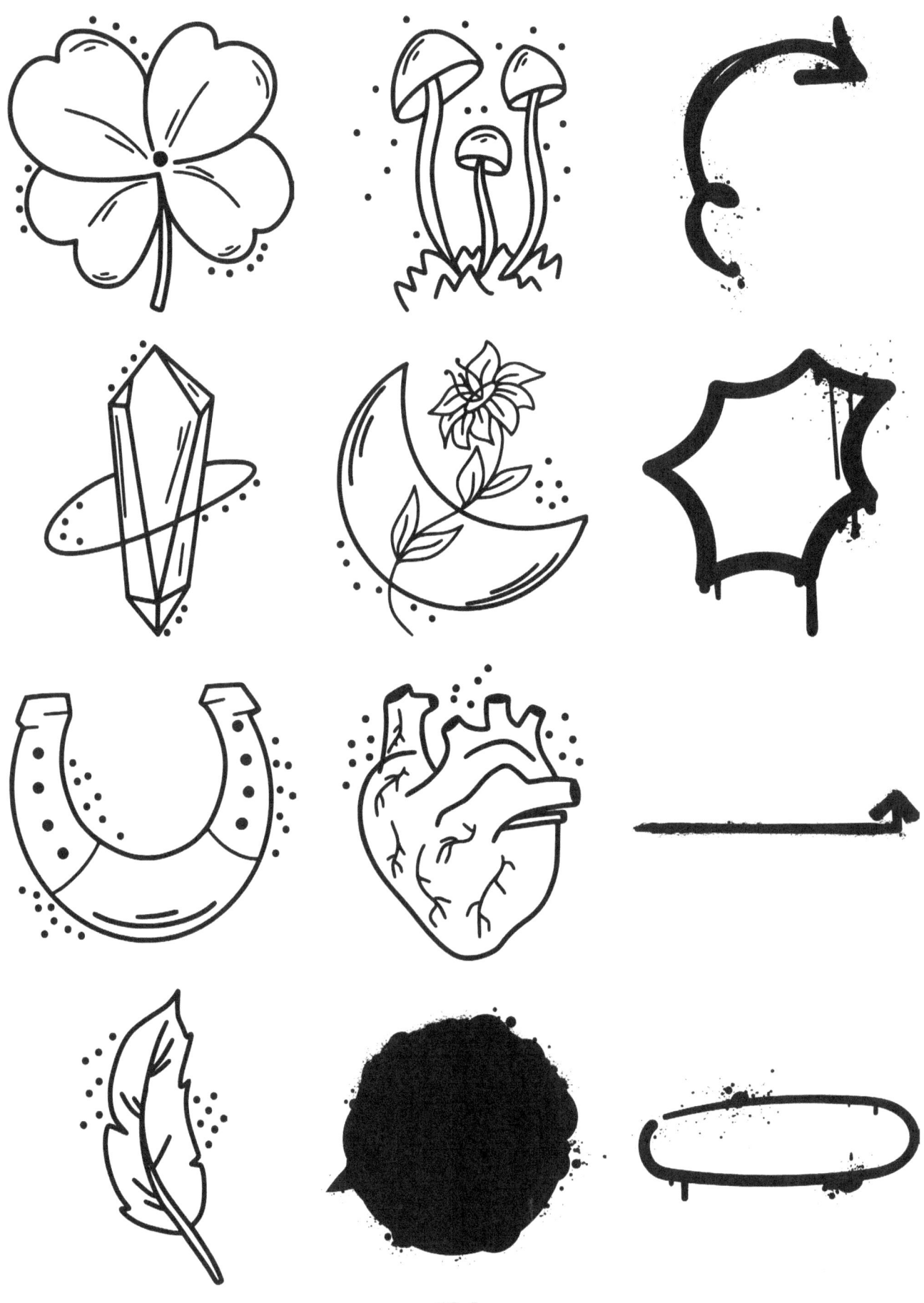

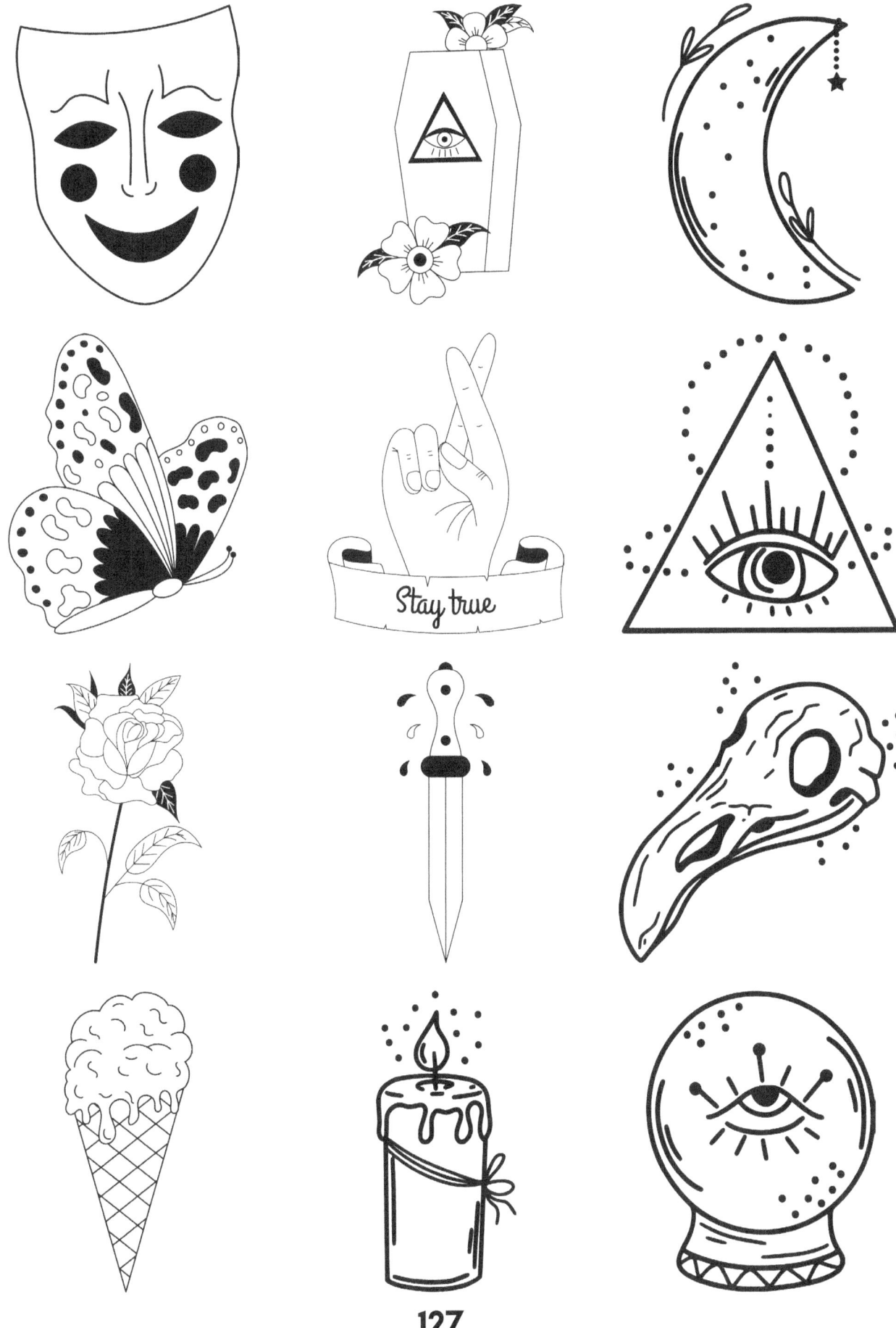

Stay true

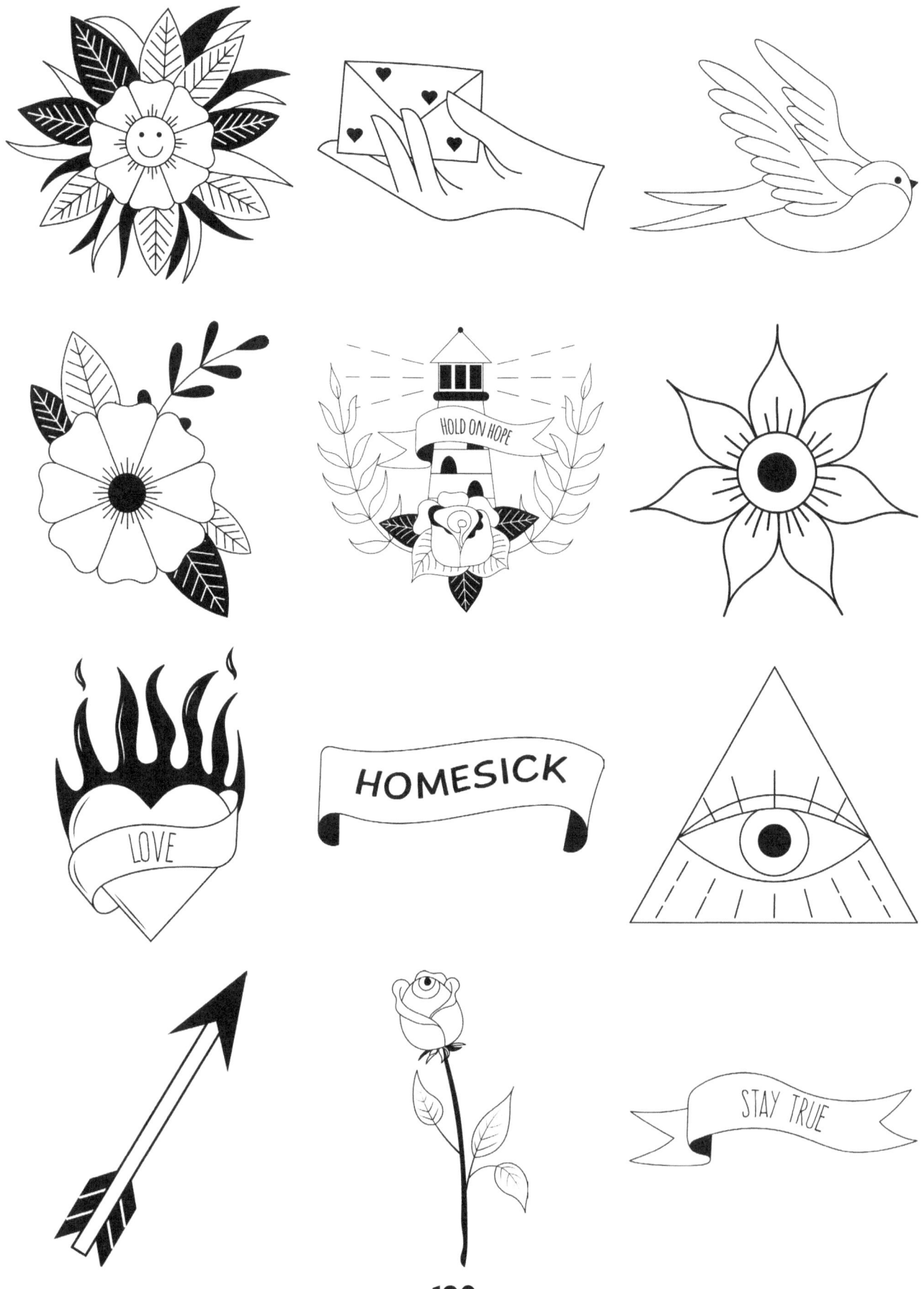

128

129

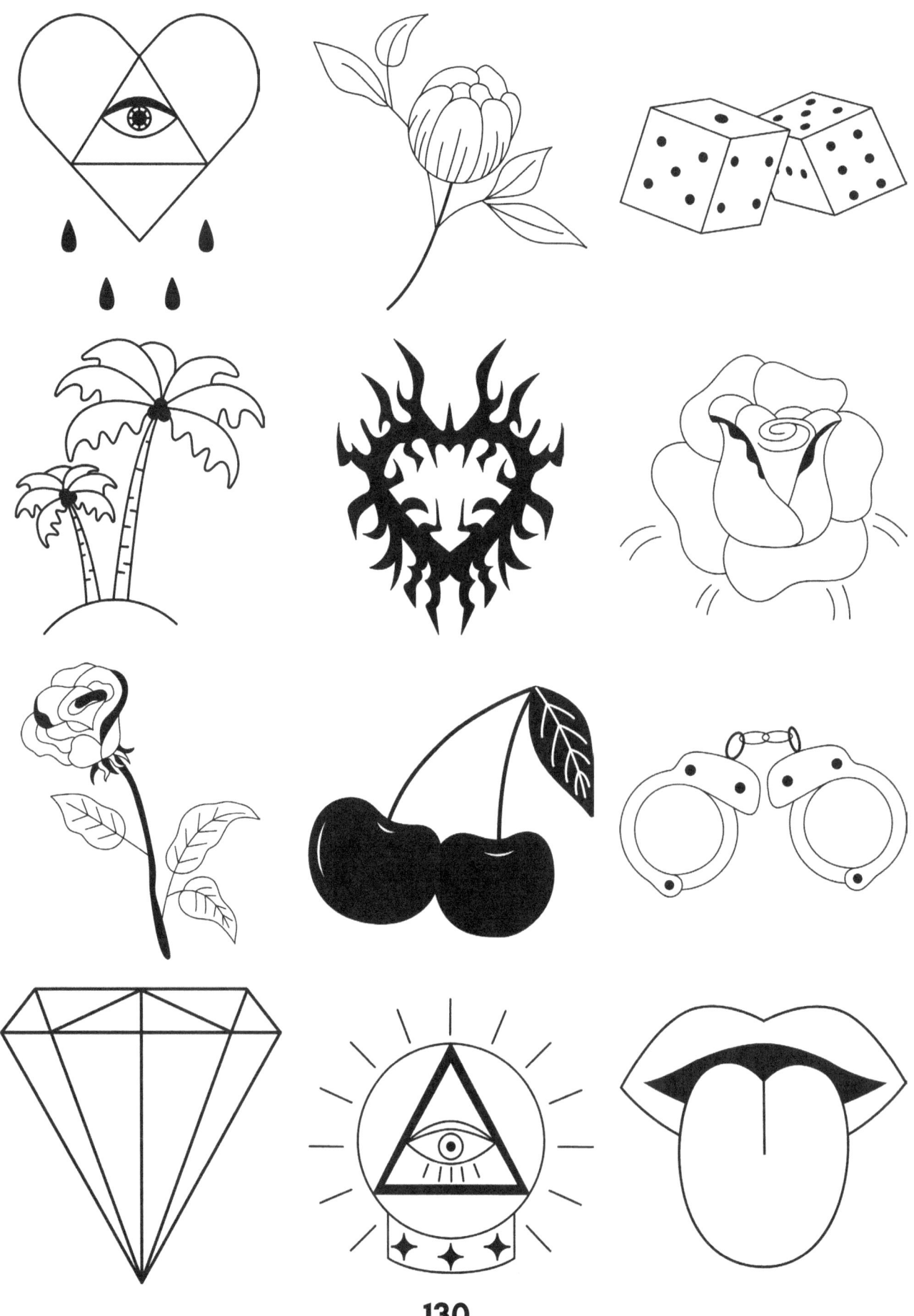

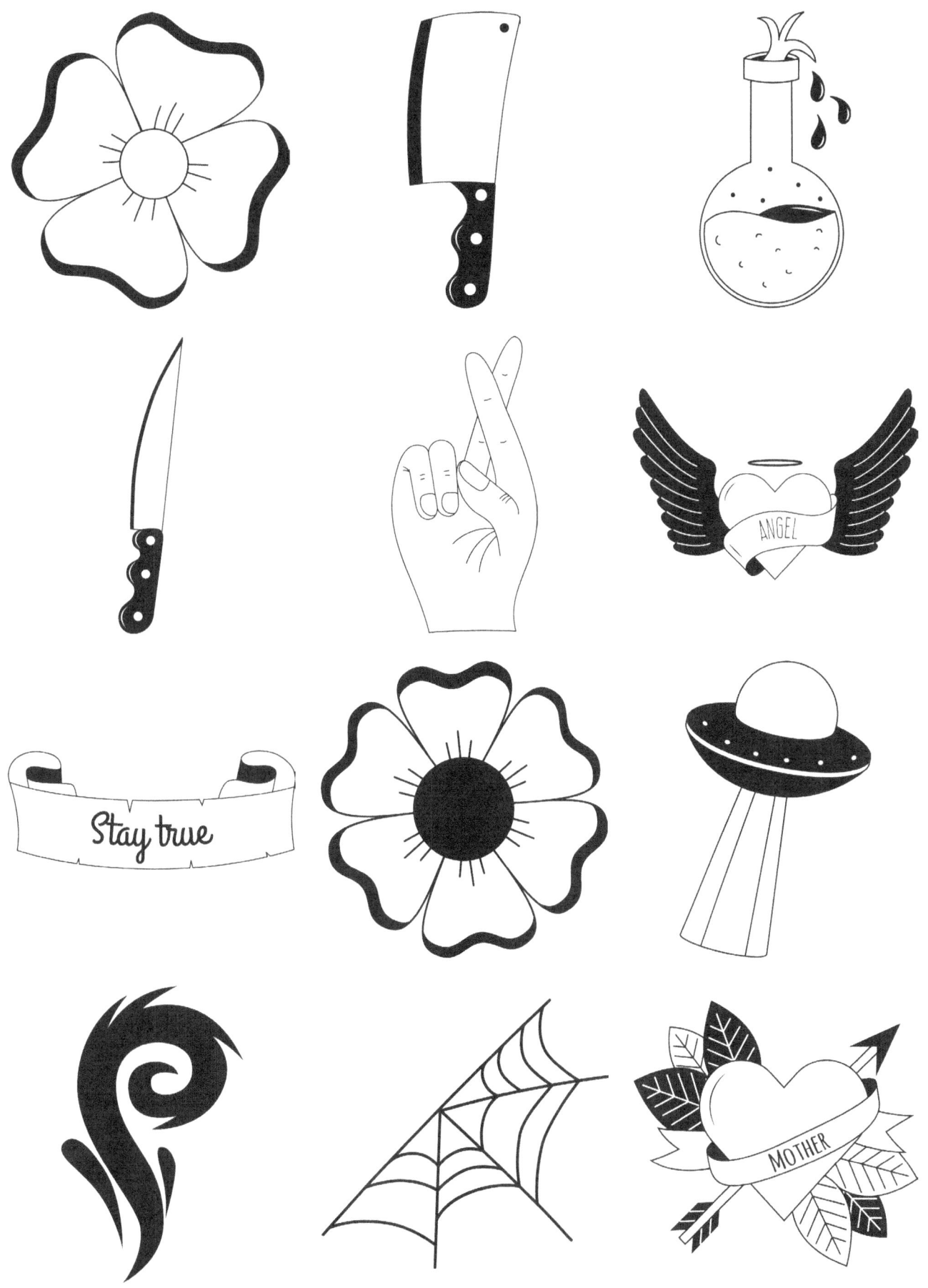

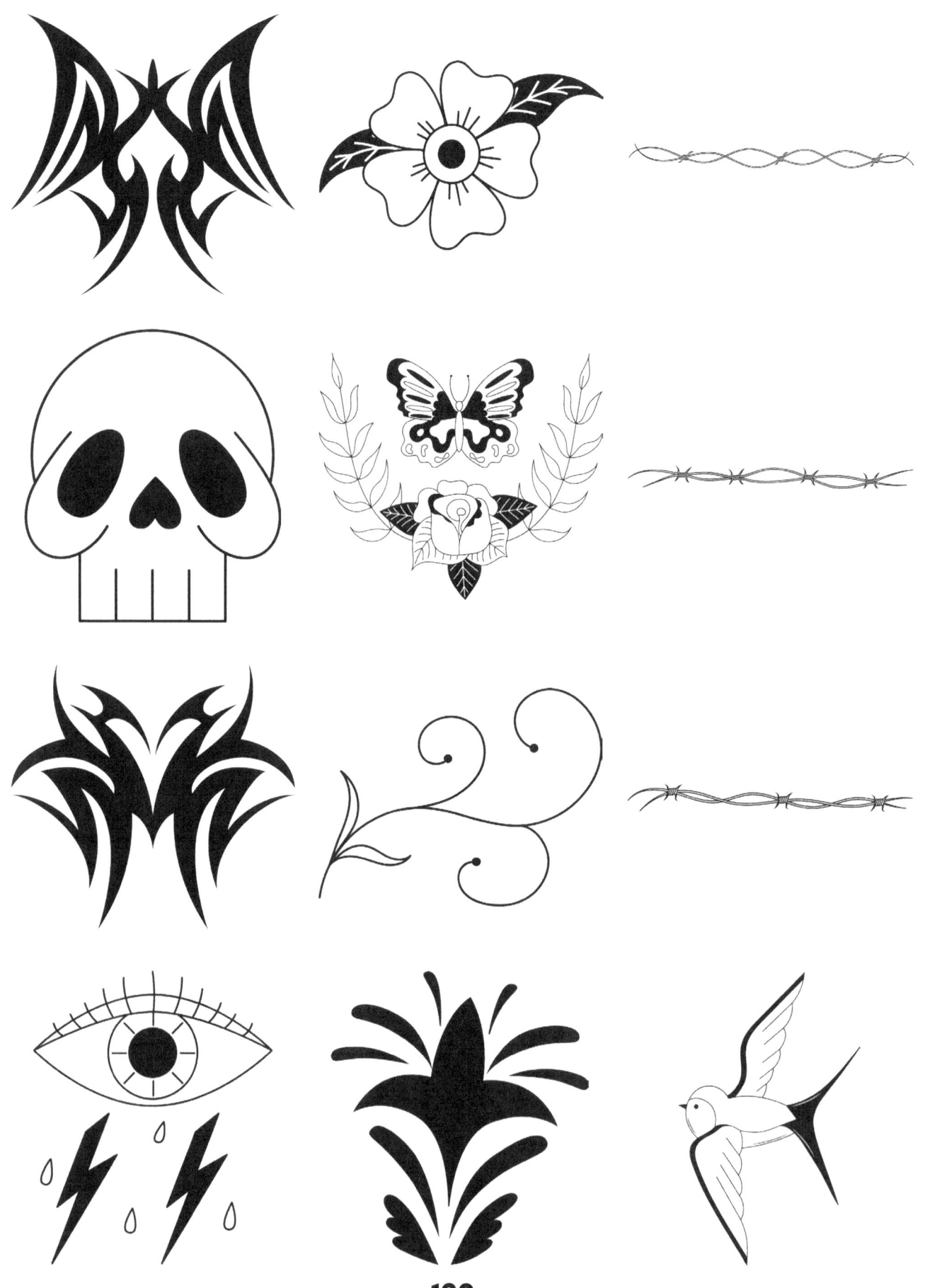

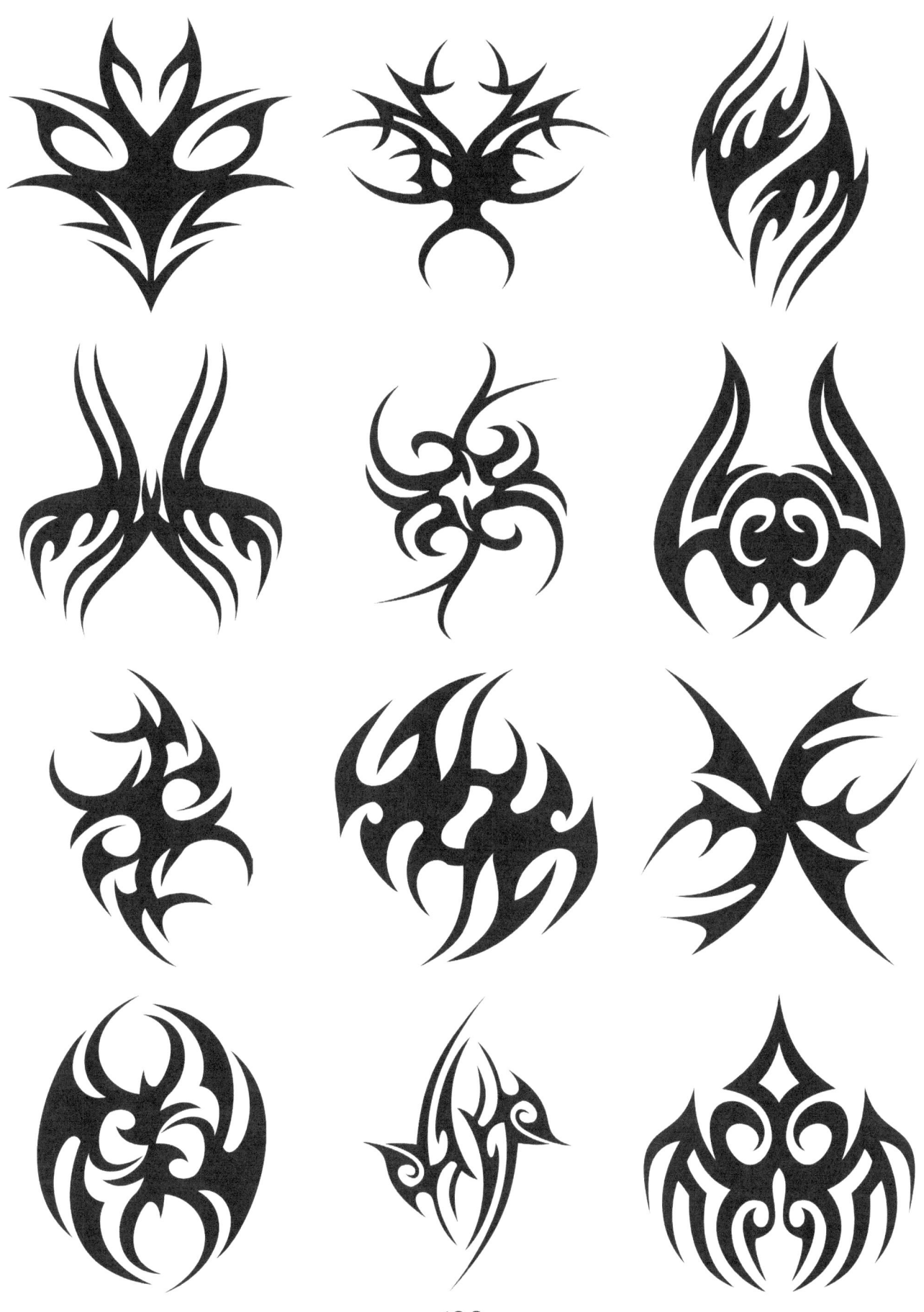

133

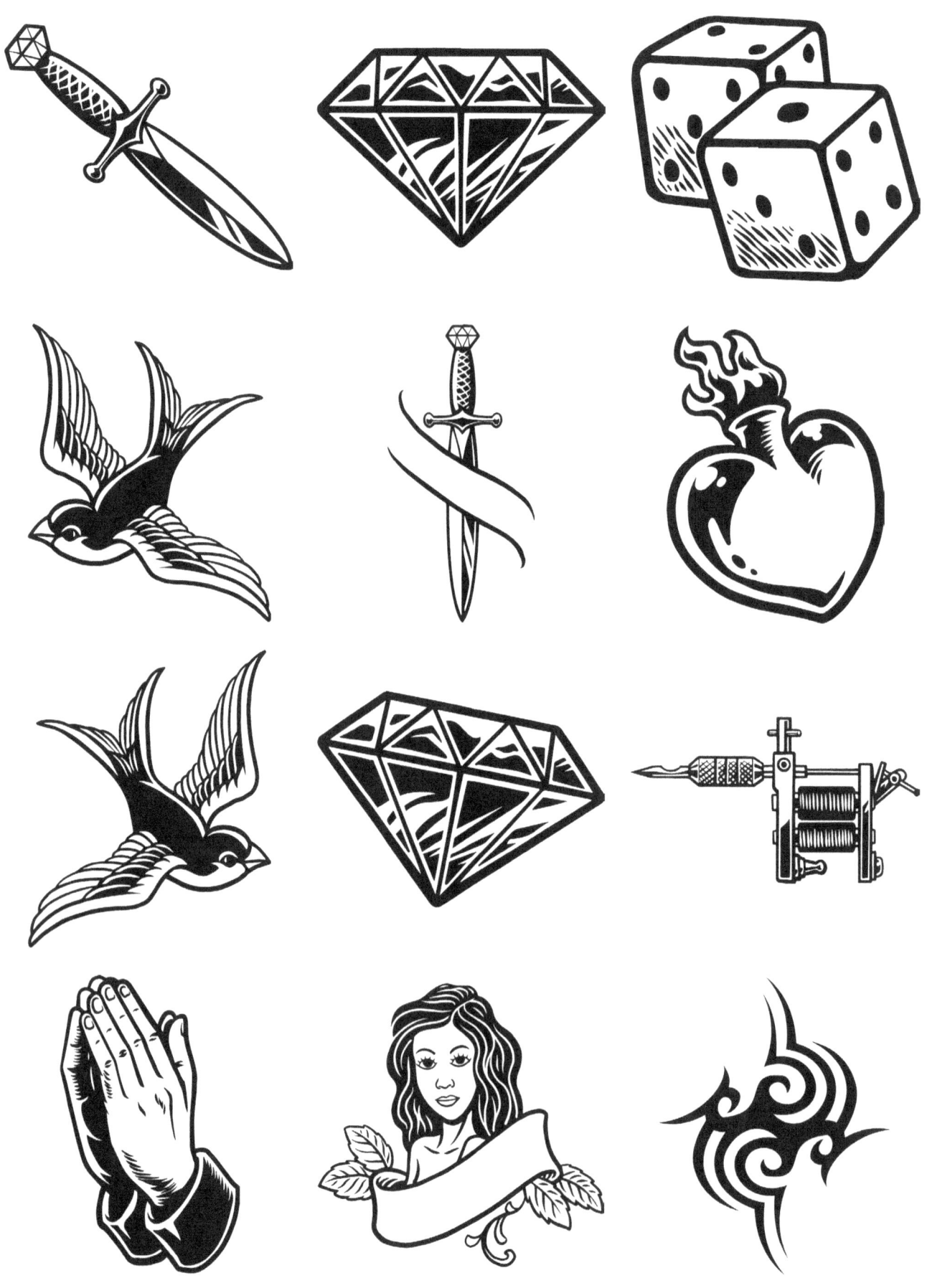

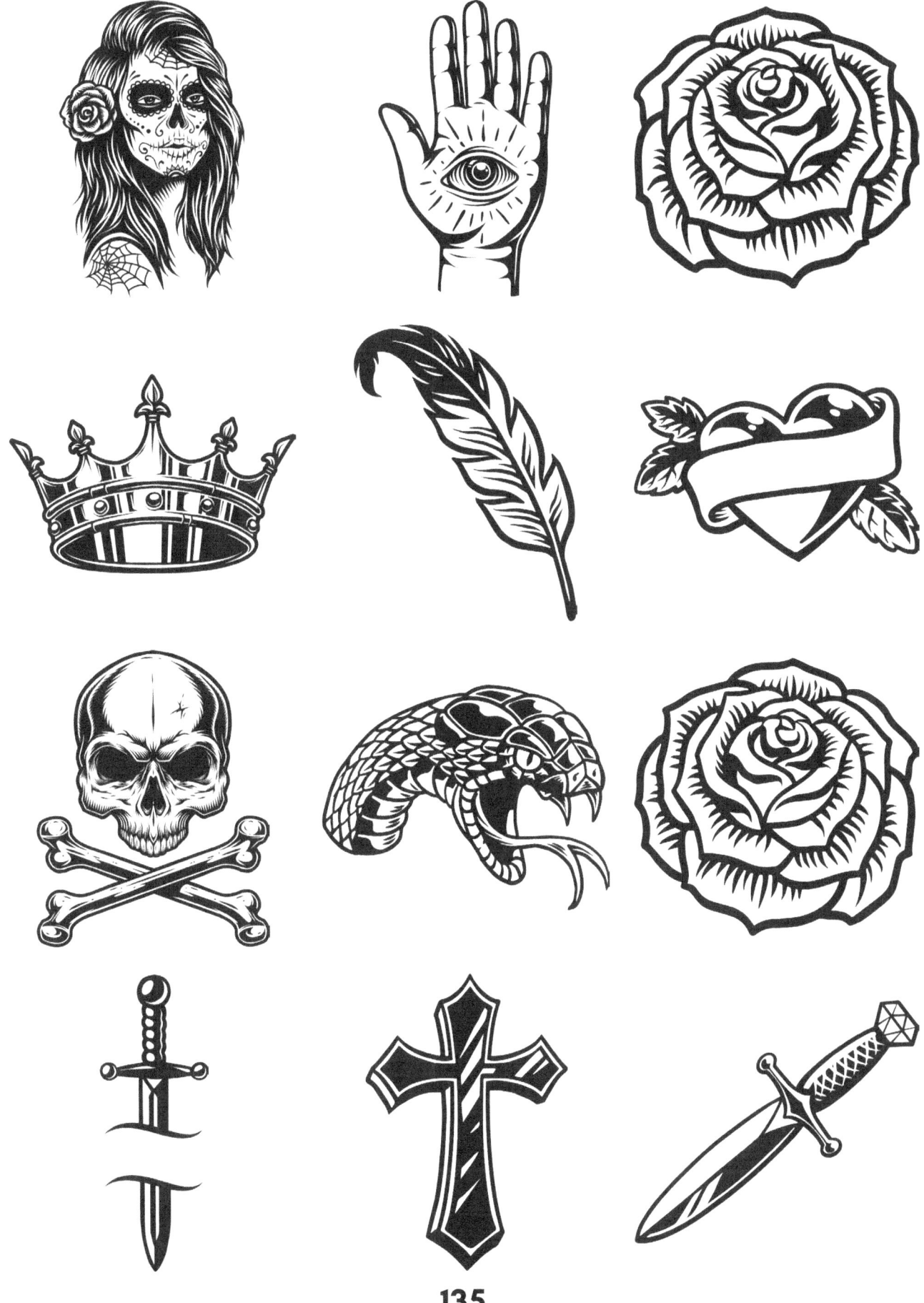

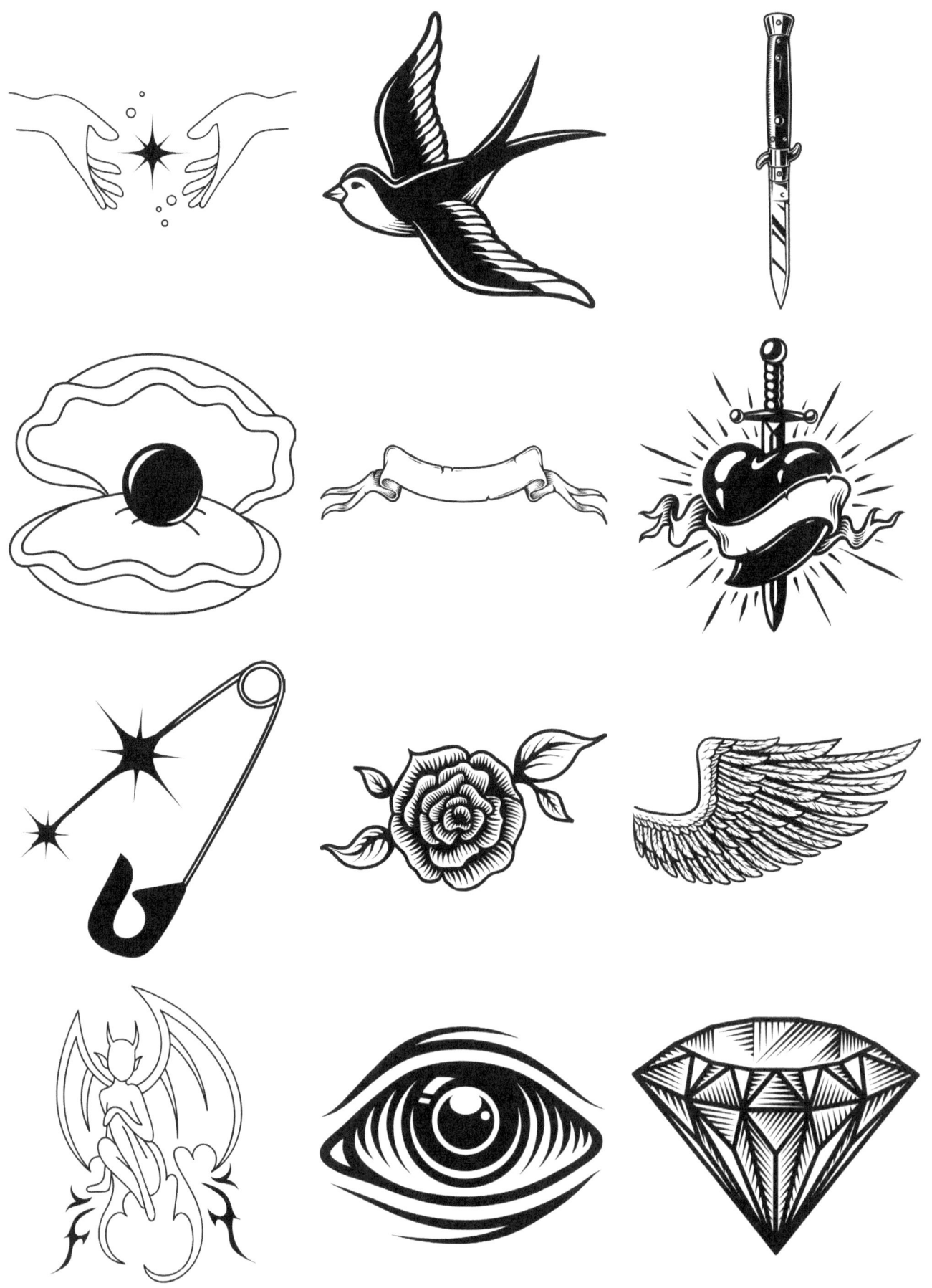

137

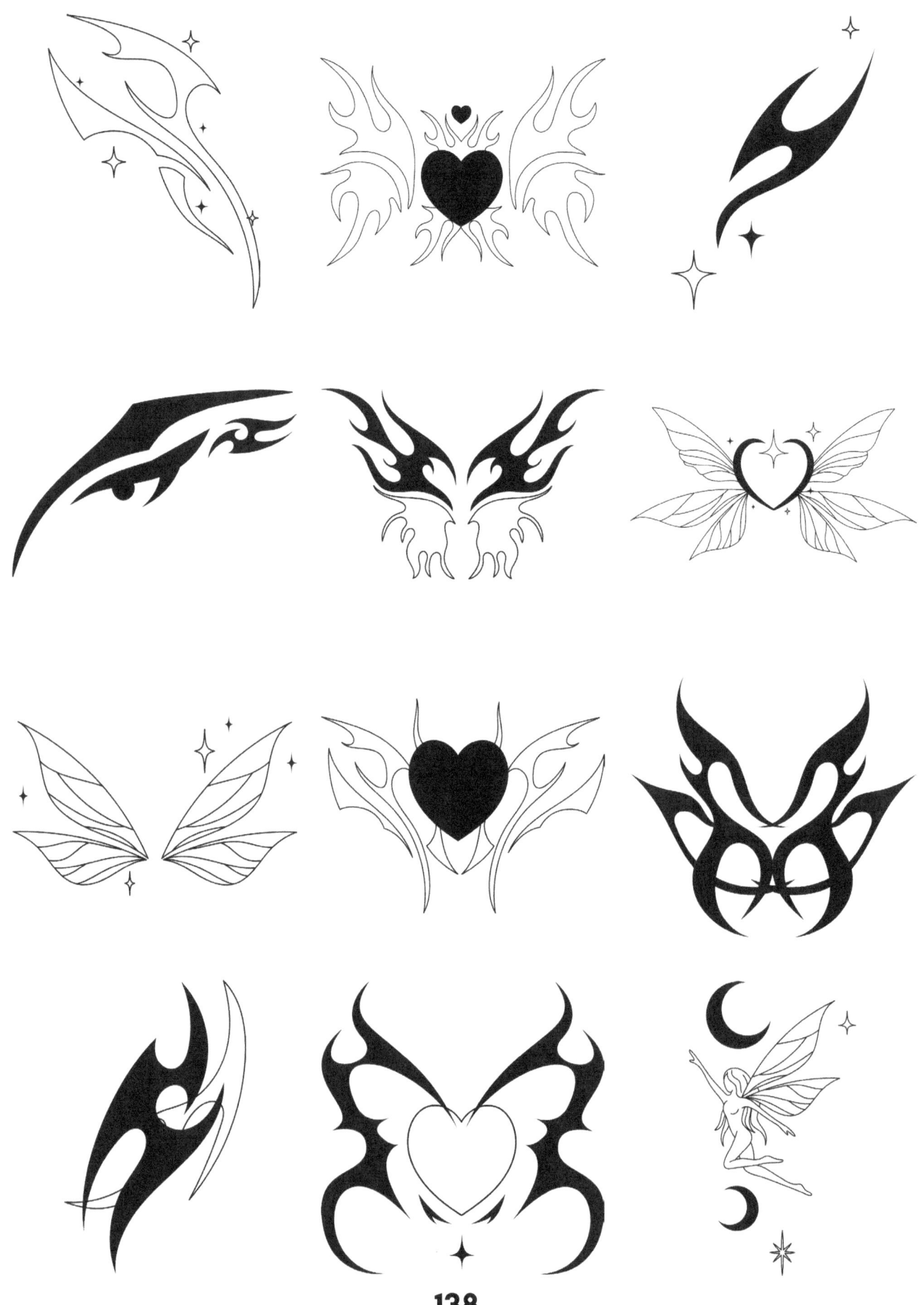

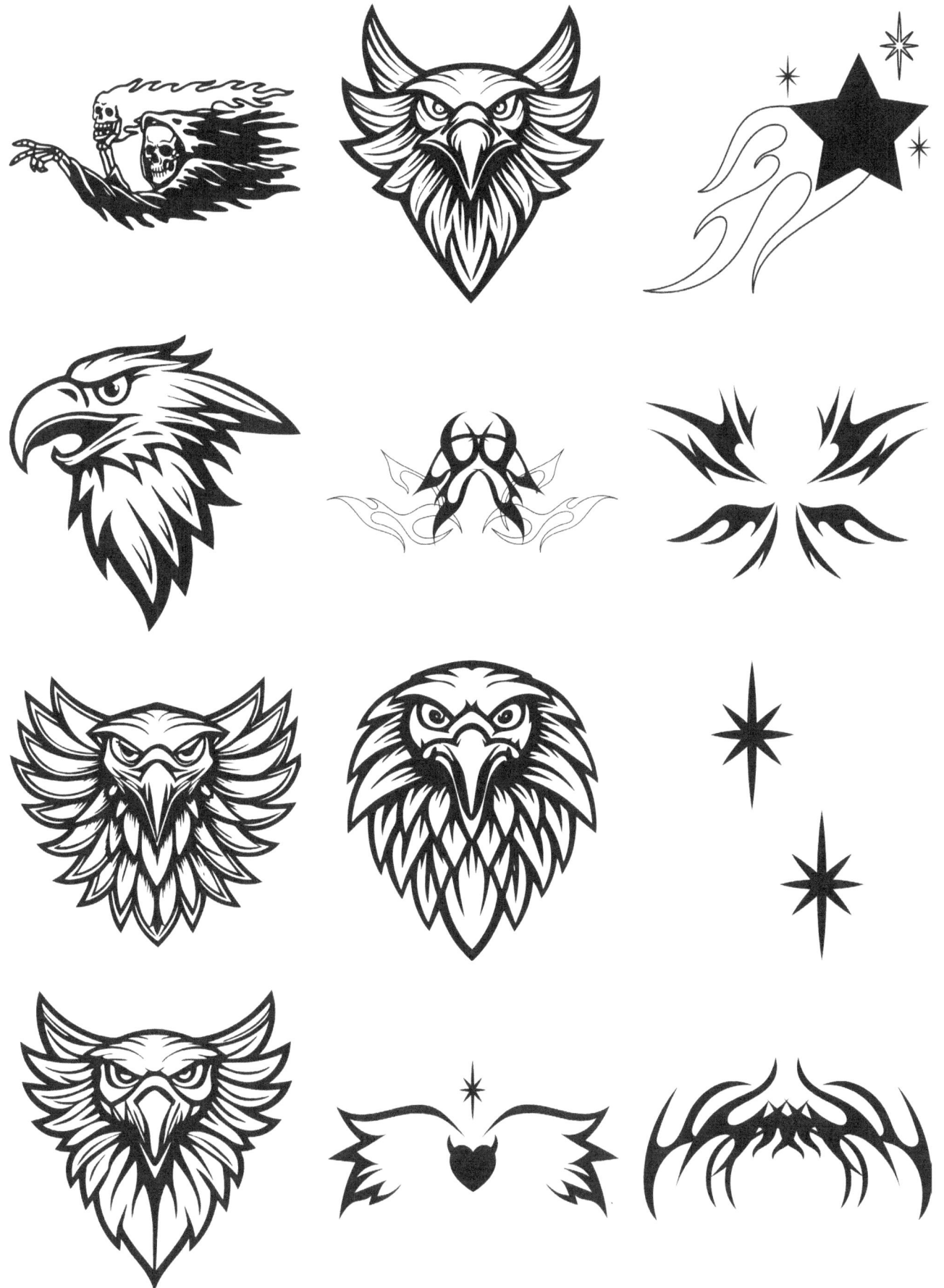

139

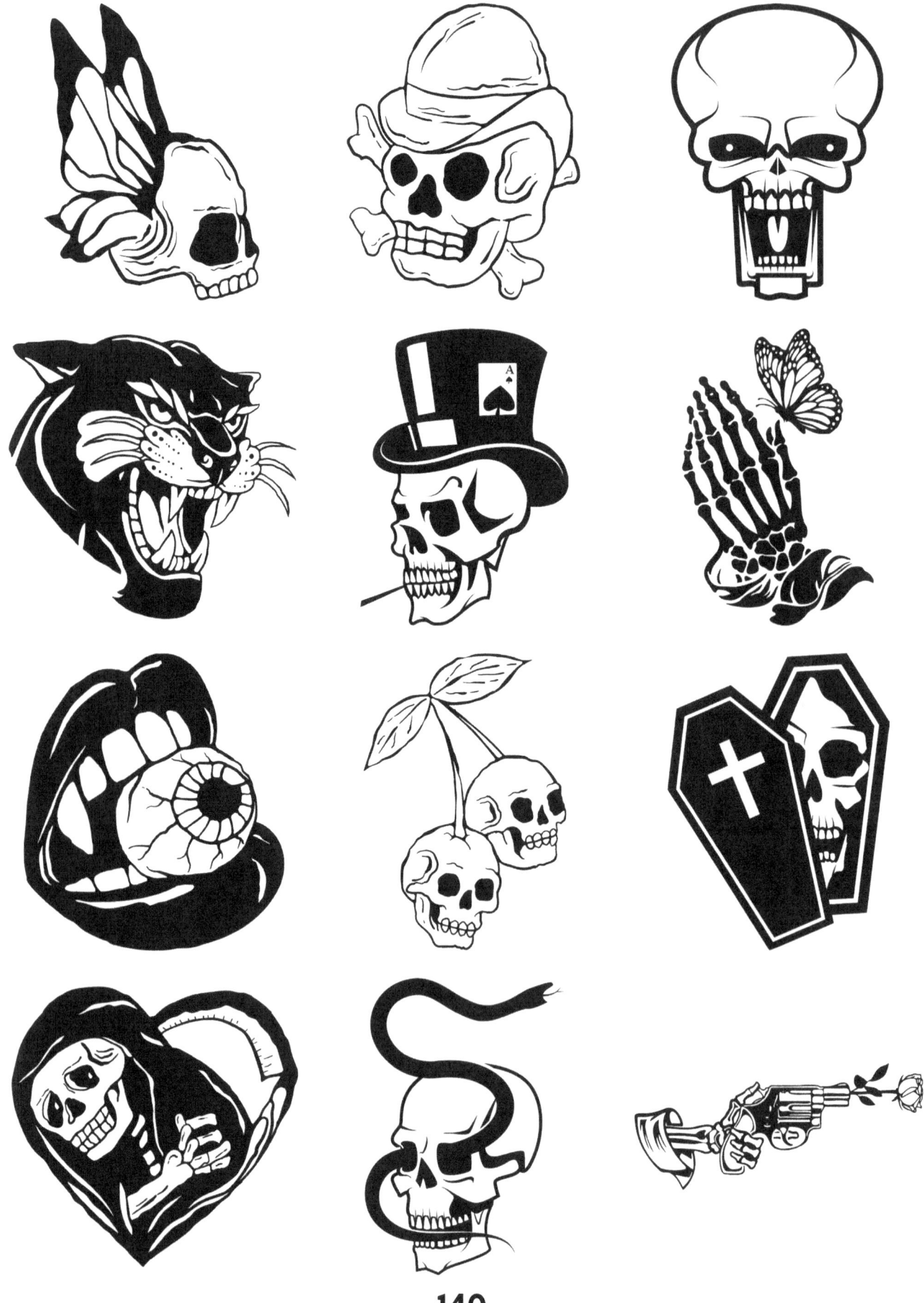

140

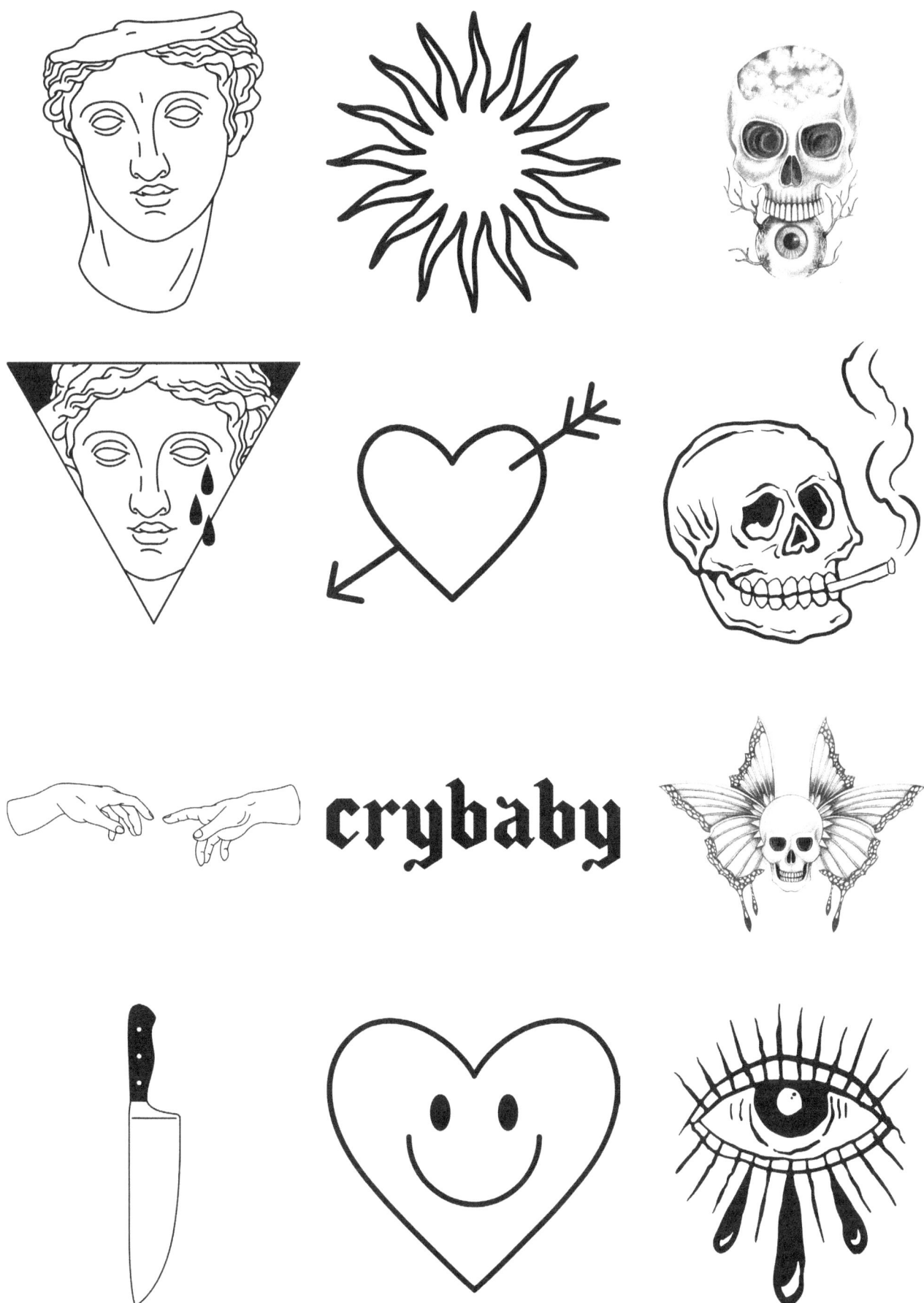

crybaby

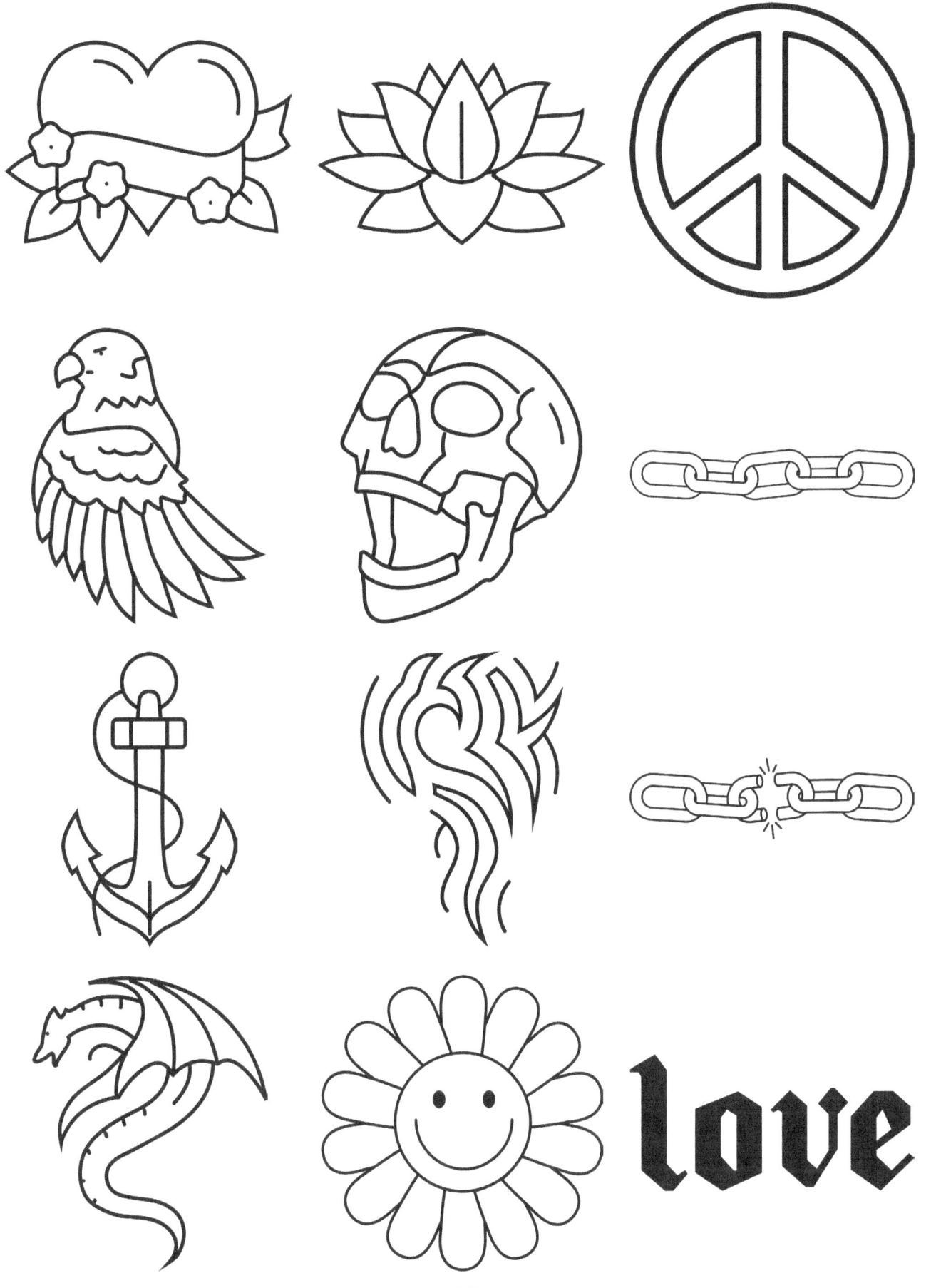

143

144

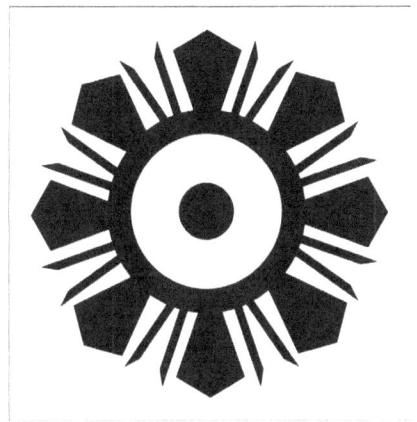
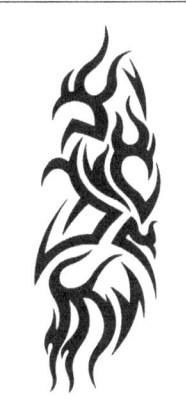
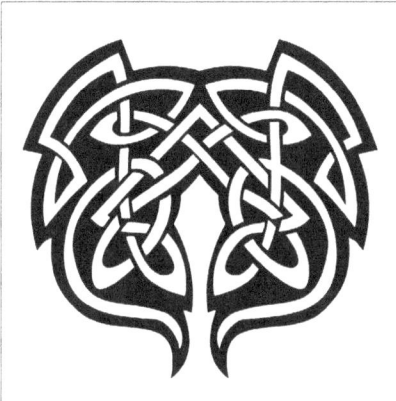
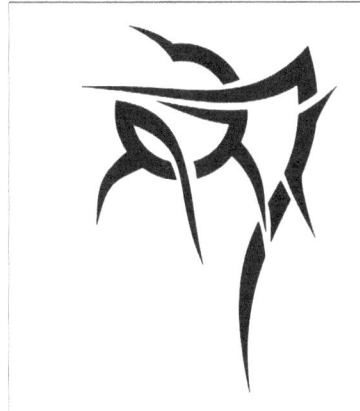
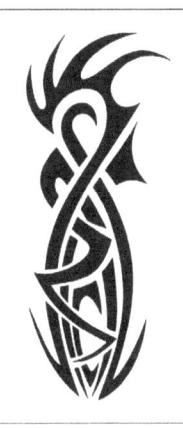
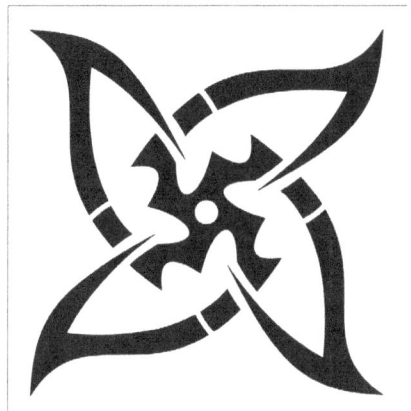
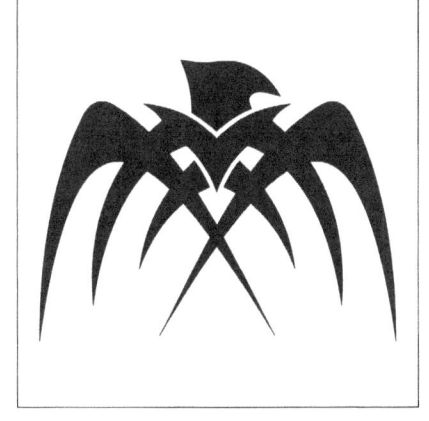
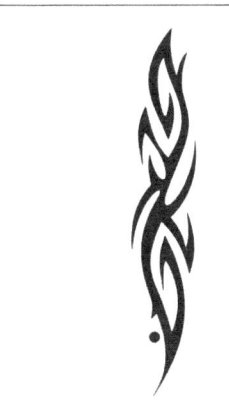
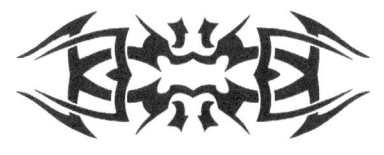
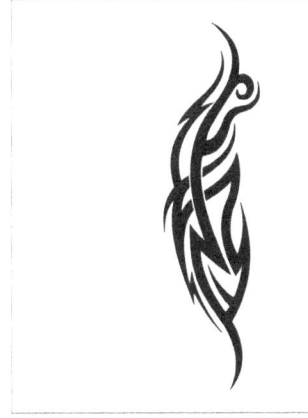
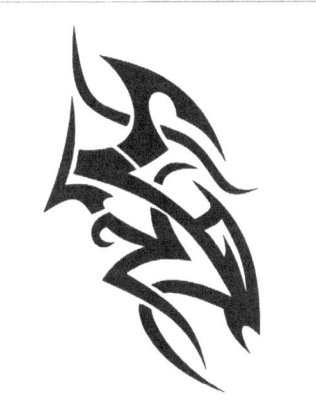
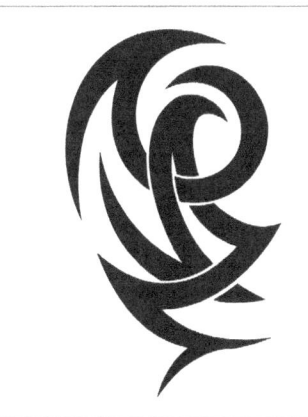

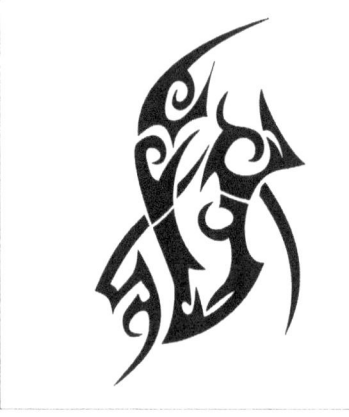
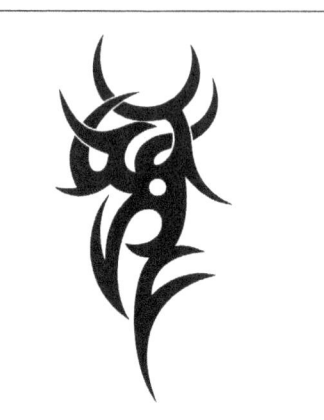
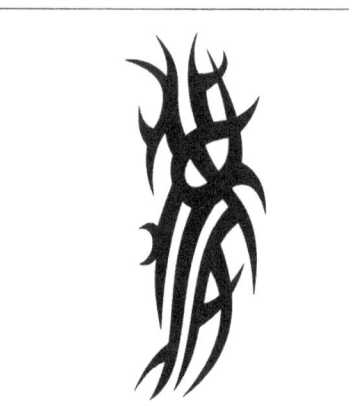
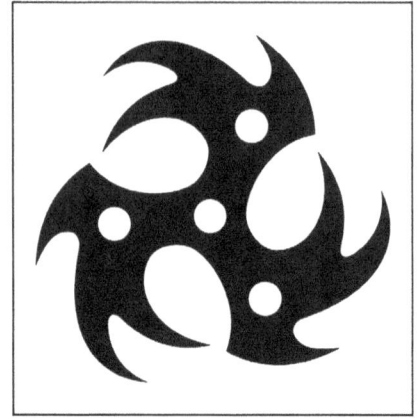
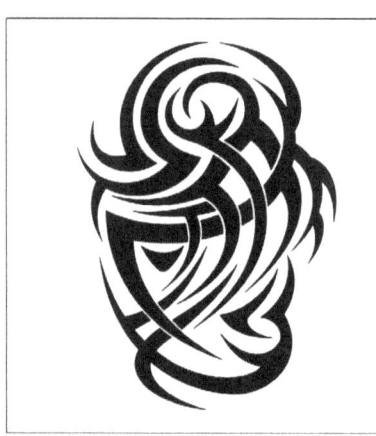
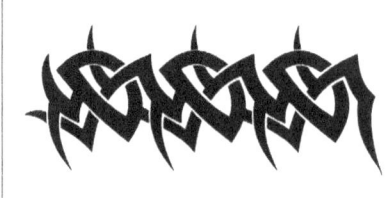

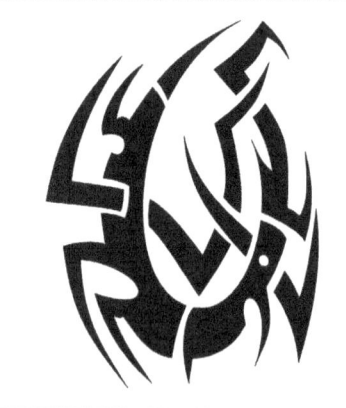
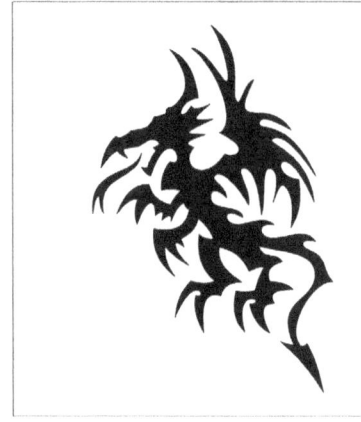
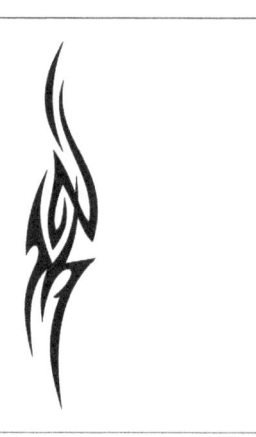
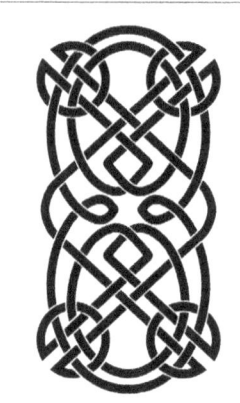

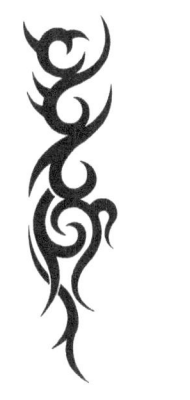
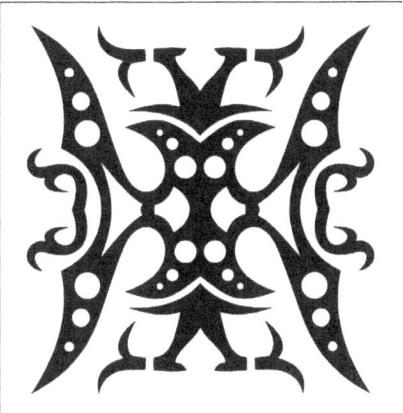
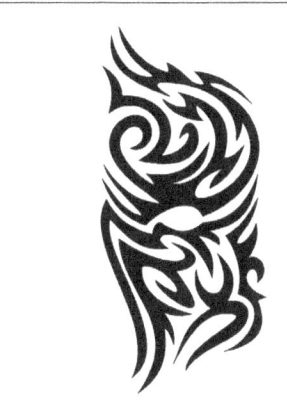
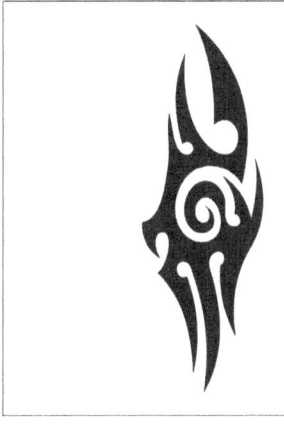
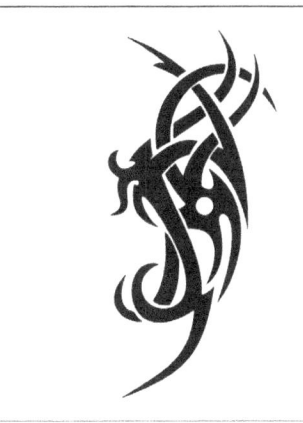
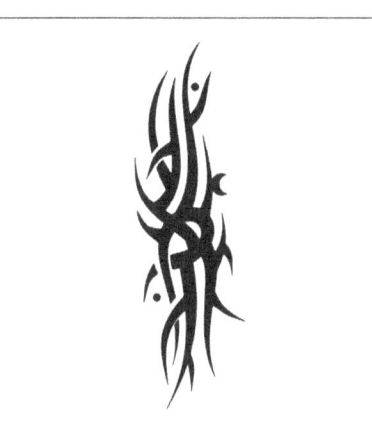
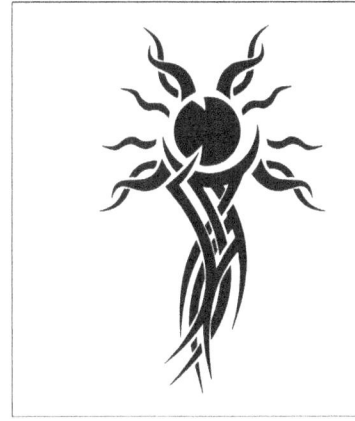
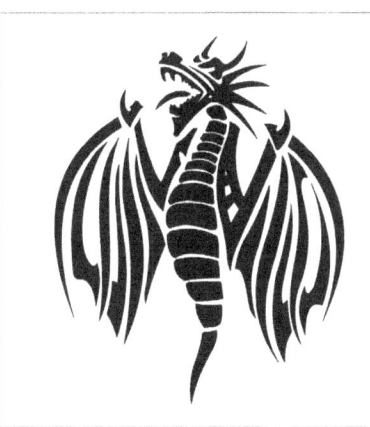
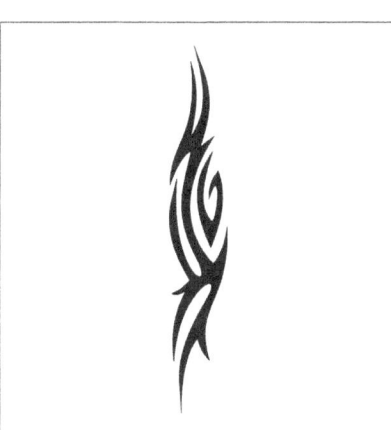
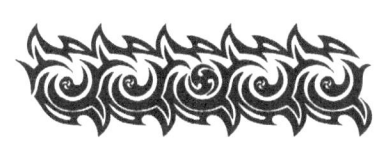
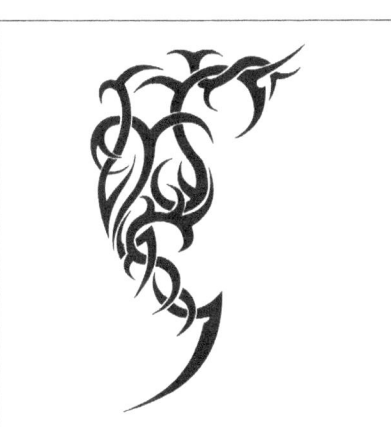
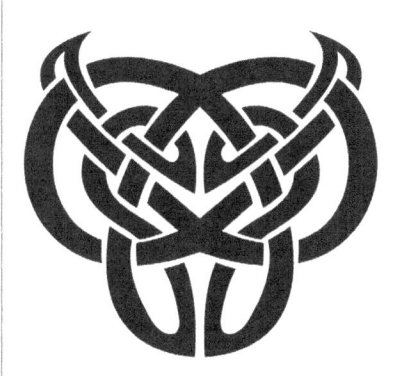

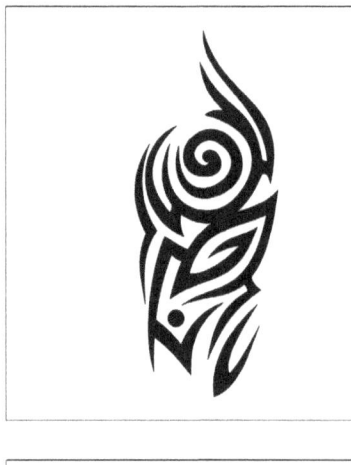
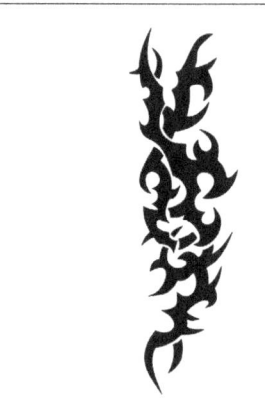
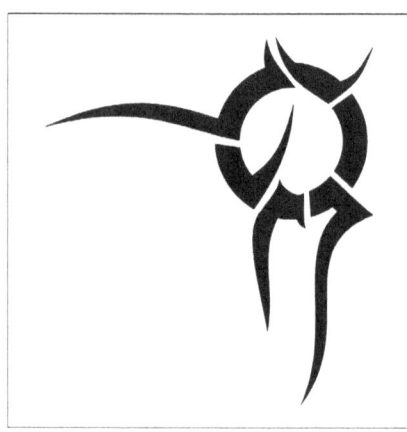

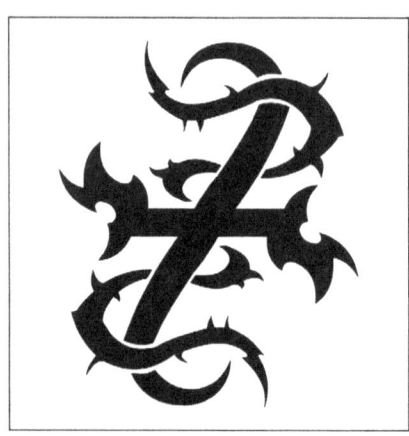
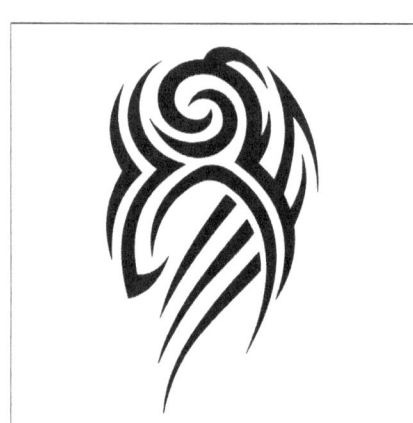
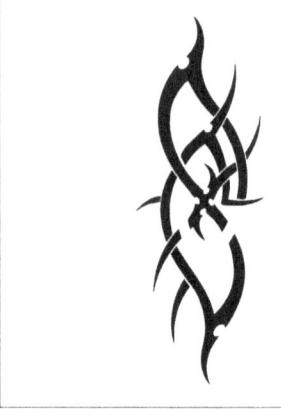
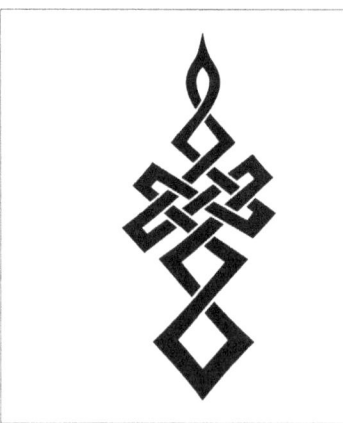
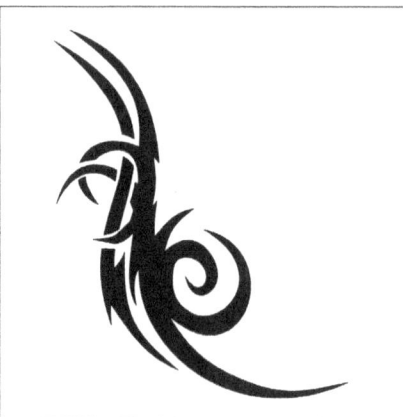
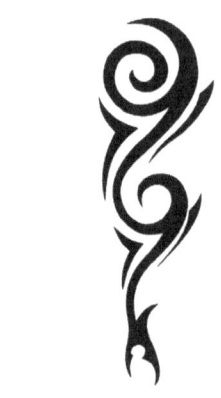
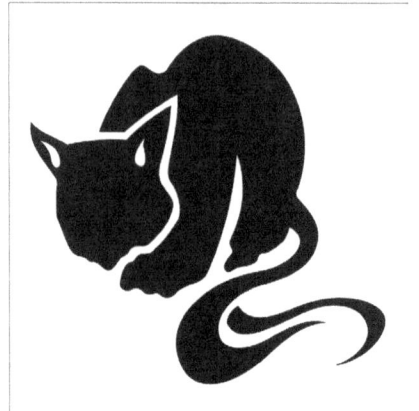
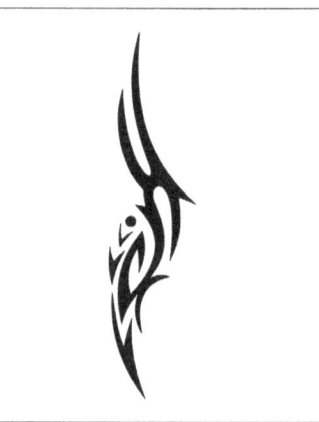

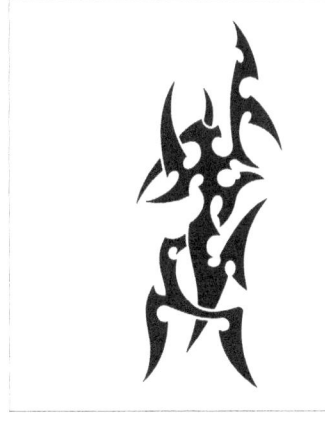

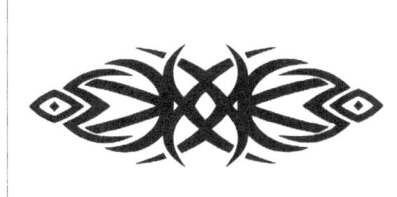
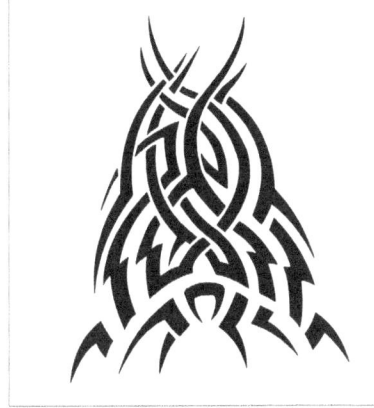
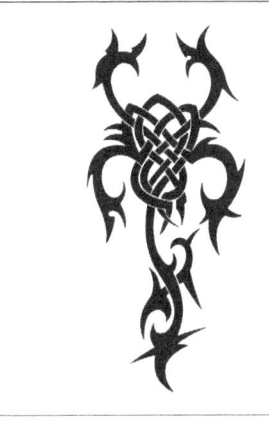
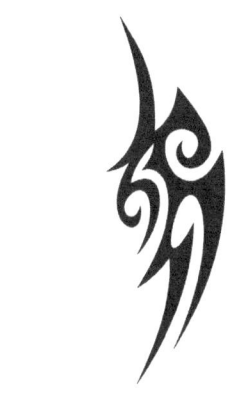
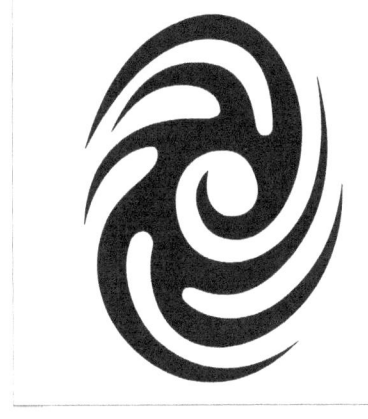
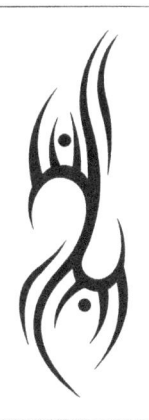
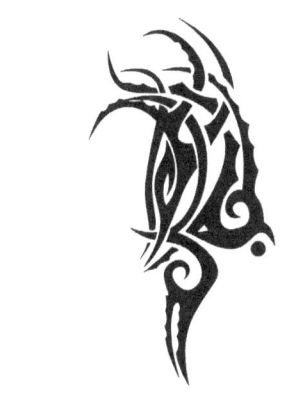
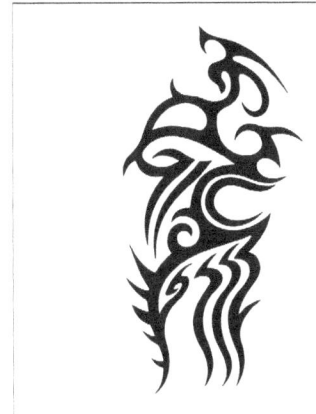
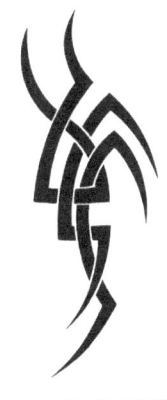
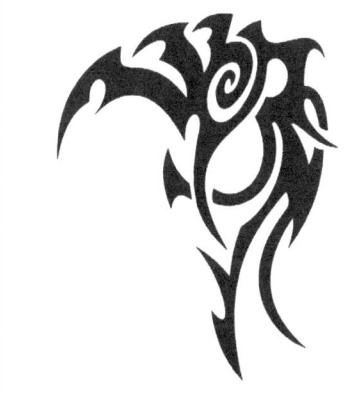

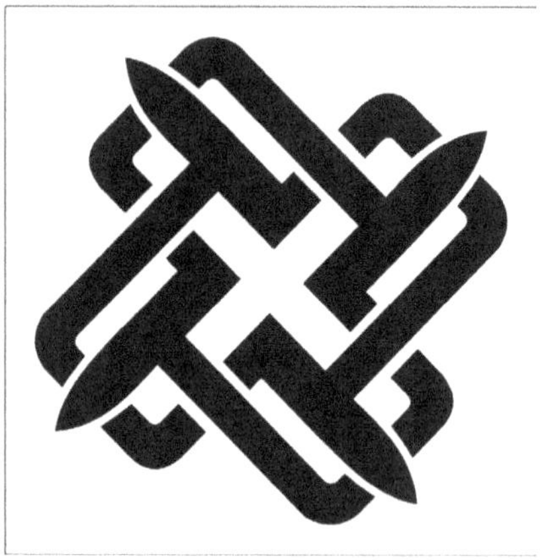

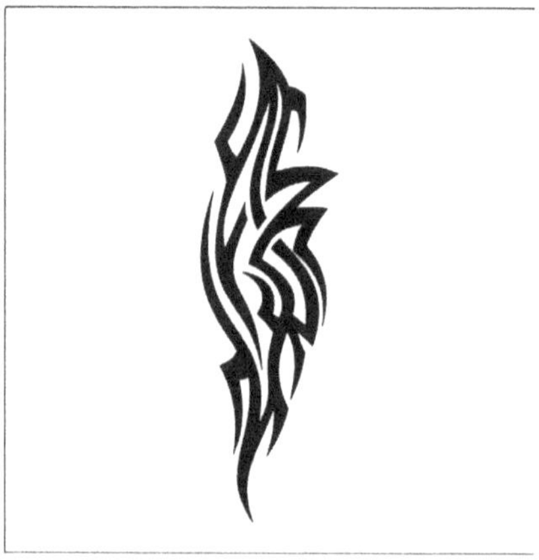

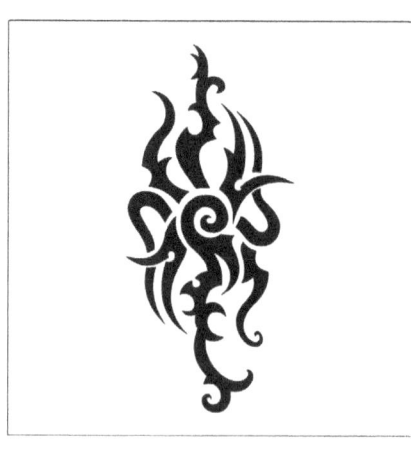

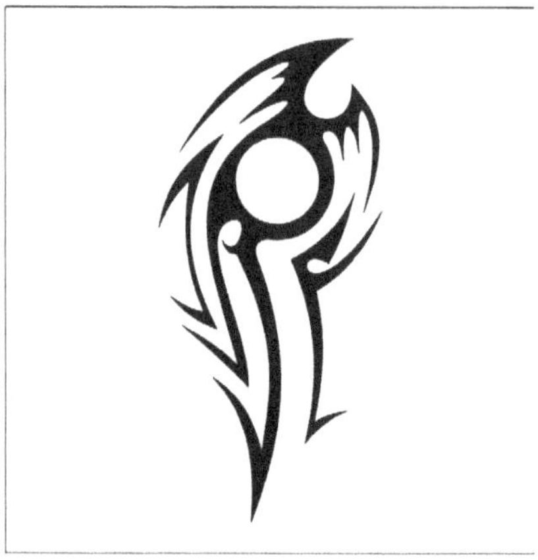

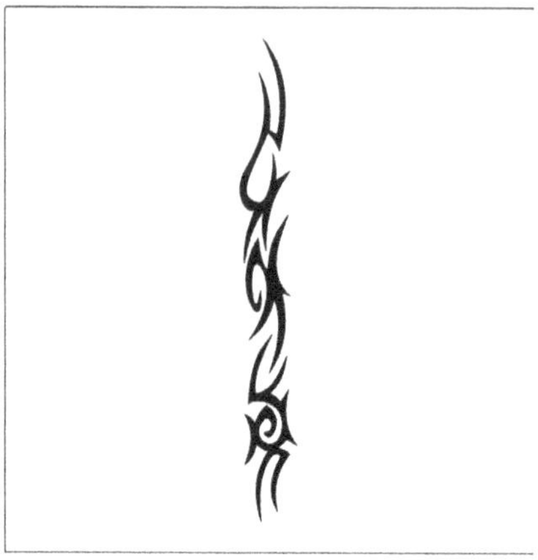

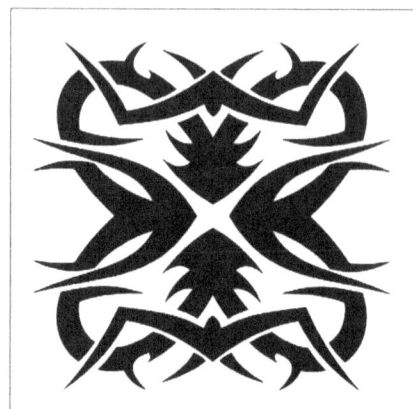

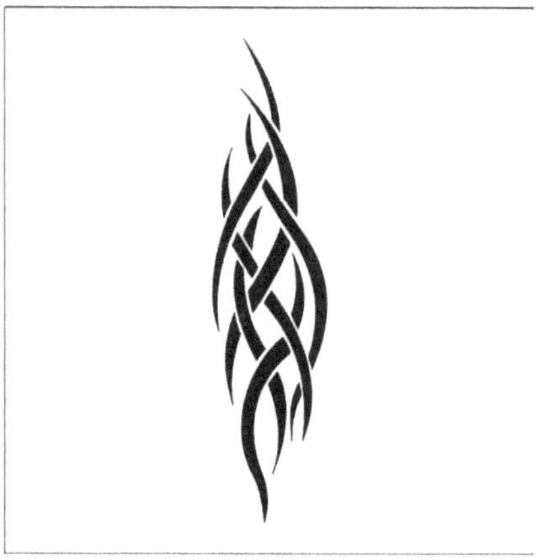

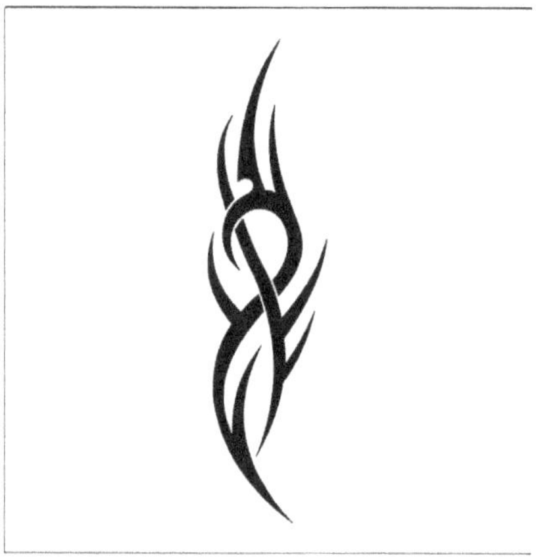

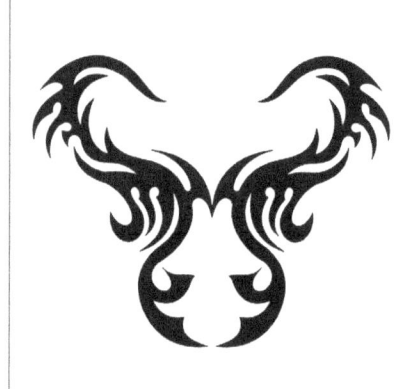

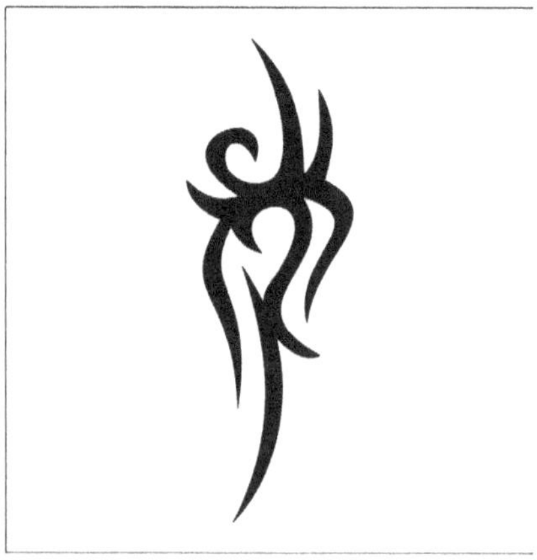

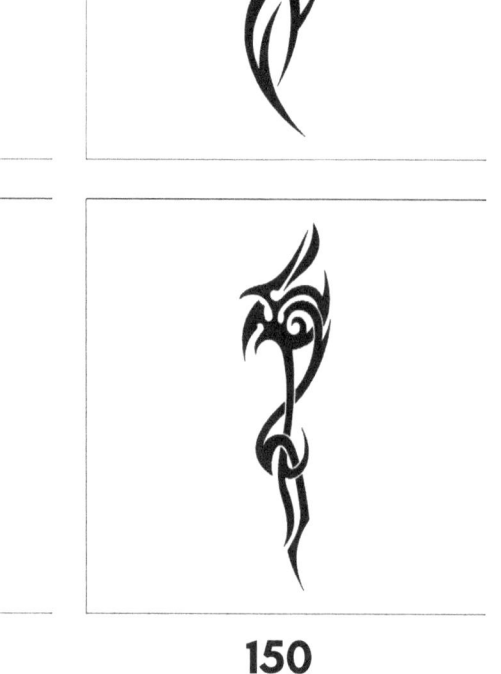

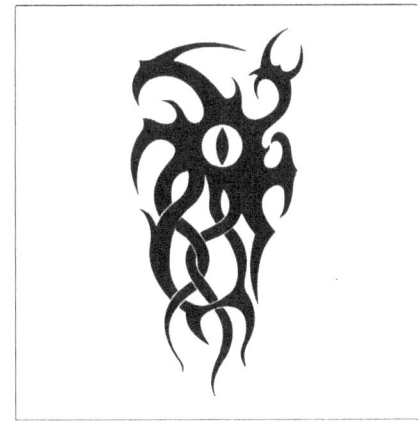 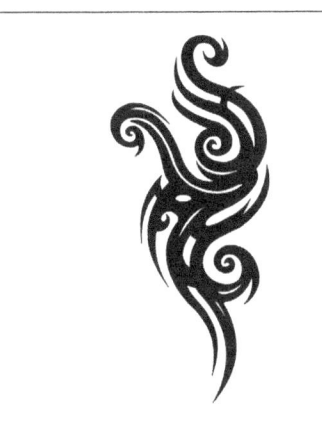 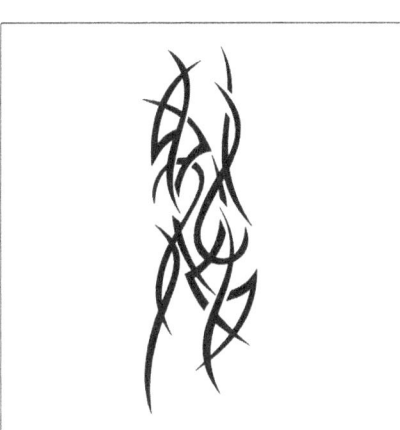

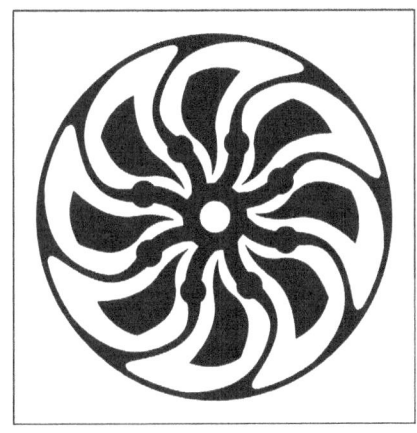 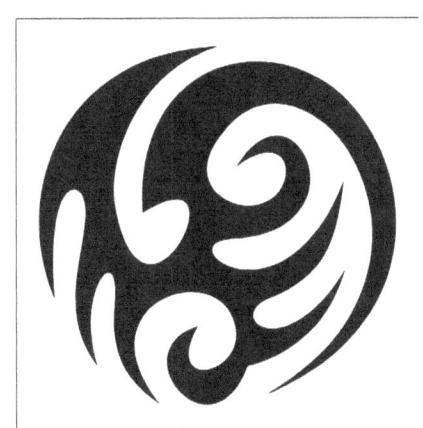 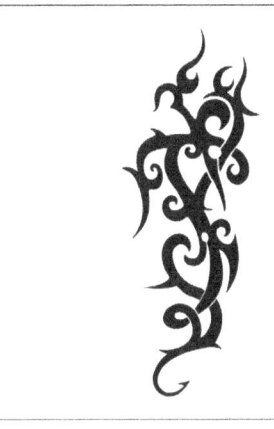

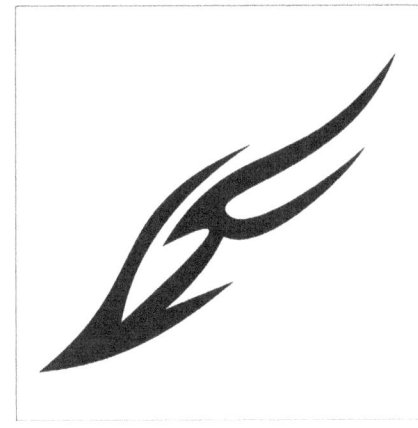 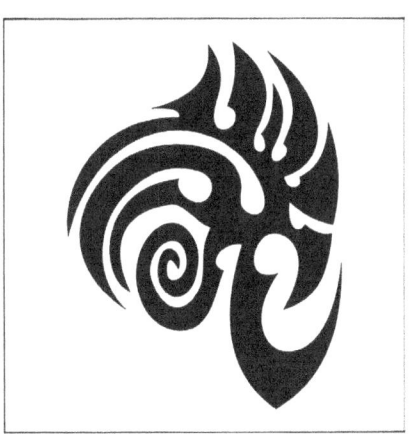 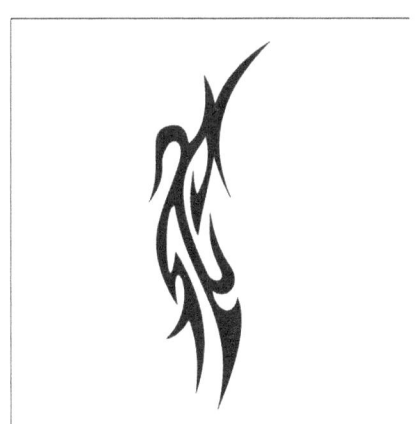

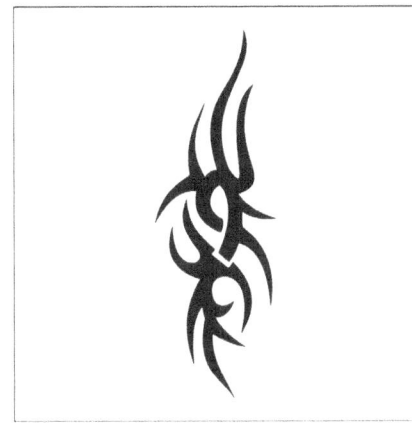 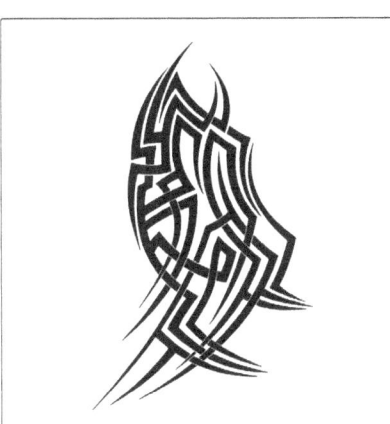 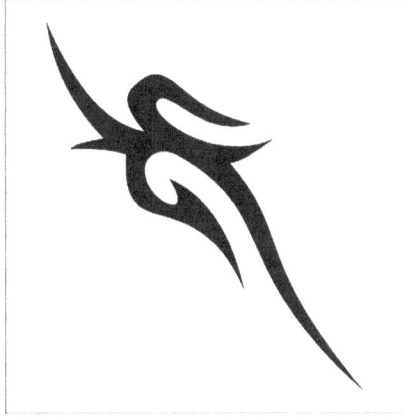

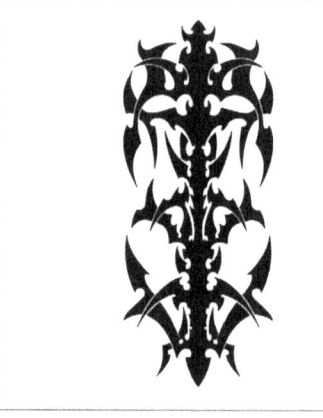

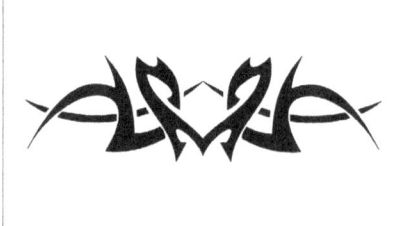

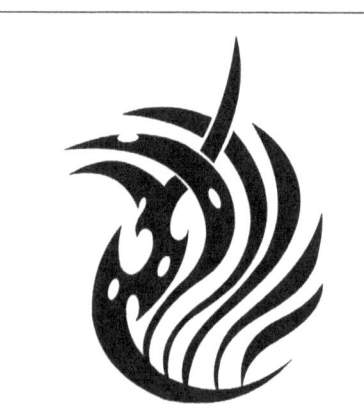

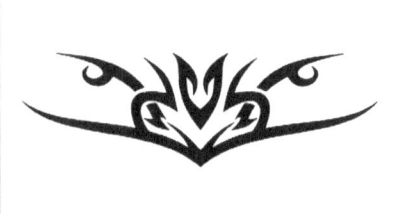

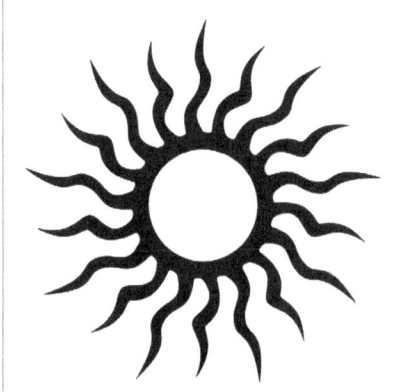

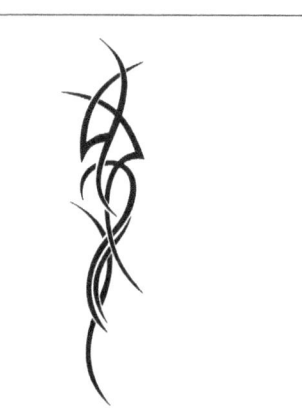

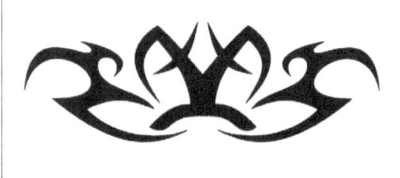

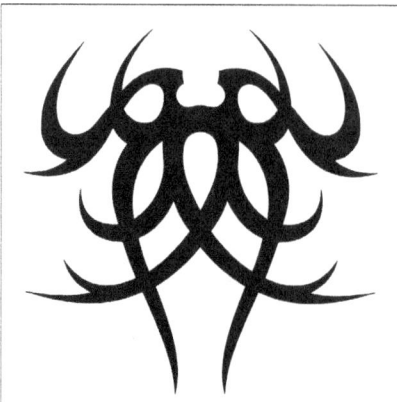

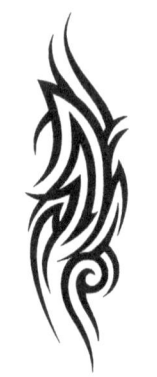

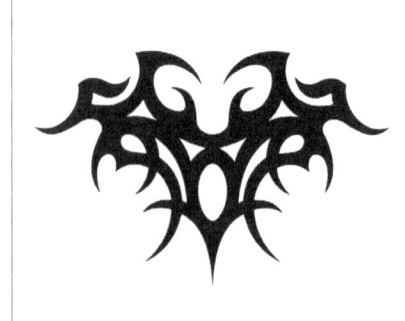

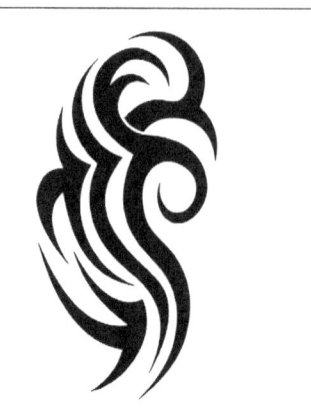

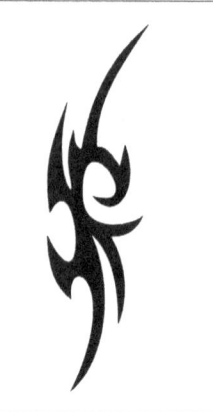

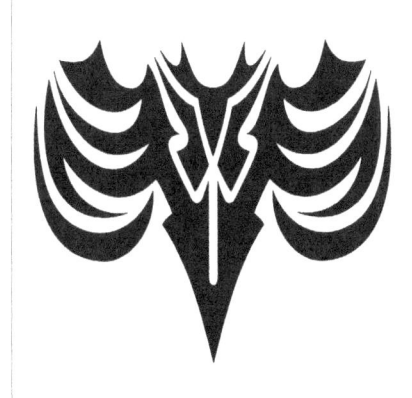 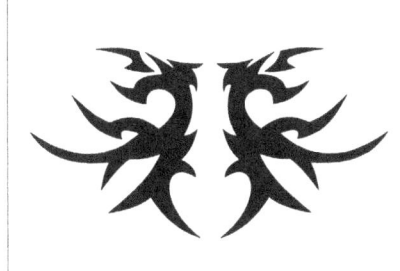 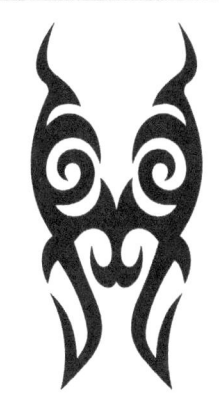

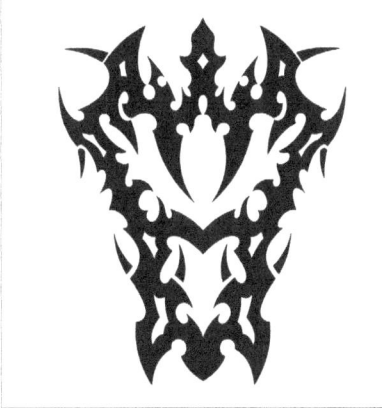 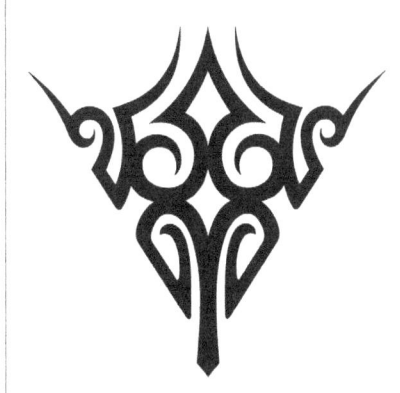 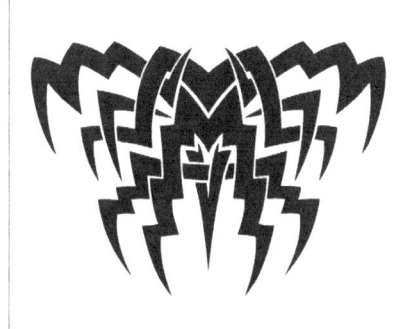

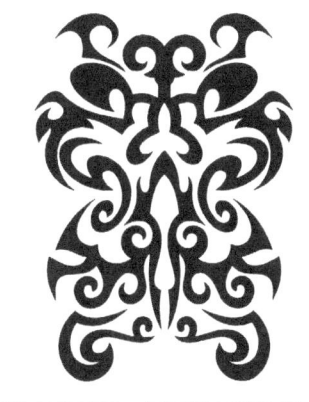 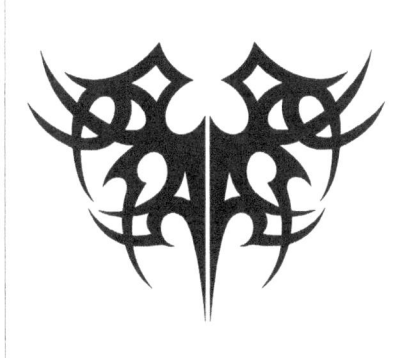 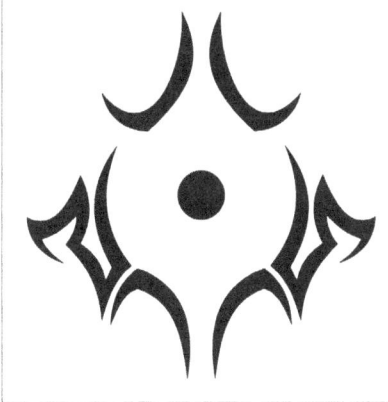

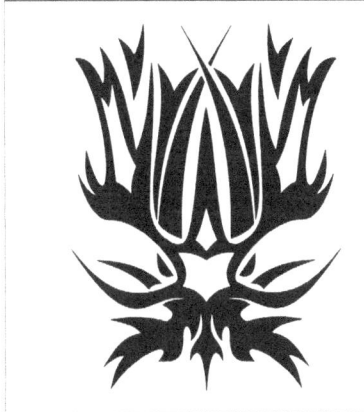 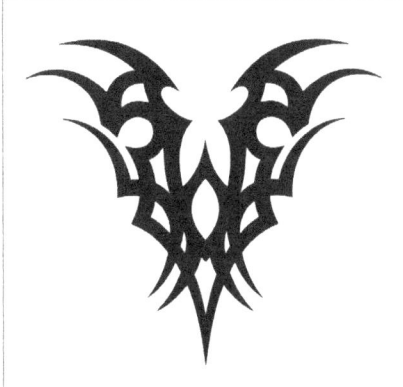 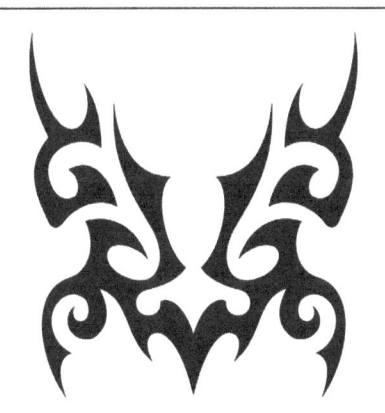

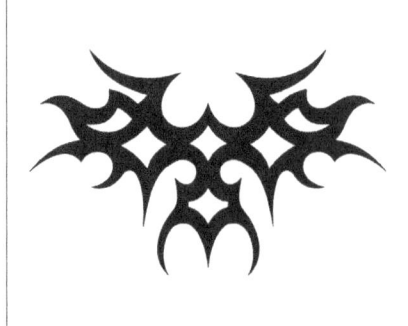
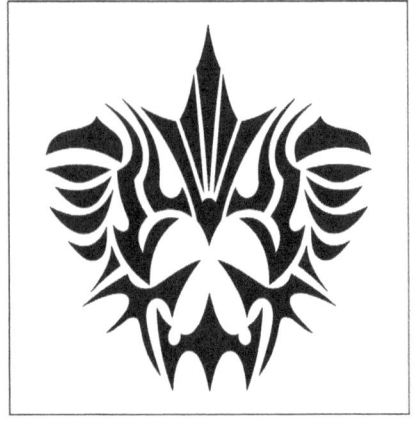
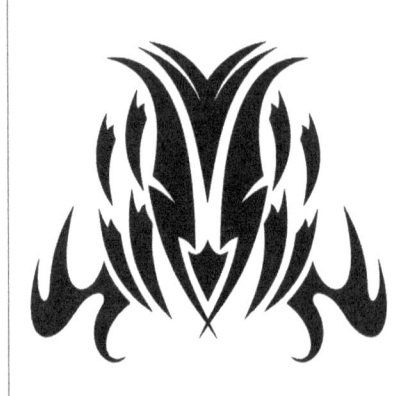
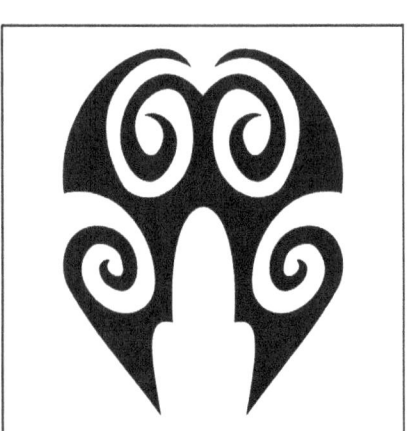

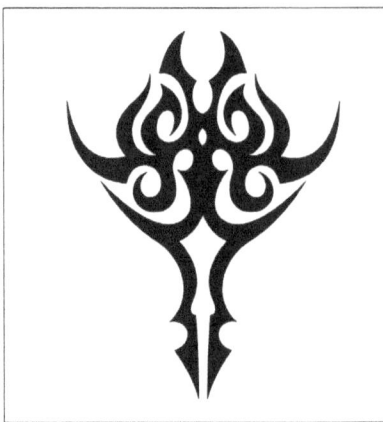
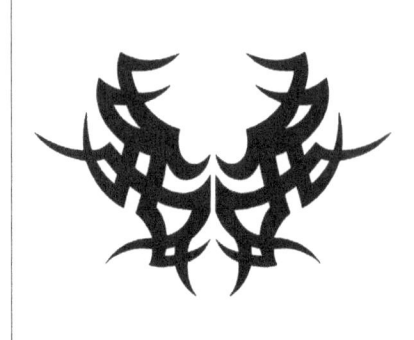
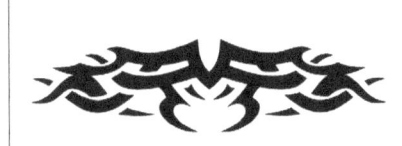
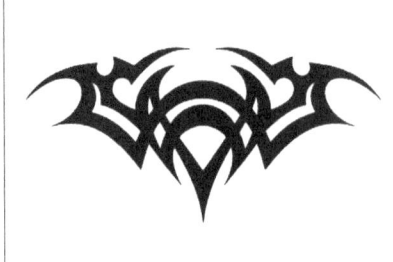
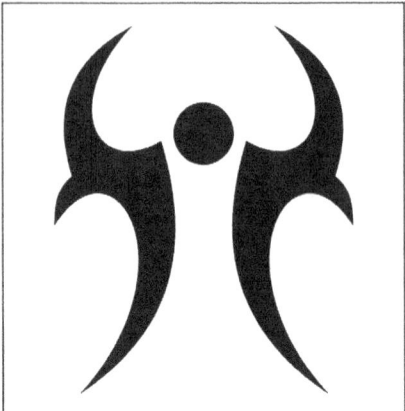

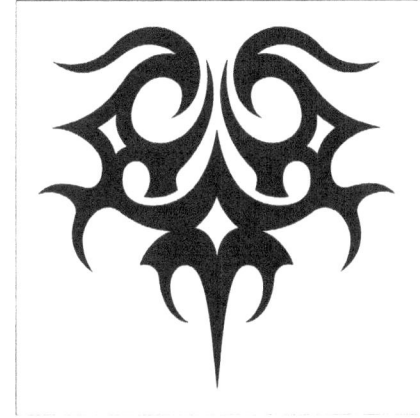

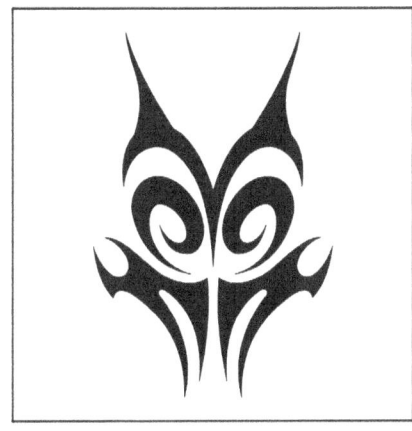
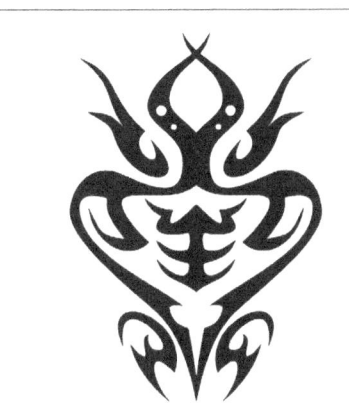
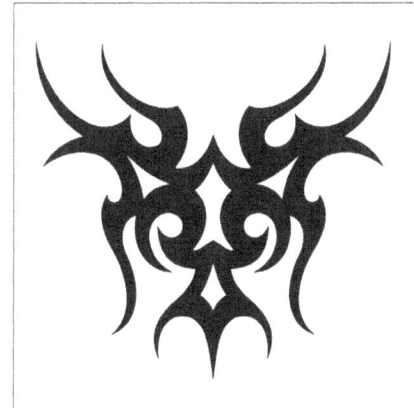
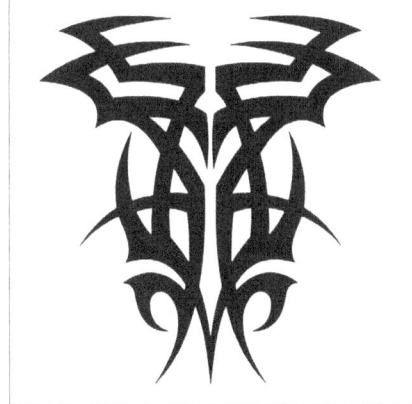
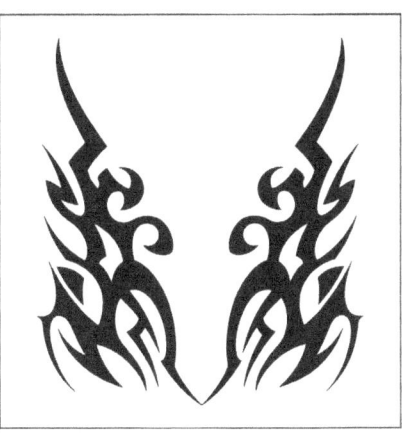
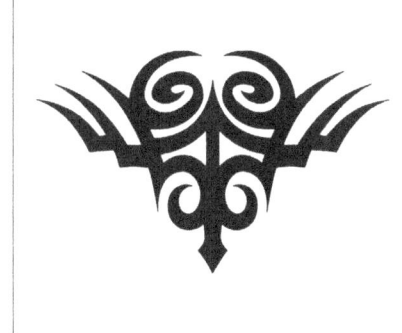
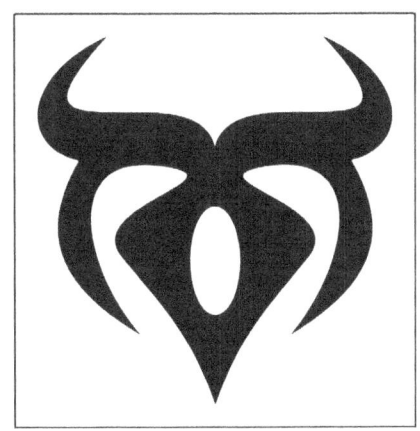

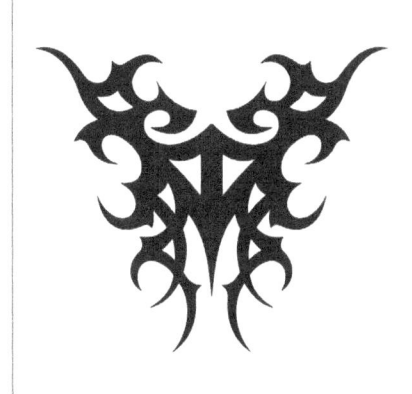

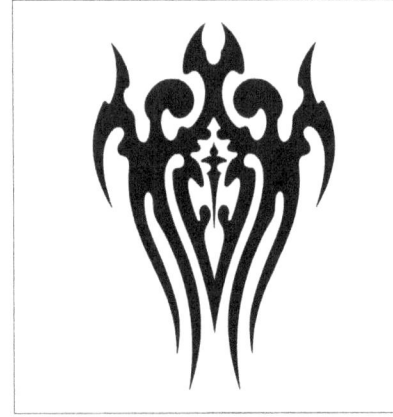
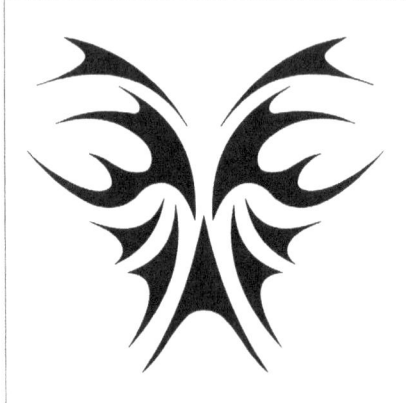
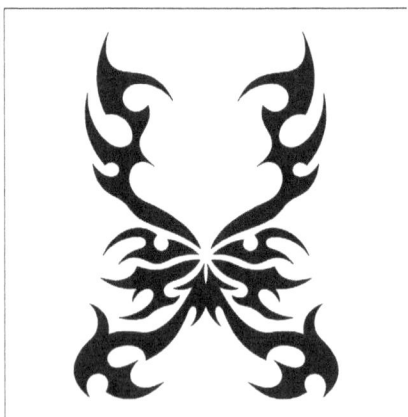
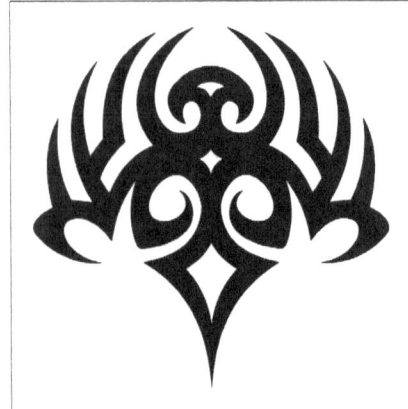
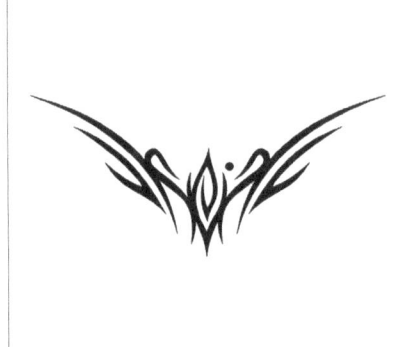

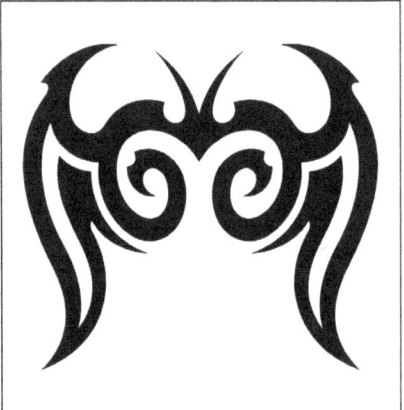
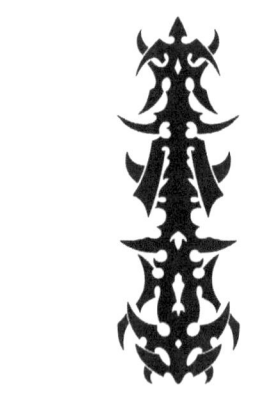
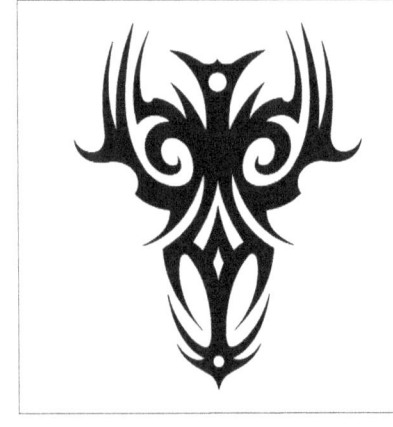
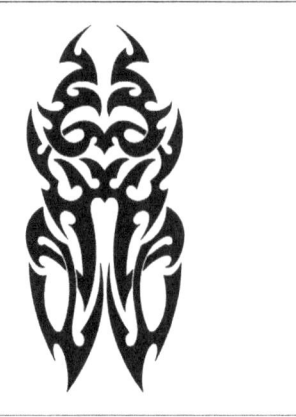

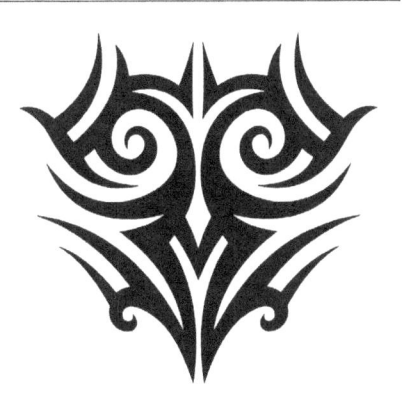
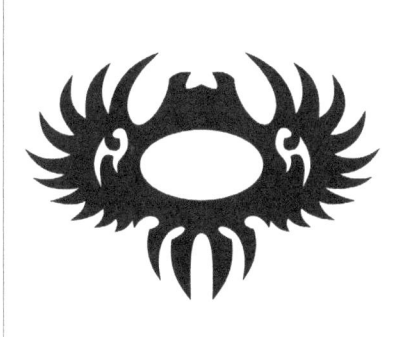

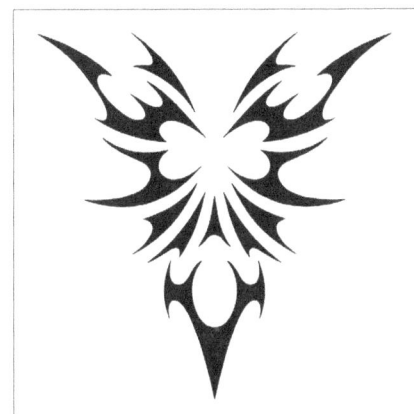

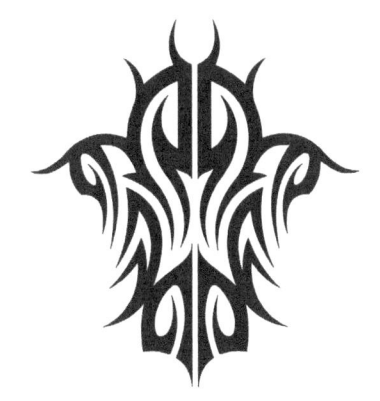

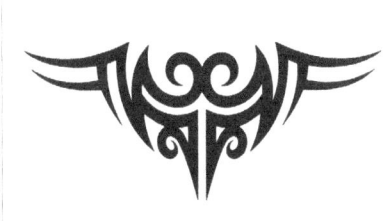
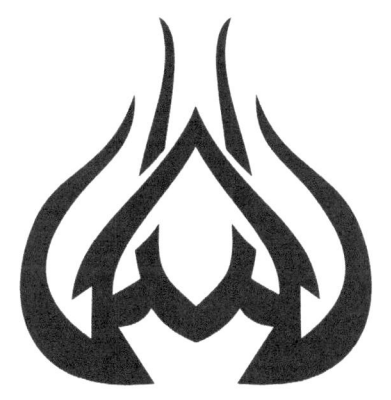

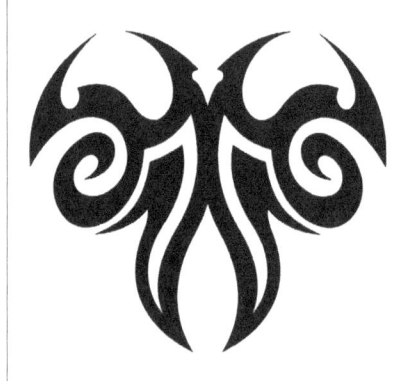

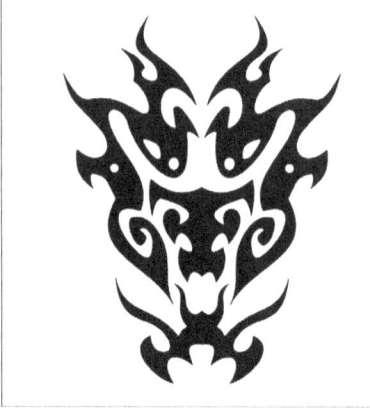
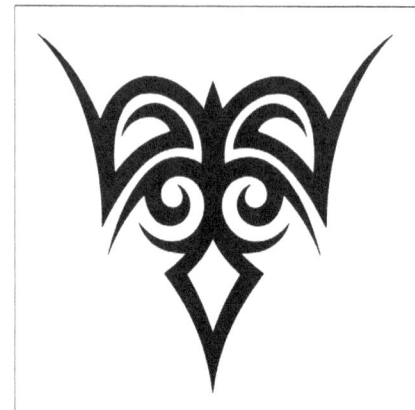
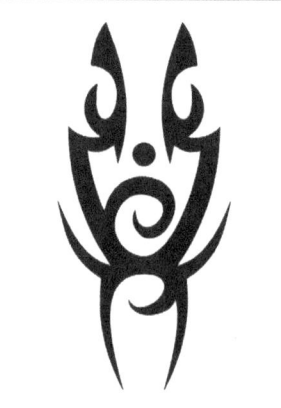
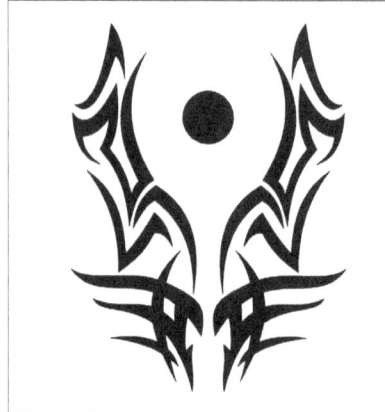

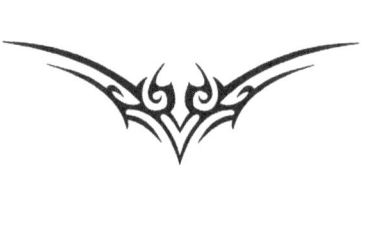
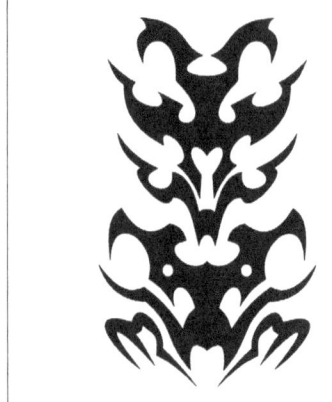
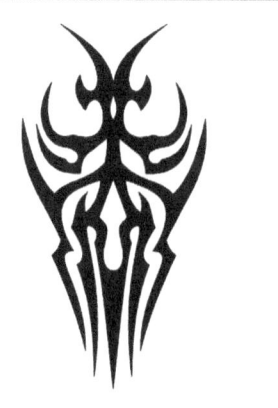
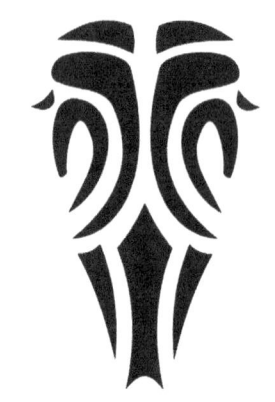

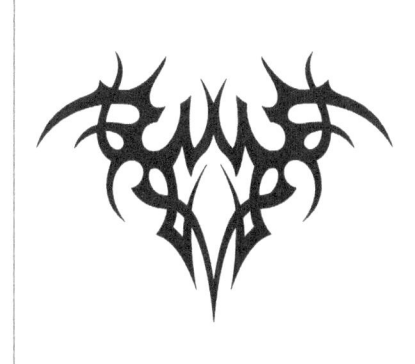

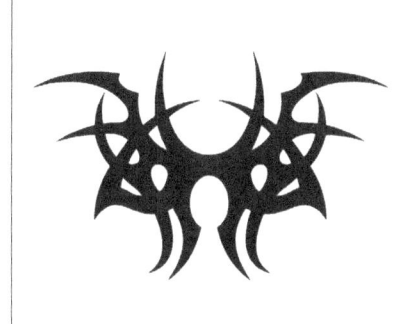
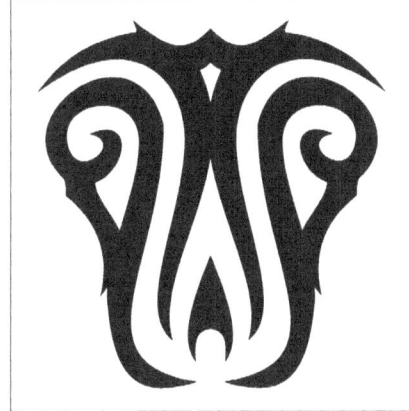

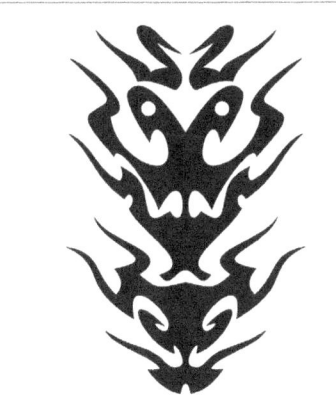
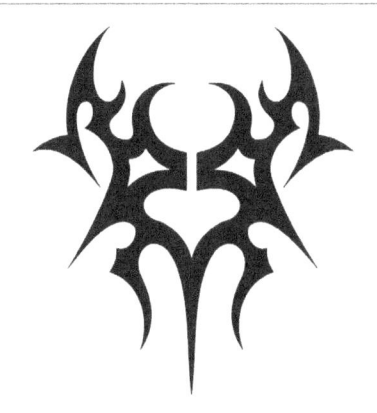
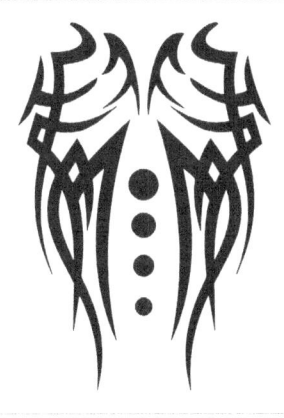

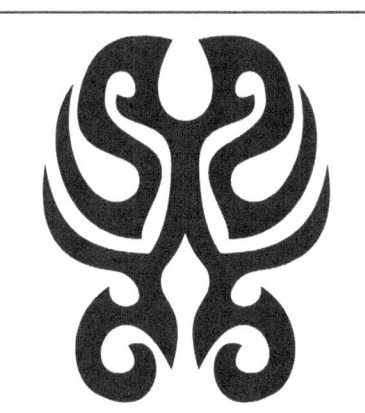

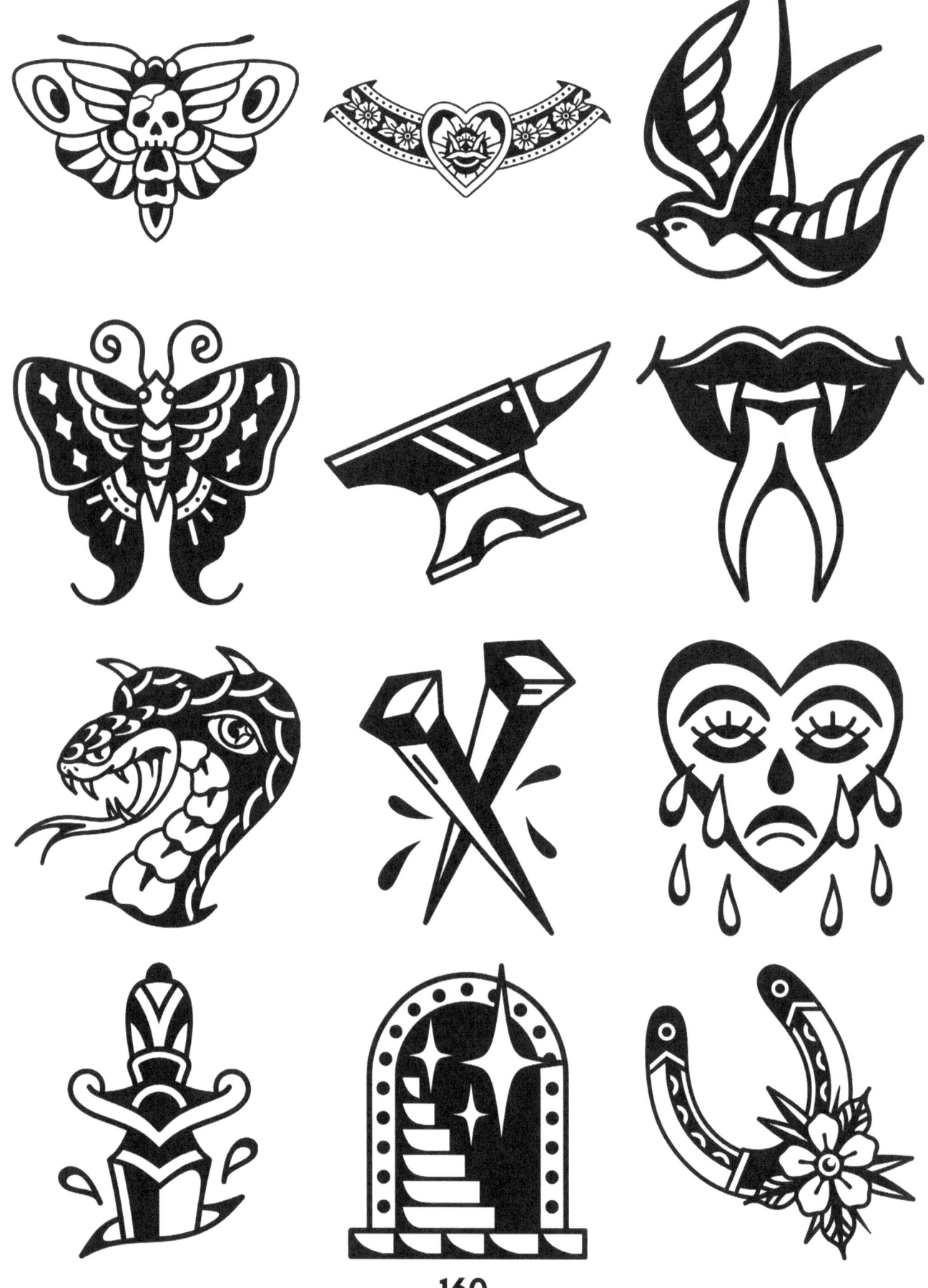

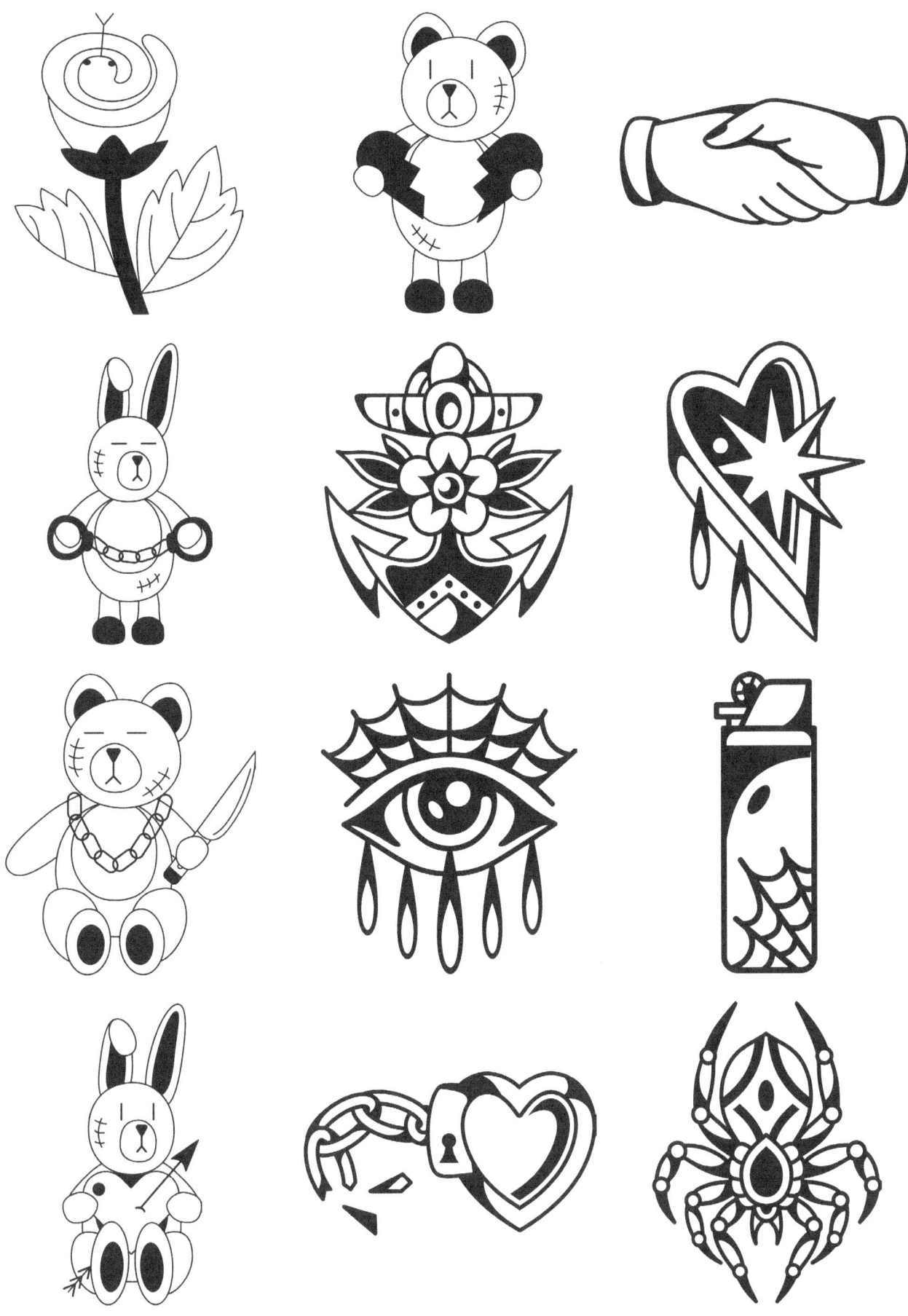

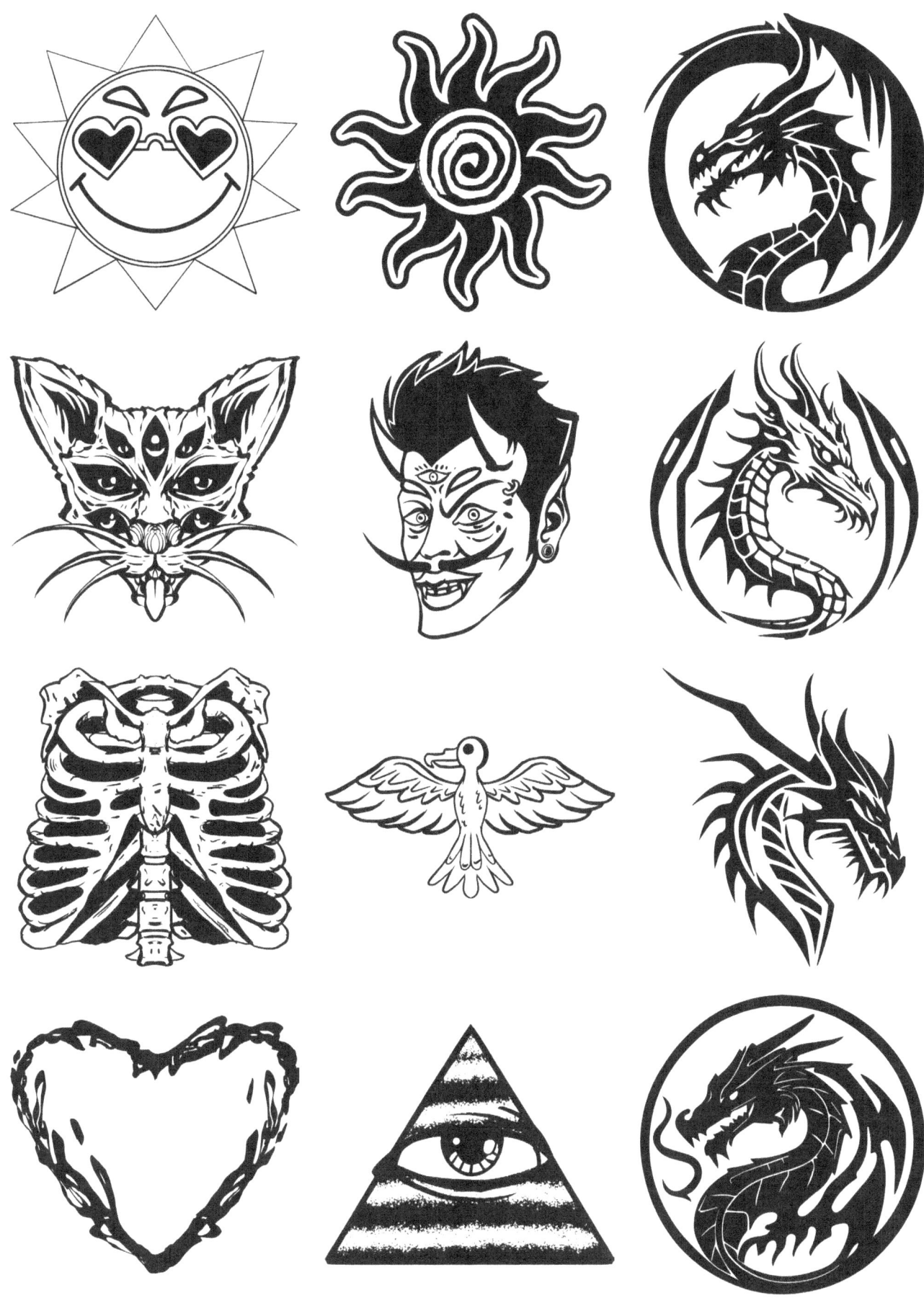

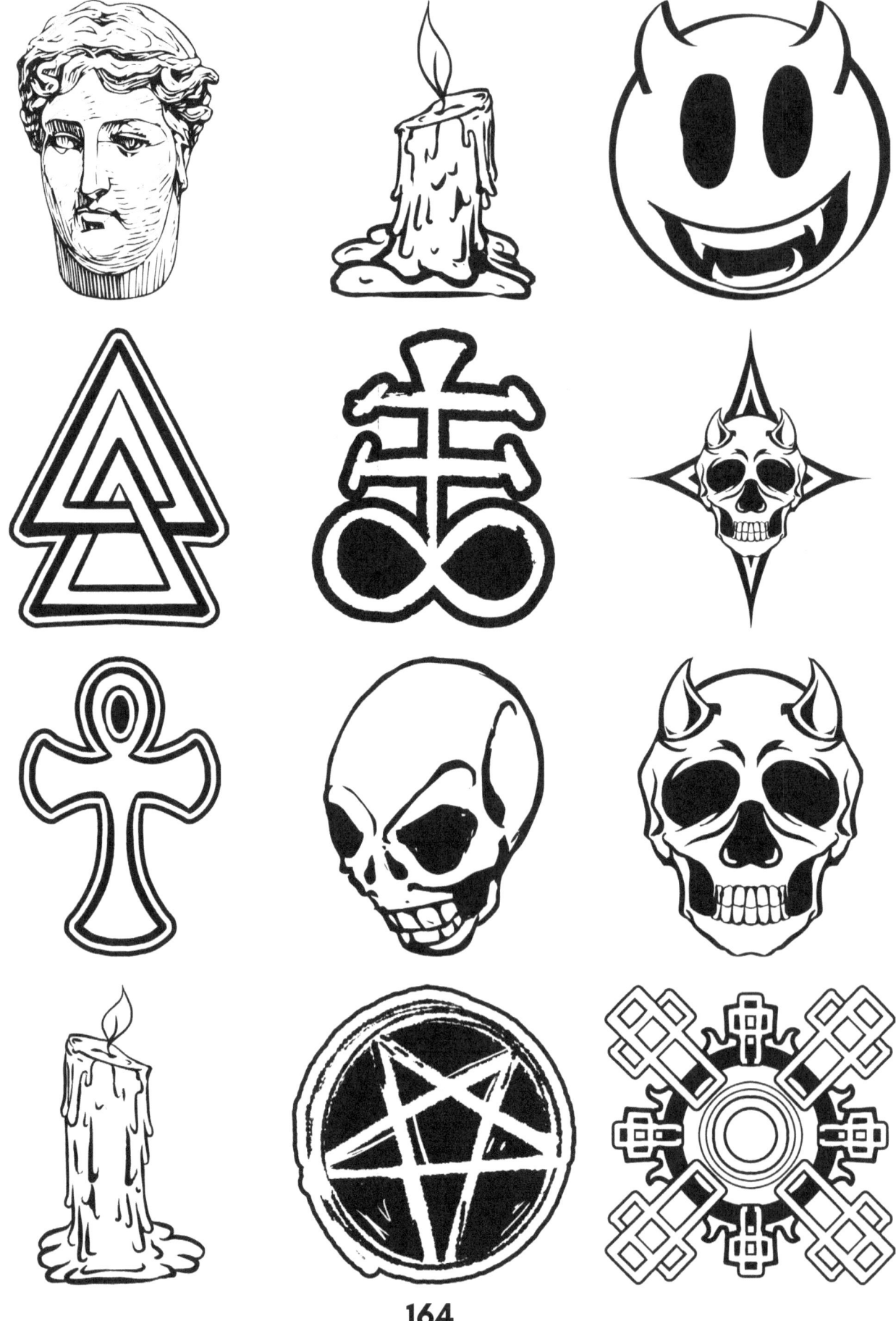

164

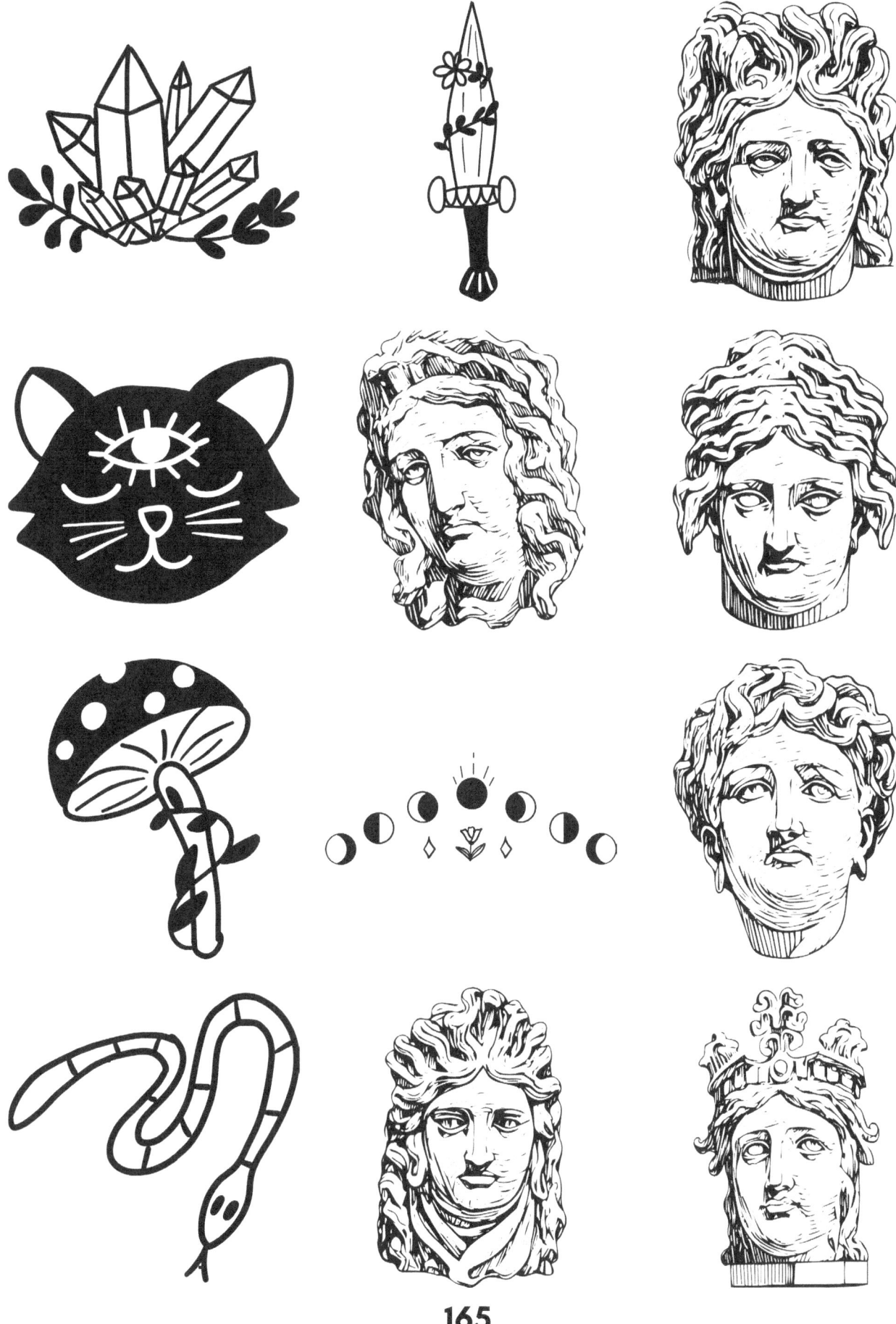

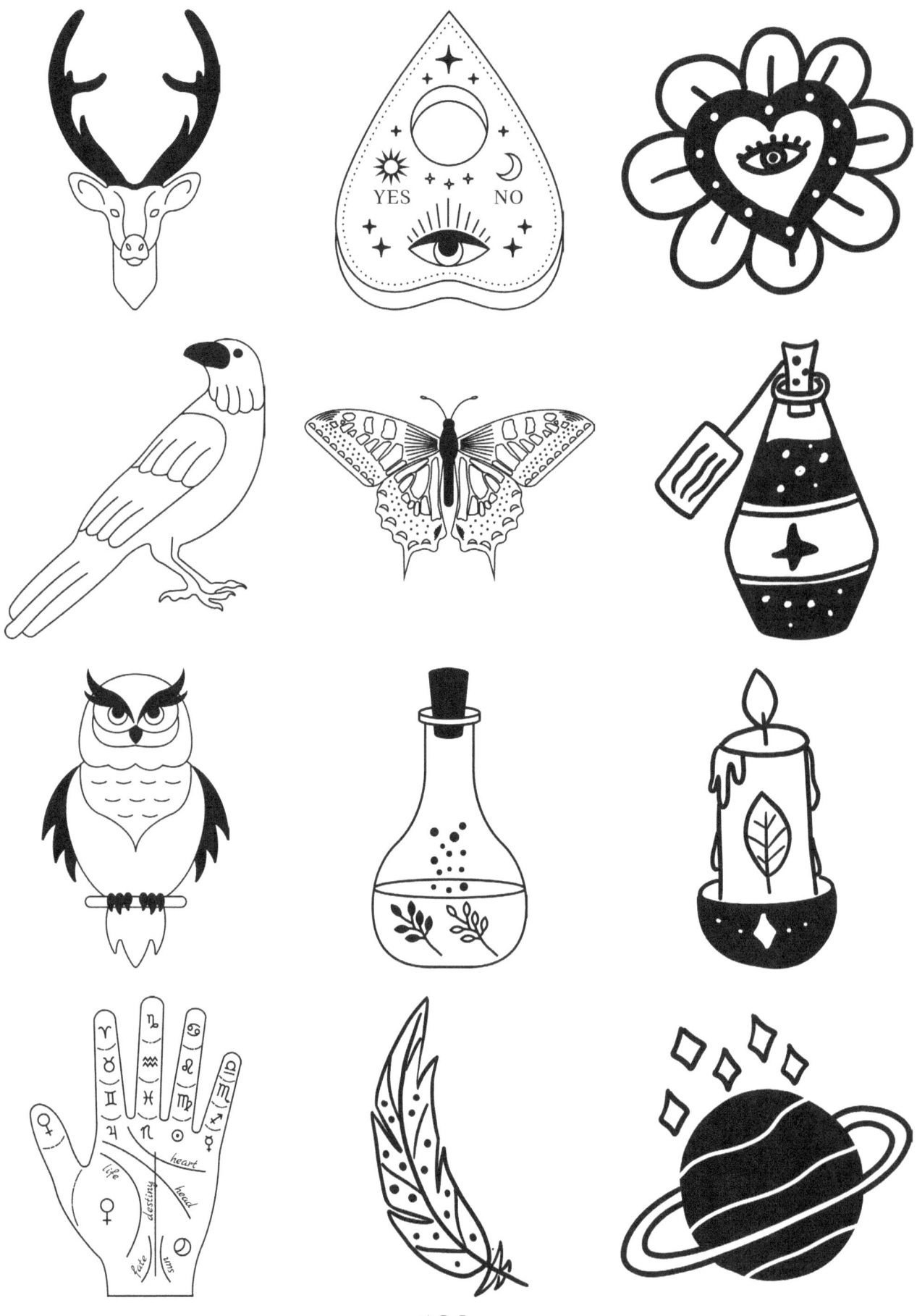

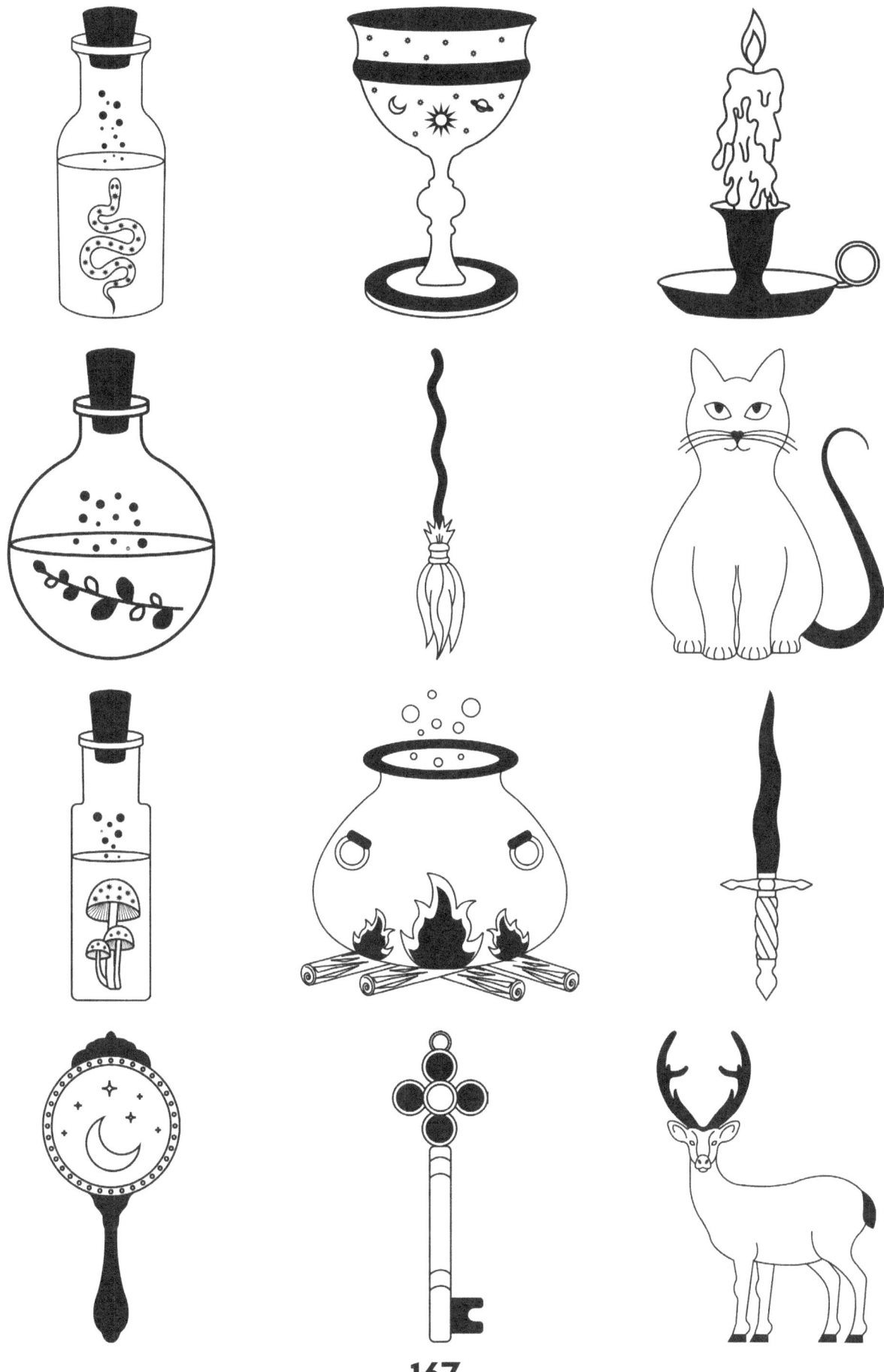

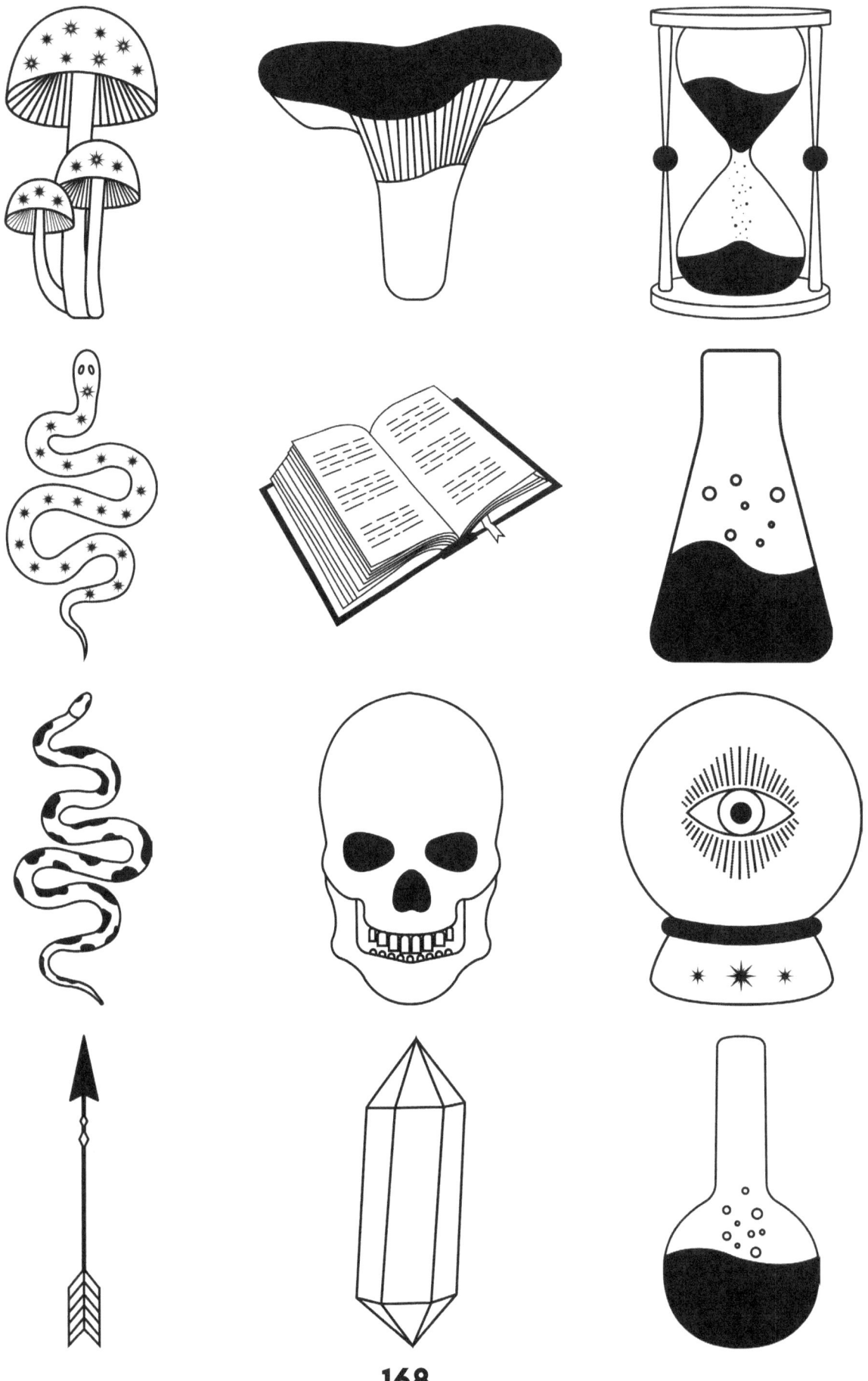

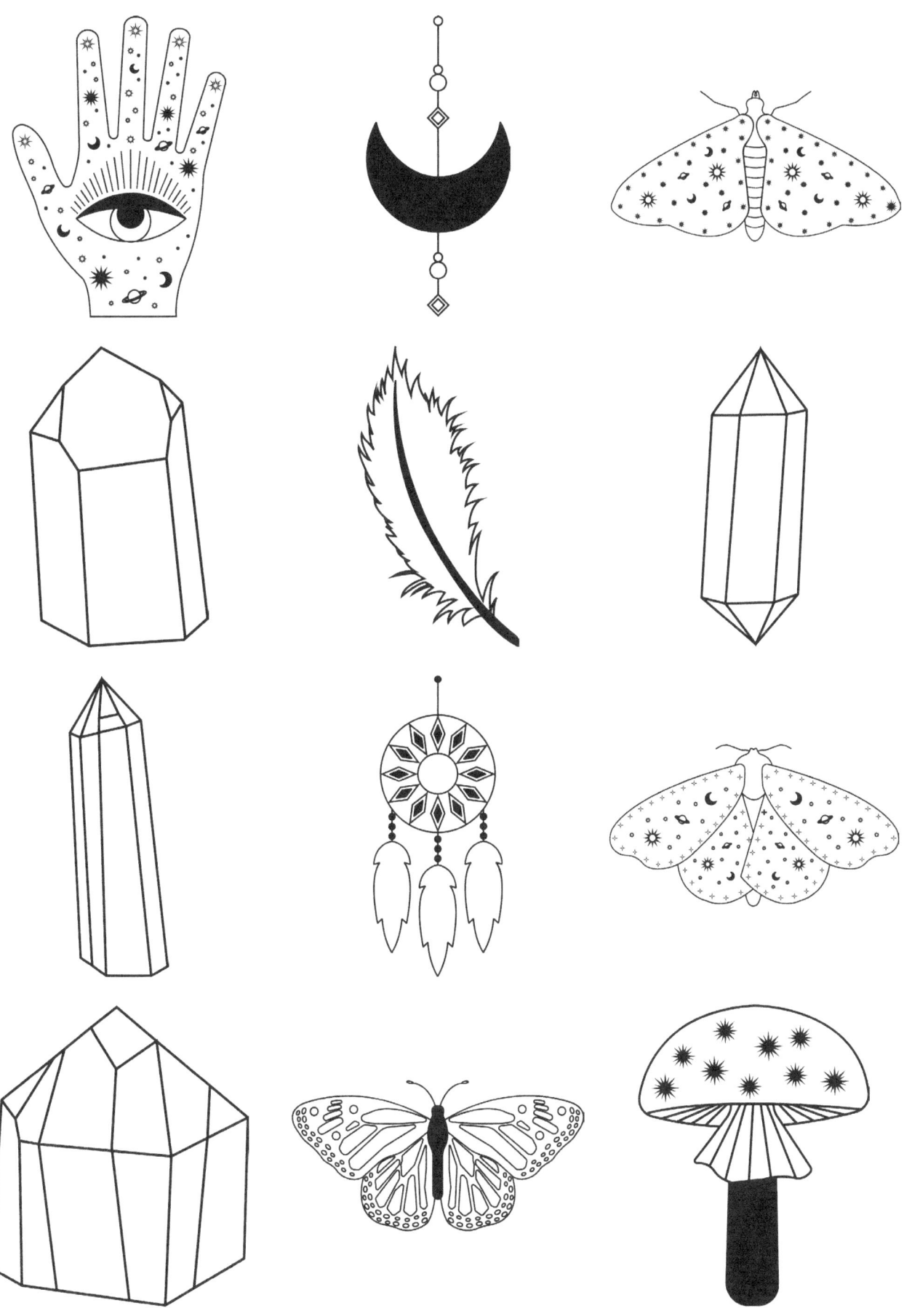

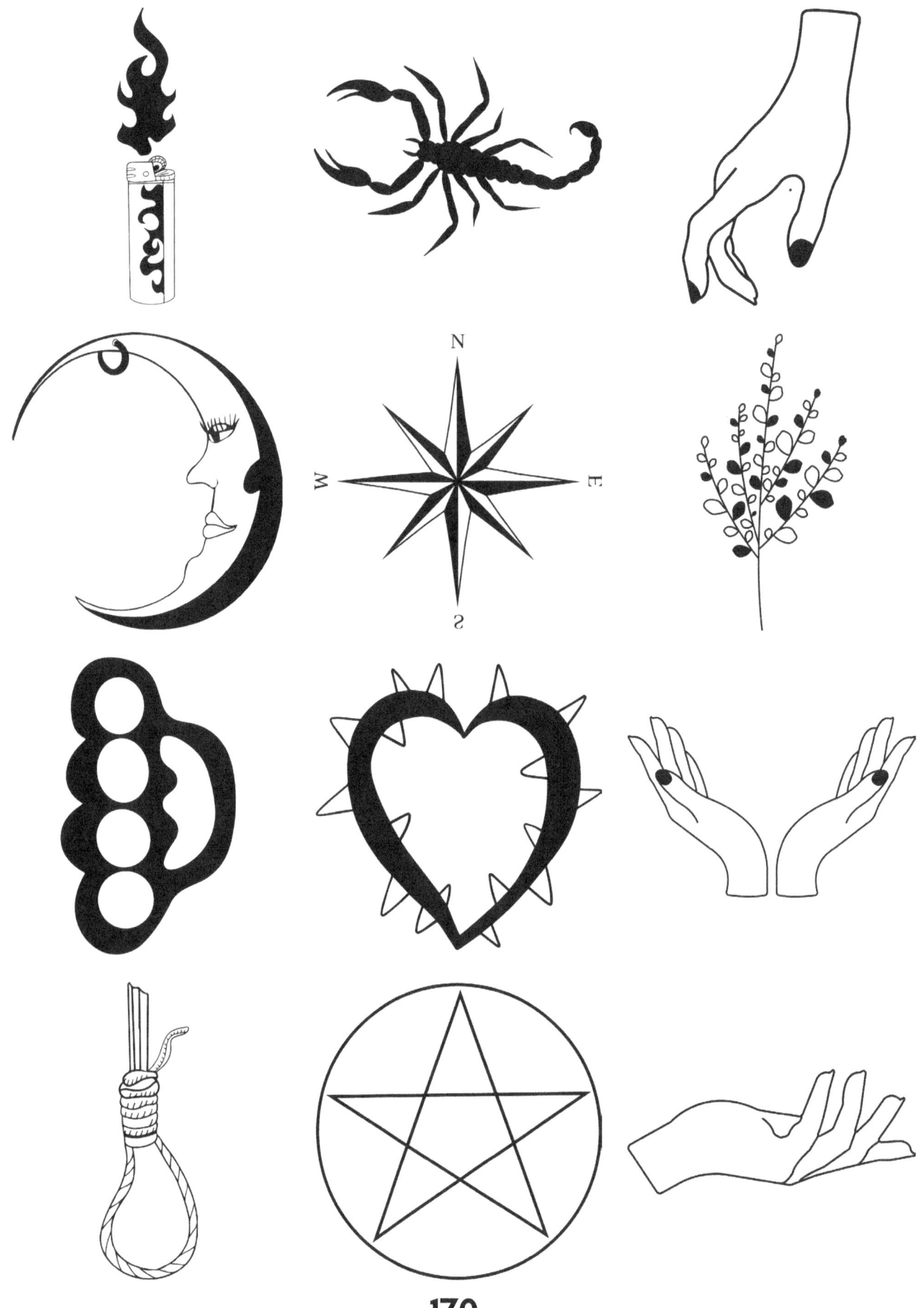